VISUAL QUICKSTART GUIDE

iCloud

Second Edition

TOM NEGRINO

Peachpit Press

Visual QuickStart Guide

iCloud, Second Edition

Tom Negrino

Peachpit Press
1301 Sansome Street
San Francisco, CA 94111
415/675-5100
415/675-5157 (fax)

Find us on the Web at www.peachpit.com
To report errors, please send a note to errata@peachpit.com
Peachpit Press is a division of Pearson Education

Editor: Clifford Colby
Production Editor: Katerina Malone
Compositor: Myrna Vladic
Indexer: Valerie Haynes Perry
Cover Design: RHDG / Riezebos Holzbaur Design Group, Peachpit Press
Interior Design: Peachpit Press
Logo Design: MINE™ www.minesf.com

ISBN-13: 978-0-321-88896-9
ISBN-10: 0-321-88896-0

9 8 7 6 5 4 3 2 1

Printed and bound in the United States of America

Dedication

To my wife, Dori, for her support and understanding of a husband who has his cranky days. Here's to fewer of those in the future.

Special Thanks to:

My patient editor, Cliff Colby, who instigated and shepherded this project to completion, made my work better, and encouraged me when a challenging schedule seemed overwhelming.

Thanks to Katerina Malone, for her excellent production work.

Thanks to the book's compositor, Myrna Vladic, and thanks to Valerie Haynes Perry for the index.

Thanks to Peachpit's Nancy Ruenzel and Nancy Davis for their support.

My appreciation to my friends and colleagues at *Macworld* magazine for doing all that testing of iCloud features and writing about it. I'd especially like to single out Lex Friedman, Dan Frakes, Dan Moren, Serenity Caldwell, Kirk McElhearn, and Ted Landau for their excellent articles. Mistakes in this book are, of course, entirely my own.

Contents at a Glance

Chapter 1	Getting Started with iCloud	1
Chapter 2	Working with Mail, Notes, and iMessages	17
Chapter 3	Working with Contacts	49
Chapter 4	Working with Calendars and Reminders	59
Chapter 5	Using iPhoto with iCloud	99
Chapter 6	Using iTunes with iCloud	115
Chapter 7	Working with Documents in the Cloud	135
Chapter 8	Backing up to iCloud	149
Chapter 9	Working with Safari	159
Chapter 10	Using iCloud to Find People and Devices	173
	Index	203

Table of Contents

Chapter 1 Getting Started with iCloud 1

What Is iCloud? 2
Hardware and Software Requirements 7
Apple ID Considerations 9
Configuring iCloud on Your iOS Devices 11
Configuring iCloud on Your Mac. 13
Configuring iCloud on Your PC 15

Chapter 2 Working with Mail, Notes, and iMessages 17

Setting up iCloud Mail Accounts on Your Mac 18
Setting up Mail Accounts on Your iOS Device 22
Working with Mail on the iCloud Website. 25
Working with Notes 40
Sending iMessages 46

Chapter 3 Working with Contacts 49

Searching, Adding, and Editing Contacts in iCloud . . . 50
Working with Contact Groups 54
Using the Action Menu 56
Setting iCloud Contact Preferences. 57

Chapter 4 Working with Calendars and Reminders 59

Setting up Calendars 60
Working with Calendars on the iCloud Website 67
Working with Events 73
Sharing Your Calendars with Others 77
Subscribing to Public Calendars. 80
Setting iCloud Calendar Preferences 83
Adding Reminders. 85
Working with Reminders on Your iOS Device 90
Managing Notifications on Mac and iOS 94

Chapter 5 Using iPhoto with iCloud 99

Setting up Photo Stream in iCloud. 100
Working with Photo Stream in iPhoto 104
Sharing Your Photo Stream. 109
Deleting Photos 113

Chapter 6 Using iTunes with iCloud 115

Configuring iTunes in the Cloud 116
Configuring and Using iTunes Match 122
Updating Your Music with iTunes Match 130

Chapter 7 Working with Documents in the Cloud 135

Configuring Documents in the Cloud 136
Storing and Working with Documents in iCloud 141
Working with iWork Documents on the iCloud Website 145

Chapter 8 Backing up to iCloud. 149

Understanding and Configuring iCloud Backup. 150
Restoring an iOS Device from Backup 153
Managing Your iCloud Storage 154

Chapter 9 Working with Safari. 159

About Bookmark Management 160
Configuring Bookmark Syncing with iCloud 161
Using iCloud Tabs and Reading List. 163
Useful Bookmarklets for iOS 169

Chapter 10 Using iCloud to Find People and Devices 173

Configuring iCloud Locating on the Mac 174
Finding and Working with Your Devices 178
Using Find My Mac 187
Using Find My Friends .193
Using Back to My Mac .199

Index 203

Getting Started with iCloud

Welcome to *iCloud: Visual QuickStart Guide, Second Edition*. This book will help you get up and running with Apple's iCloud online service, which allows your iOS devices (the iPhone, iPad, iPad mini, iPod touch, and Apple TV), your Macs, and your Windows PC to work together in ways that couldn't be done before.

The iCloud service doesn't do just one thing; it's a collection of tools that allows you to better manage your mobile devices, automatically synchronizing your personal information, including calendars, contacts, photos, music, and documents with all your devices. You can use iCloud to find the location of friends, family, and your devices, should those devices (or people) go missing. And iCloud also has added small benefits, such as freeing you from the tyranny of your wireless carrier's overpriced text messaging plans.

In this book, I'll show you how to get the most out of iCloud's various services, allowing you to use your computers and devices and more efficiently. Let's get started.

In This Chapter

What Is iCloud? 2

Hardware and Software Requirements 7

Apple ID Considerations 9

Configuring iCloud on Your iOS Devices 11

Configuring iCloud on Your Mac 13

Configuring iCloud on Your PC 15

What Is iCloud?

iCloud is Apple's online service that is, more than anything else, devoted to automatically and seamlessly synchronizing your personal data between all of the devices you may happen to use. First, let me clarify one bit of terminology I'm using in this book. When I refer to a "device," it could be a Mac desktop computer, a Mac notebook computer, or any iOS device, such as an iPhone, iPad, iPad mini, iPod touch, or the Apple TV. It could even be a Windows PC.

Things have changed quite a bit from the world in which we were tied to our desktop, or even laptop computers. With the advent of the iPhone and the iPad, you might want to check your mail, add to your calendar, edit a contact, or snap a photo when you're away from your computer, and if you have more than one computer, or more than one mobile device, it would be nice if changes you made on one device automatically appeared on all your other devices.

Essentially, that's what iCloud is all about. It liberates you from needing to worry about where your data is. There is no wondering about "Did I take my iPhone photos off the phone and put it on my computer?" or "Did I remember to take that appointment I entered on my iPad and put it on my iMac?" With iCloud, these things simply happen, in the background, and you never have to worry about them. Ideally, all your important data and documents are pushed to all your devices. It's a way to make sure that not just your digital life but your entire life is with you wherever you happen to be.

But really, I tend to think of iCloud as "plumbing in the sky." It doesn't so much do things itself as it enables devices and software to interact with one another in ways that make your life easier.

If, like me, you've been using the Mac for a long time, and you used previous Apple online services such as .Mac and MobileMe, you might be tempted to think that iCloud is just the newest flavor of those services. However, I think that's the wrong way to think about it. Those older services weren't built from the ground up, as iCloud has been, with the idea that your personal information and the documents you create should be ubiquitous and available no matter what device you have within reach.

So let's take the 10,000 foot view of what iCloud can do for you, and I think you'll see that in most cases, it does things that make excellent sense for most of us. And since most of the time, iCloud is free, the price is certainly right.

- **Wherever you go, your stuff is there.** In the early days of OS X, there was a program called iSync that allowed you to manually synchronize information (mostly contacts) between mobile phones and a Mac, connected by a wire (or sometimes via Bluetooth). Compared to iCloud's capabilities, you can think of iSync as roughly equivalent to a stone ax. With iCloud, you can wirelessly synchronize contacts, calendars, email, browser bookmarks, photos, music, apps, documents, and more. You don't have to "initiate a synchronization," and you don't have to do any manual copying, either. All you need do is make or edit something, and it automatically appears on the rest of your devices within a minute or so. So you can shoot a picture on your iPhone, get a decently large-sized view of it on your iPad, then move immediately to your Mac and touch up the photo.

- **You don't need to carry all your stuff with you.** The last time I bought an iPhone, I bought the model with 16 GB of storage. Why that instead of the fatter 32 or 64 GB models? Because I didn't want to spend the extra $100 or $200 to increase the storage. I knew that most of the storage space used on an iOS device is taken up by music and video, and I knew that my iTunes library was already far larger than any device I could buy, so I knew that I would always be carrying a subset around with me. Little did I know that Apple was already working on ways to make all of my data available to me, whether I chose to put it on my device or not. With a decent Wi-Fi connection and an optional service called iTunes Match, you can stream the contents of your iTunes library to your iOS device, whether or not you have purchased that content from Apple. You'll find more about using iTunes with iCloud in Chapter 6.
- **Your information is safer, even if you forget.** One of the best things you can do with iCloud is have it automatically back up your iOS devices to Apple's servers, once a day, as long as you have a Wi-Fi connection. That means that if your device is tragically either lost or stolen, you'll be able to purchase a replacement device, run through the setup process, and restore from the latest backup, without a lot of manual torment. You simply run through the restore process, and your device is in the same state it was the last time iCloud backed it up for you. The process isn't entirely seamless—you'll need to reenter some passwords and such—but it's way easier than reinstalling and reconfiguring things from scratch. And from any other iOS device or from the iCloud website, you can remotely lock or erase the data on your wayward device. Don't get me wrong; losing a device is still a pain. But with iCloud, at least it's a pain in your wallet, rather than the pain of identity theft. You'll find more about backing up with iCloud in Chapter 8, and more about remotely locking and erasing an iOS device in Chapter 10.
- **There's less need for wires.** Because iCloud can synchronize many kinds of data and backup your device over a Wi-Fi connection, most of the time you'll only need a USB-to-Dock connector cable to charge your iOS device. Even upgrading to a new version of iOS (once you're on iOS 5 or later) can be done wirelessly; one of the nice little features introduced in iOS 5 are "delta updates," which upgrades only the portion of the operating system that needs it, rather than requiring the whole thing to be downloaded. But in a big conceptual shift, Apple has cut the cord when it comes to iOS devices, meaning that you no longer need a Mac or PC to set them up or maintain them. With modern versions of iOS, the days of needing to plug your iOS device into a computer running iTunes to set it up are gone; a Setup process runs right on the device.

Whether you use the bare minimum of iCloud's services, or you jump in with both feet, iCloud has the ability to blur the location of your data. And that's a good thing. The important thing to understand is that you, personally, won't be dealing so much with iCloud as you will be dealing with the apps on your devices (or, if you prefer, with the iCloud website).

Let's talk a little more about the specific features that iCloud enables. Many of these are familiar, either as apps on your devices, or from use with MobileMe. These features include:

- **Email.** An iCloud account comes with an `icloud.com` account (if you previously had a `mac.com` or `me.com` account, they will work too; in fact, they are treated as the same account), and email from that account appears on all your devices. iCloud also deals with notes and text messages. You'll find more information about all of these functions in Chapter 2.
- **Contacts, Calendars, and Reminders.** Your address book, calendar, and reminder information can be shared not only with your own devices but also with other people for whom you give permission. I cover these features in Chapters 3 and 4.
- **Photos.** Part of iCloud is a service called Photo Stream, which pushes the contents of your iOS device's Camera Roll up to the cloud and down to your other devices. You can keep your Photo Stream to yourself, or share parts of it with other people. Look for more about that in Chapter 5.
- **Music.** iCloud allows you to keep your music (the music you bought from the iTunes Store, music you've ripped from your CD collection, and music you've picked up over the years) available to all your devices. You can download whatever subset of your music library you want onto your mobile device. I'll be talking about that in Chapter 6.
- **Synchronized Documents.** In iCloud, you can share documents created in other applications, for example Apple's iWork applications: Keynote, Pages, and Numbers. Documents that you create or edit on one device can update automatically on all your other devices, so no matter what device you're working on, you're always up-to-date. Apple calls this feature Documents in the Cloud, and it's not limited to just Apple's own programs; third-party programs can take advantage of the feature as well. You'll find more information about that in Chapter 7.
- **Browser Bookmarks.** If you like, you can synchronize your Safari (or on Windows, your Internet Explorer) browser bookmarks via iCloud. You'll find more information about that in Chapter 9.
- **Location Services.** Using iCloud, you can find the location of people and devices. Again, turn to Chapter 10 for more information on finding and working with people and devices.

All of these services are tied together using storage on Apple's servers. With every iCloud account, you get 5 GB of storage for free, and you can purchase more storage on a yearly basis if needed (up to 50 GB). Some items, such as anything you buy from the iTunes Store (whether it be music, podcasts, apps, books, movies, or television episodes) and photos in your Photo Stream, don't count against the 5 GB storage quota. What you'll mostly find using up your iCloud storage quote is your iCloud email, your documents and data used by applications (usually preferences and the like).

MobileMe Services Missing in iCloud

Apple provided a variety of features in their online services as it evolved, from .Mac to MobileMe and now to iCloud. Some of the original .Mac features were already long gone (anyone remember the iCards online greeting cards? Ironically, they've been resurrected as Cards, a free iPhone or iPod touch app from Apple that lets you shoot pictures on your device and add a note, and Apple prints and mails a physical card for you), including a general backup service that worked with your Mac.

When Apple announced iCloud, it also heralded the end of MobileMe. Apple turned off access to MobileMe services forever on June 30, 2012.

Besides the end of MobileMe in general, some of its services also permanently ended with its demise. Here's a rundown of these services, with my suggestions for alternate services:

- **iDisk** online storage space (partially offset by iCloud's 5 GB of storage, but less flexible, since you can't mount iCloud storage as a network disk, as you could with iDisk). Instead of iDisk, I recommend you use Dropbox (**`www.dropbox.com`**), which allows you to create a folder on your computer's disk that is automatically synchronized between your different computers and that also makes files and folders available for download to your iOS devices. Other good services for online storage and (light-duty) backup are Google Drive (**`drive.google.com`**); Microsoft SkyDrive (**`skydrive.live.com`**), and Box (**`www.box.com`**). All offer a free amount of storage (at least 5 GB), with more if you pay.
- **iWeb site publishing.** This was used by people who used iWeb, part of Apple's iLife software suite, who either lost their iWeb sites or found alternate web site hosting (iWeb allows you to use any Web hosting company). Apple quietly ended development of iWeb in 2011; it hadn't been significantly updated since iLife '09, and the program didn't join in the transition of the other iLife programs into versions sold on the Mac App Store. If you have little in the way of Web building skills, and you need a free solution, two good template-based sites are Weebly (**`www.weebly.com`**) and Jimdo (**`www.jimdo.com`**). If you're more experienced with building web sites and need Web site hosting, I strongly suggest you pay for it (and don't use iWeb); there are thousands of Web hosts out there. Personally, I use Dreamhost and Pair Networks for hosting, and WordPress and Dreamweaver to build sites, but the decision as to what host and software to use can be complex.
- **Gallery.** One of the photo sharing destinations in iPhoto was MobileMe Gallery, which hosted your pictures on the web. iCloud's Photo Stream isn't a substitute, since you can't view items in the Photo Stream in a Web browser. Instead of the MobileMe Gallery, iPhoto allows you to share photos on Flickr (**`www.flickr.com`**), which is actually a better service; Gallery had been languishing in features and interest for several years. Besides Flickr, which is my first choice, my photographer buddies seem to like Photobucket (**`www.photobucket.com`**) and SmugMUG (**`www.smugmug.com`**).
- **OS X system synchronization.** MobileMe allowed you to synchronize keychains (which contain your system and web passwords), Dock items, System Preferences, Mail accounts, Mail Rules, Mail Signatures, Smart Mailboxes, and Dashboard widgets. A good replacement for keychain synchronization (and the one that I've used for years, because it offers many more features than Apple's old solution) is AgileBits' 1Password (**`www.agilebits.com`**).

continues on next page

MobileMe Services Missing in iCloud *continued*

- **Third-party software synchronization.** Many programs, such as Microsoft Entourage, Bare Bones' Yojimbo, The Omni Group's OmniFocus, and Panic's Transmit, used MobileMe to synchronize their settings or documents, and when you make the change to iCloud, you'll lose those synchronization services, because the iCloud migration turns off all MobileMe sync features. If you use a program that used MobileMe for synchronization across devices (you can tell because the program will be listed in the Sync tab of the MobileMe preference pane), you should check with the software maker for alternatives, if available. For example, OmniFocus allows you to use Omni's own synchronization server, or any WebDAV server (if you want to handle your own sync server). But as of this writing, Panic hasn't released any alternative for Transmit's synced Favorites. Some programs have instead embraced Dropbox to store their shared preferences; 1Password does, as do Smile's TextExpander, Bare Bones' BBEdit, and more.

Ⓐ On your Mac, you must be running OS X Lion 10.7.2 or Mountain Lion to use iCloud.

Ⓑ You'll need to be using iOS 5 or preferably iOS 6 on your mobile devices to use iCloud features.

Hardware and Software Requirements

In order to use iCloud, Apple required users to break with past operating systems and start anew with the latest versions of both their desktop (OS X) and mobile (iOS) operating systems. iCloud also works on recent versions of Microsoft Windows, though many iCloud features work best with or require a Mac.

On the Mac, using iCloud requires that you be running OS X 10.7.2 Lion or later, including all versions of 10.8 Mountain Lion, which is the latest OS X version as I write this Ⓐ. That means that iCloud on the Mac has the same hardware requirements as Lion. A Mac requires an Intel Core 2 Duo, Core i3, Core i5, Core i7, or Xeon processor. For portable machines, that includes most of the Intel-based MacBooks (excluding only the original 2006 model); MacBook Pro (if introduced after October 2006); and all models of the MacBook Air. For desktop machines, it includes the Mac mini (mid 2007 or later); iMac (after September 2006); and all versions of the Mac Pro. Your computer needs at least 2 GB of memory (as usual with a Mac, you'll get better performance with more memory), and at least 7 GB of available storage space. 10.8 Mountain Lion dropped a few early models throughout the Mac line, so double-check your older machine's specs with the excellent, free Mactracker (available on the Mac App Store), which has a comprehensive listing of Apple hardware and software back to 1984.

On an iOS device, you must be running iOS 5 or later, including iOS 6 Ⓑ (as I write this, iOS 6.1 is the latest release); iCloud comes free as part of iOS 5 or 6. In fact, much of the amazing things that you can do with iCloud are completely dependent on the features in iOS 5 and 6. In terms of hardware, most, but not all, iOS devices are compatible with iOS 5 and 6. Any iPhone from the iPhone 3GS or later; any iPad or iPad mini; and the iPod touch third generation or later can run iOS 5, and therefore use iCloud. The second- and third-generation Apple TV, which is a modified iOS device, can use iCloud's Photo Stream and iTunes Match services, but the original Apple TV cannot.

In general, I always recommend you upgrade to the latest versions of both OS X and iOS your hardware can handle.

I wrote this book using Mountain Lion on my Macs and iOS 6 on my mobile devices, and the book's screenshots reflect those operating systems. I'm also using iTunes 11 in screenshots.

On a Windows PC, you can install the iCloud control panel on any version of Windows 7, or Windows Vista with Service Pack 2 or later.

On any platform, you can do some interaction with iCloud services with nothing more than a web browser **C**. I'll discuss the interaction on the iCloud website in each of the chapters that relates to that section of the website.

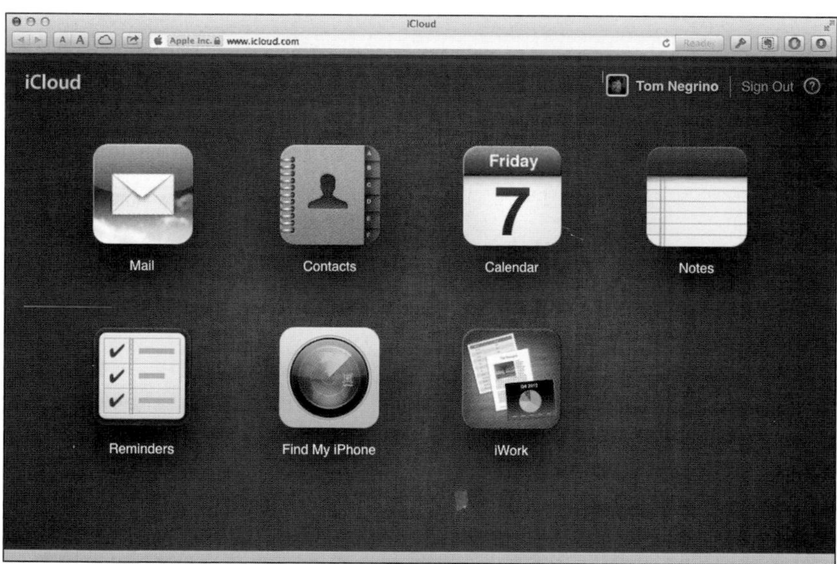

C The iCloud website allows you to access and work with much of your iCloud data.

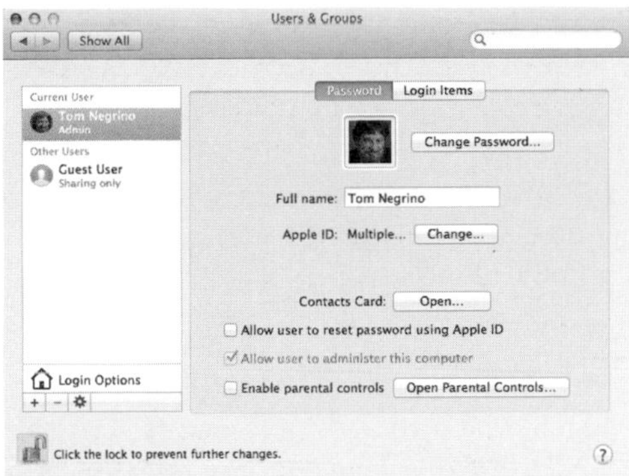

A In Lion and Mountain Lion, there is now an entry for Apple ID in the Users & Groups preference pane.

Apple ID Considerations

Before you can move to iCloud, you'll need one crucial bit of information: your Apple ID and password. The Apple ID is the glue that holds all your iCloud information together. You may already have an Apple ID, because one is required if you've ever bought anything from the iTunes Store or Mac App Store. And OS X users have been prompted to create an Apple ID when they set up their Macs for years.

The Apple ID must be a valid email address, and is usually a me.com (for older accounts) or icloud.com address, which Apple will give to you for free. You'll create and sign into your iCloud account using a single Apple ID, which will then be the Apple ID you use for all iCloud services (but there are caveats; see the "Dealing with Multiple Apple IDs" sidebar later in this section).

Beginning with OS X Lion, your Apple ID can serve as an alternate set of credentials to your usual username and password for services such as file sharing, screen sharing, and account recovery. In Lion and Mountain Lion, the Apple ID is integrated into the Users & Groups preference pane **A**.

It's worth pointing out that if you have previously been sharing your Apple ID with others (perhaps because you have been sharing your iTunes library using Home Sharing, or to share purchases from the iTunes Store), those people now have access to your account on a Mac, either over a local network or remotely via Back to My Mac. Before you begin using iCloud, it's a good idea to reflect upon your security requirements, and if necessary, change the password associated with your Apple ID. Along the same lines, now is the time to think about how secure your Apple ID password is. If it is easily guessable, a word that is in a dictionary, a consecutive sequence of numbers or letters, or otherwise weak, I strongly recommend you change it to a stronger password before moving to iCloud. A quick Google search using the phrase "making a good password" will lead you to much good advice.

If multiple people use a single Apple ID (for example, if your entire family has been using your Apple ID for iTunes Store purchases) you can still do so for that purpose, but each person will have to create a separate Apple ID/iCloud account for syncing and backup of their personal devices.

TIP When I wrote this book, rather than blur my Apple ID in the book's many screenshots, I chose to leave it in readable form. But before the book went to print, I changed the password (which was already pretty good) to an even more secure password.

TIP If you click the Change button in the Users & Groups preference pane under Lion or later, it's possible to associate your user account with more than one Apple ID. You can see this in A; next to Apple ID, it says Multiple,,,

Dealing with Multiple Apple IDs

Over the years, you may have created more than one Apple ID. For example, you may have created and used a particular Apple ID with the iTunes Store (say, the email address you got from your ISP), and you had a MobileMe address. Both of those can count as Apple IDs. In the fall of 2012, Apple began offering `icloud.com` addresses. If you previously had a .Mac account, you may have both a `me.com` account and a `mac.com` account, which are aliases of one another and of the `icloud.com` address. And any of them can be used as an Apple ID.

The obvious solution would be for Apple to offer the ability to consolidate multiple Apple IDs into one. Unfortunately, if you already have multiple Apple IDs, Apple simply isn't offering that ability as of yet. You do have the option of creating, managing, and resetting the password of your Apple ID account by going to `http://appleid.apple.com`. But by not allowing a person to consolidate multiple Apple IDs they may have picked up over the years, Apple is throwing the management burden onto that person; not exactly consistent with Apple's vaunted philosophy of simplicity.

A During iOS setup, you'll be prompted to sign in with an existing Apple ID, or create a new one.

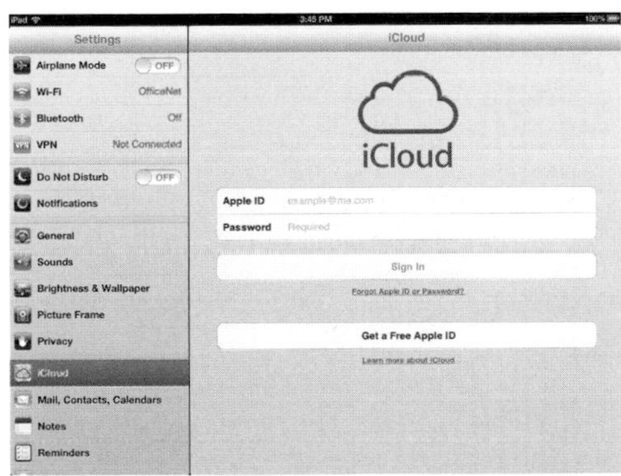

B You can sign in to iCloud in the iCloud pane of the iOS Settings app.

Configuring iCloud on Your iOS Devices

It's easy to set up iCloud on your iOS device. You can either set it up when you set up your mobile device for the first time, or you can turn it on at any time. In either event, you'll need an Apple ID. If you don't already have an Apple ID, you can create one during the process.

If you previously had a MobileMe account, there are some other important considerations before you turn on iCloud on your iOS devices. Before you continue in this section, you should first read the "Migrating to iCloud from MobileMe" section, later in this chapter.

To set up iCloud on your iOS device:

1. During iOS initial set up, one of the screens that you will see is the Apple ID screen **A**. If you have already gone through the iOS setup process, skip to step 4.

   You'll need to be connected to a Wi-Fi network during the setup process.

2. Tap Sign In with an Apple ID if you already have an Apple ID.

   or

   If you need an Apple ID, tap Create or Get (depending on the device) a Free Apple ID. You'll be prompted through the sign-up process, where you'll get an `icloud.com` email address and enter a password.

3. On the Apple ID screen, enter your Apple ID and password, then complete the setup process.

4. In the iOS Settings app, tap iCloud **B**.

continues on next page

5. Enter your Apple ID and password, then tap Sign In.
6. In the iCloud Settings panel, turn on the services you wish to use (C and D).

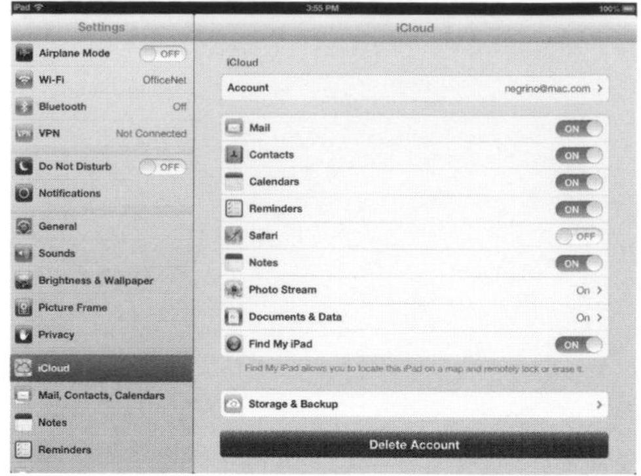

C Once you are signed in to iCloud...

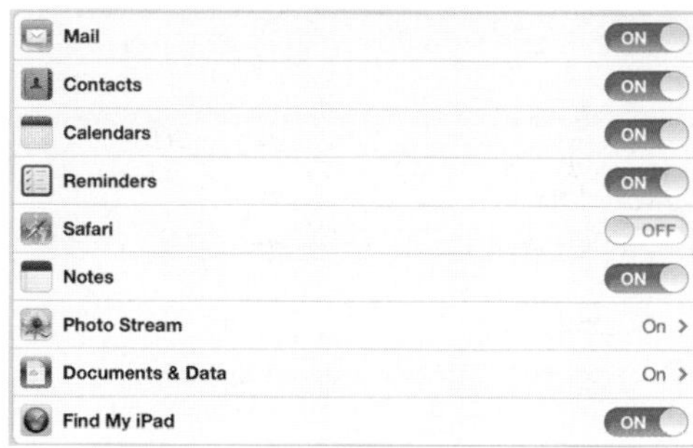

D ... you can turn on the specific services you want to use.

iCloud and the Apple TV

The Apple TV is the set-top box that lives near your television, and plays audio and video at quality up to 1080p, streaming it from your home network using either Wi-Fi or Ethernet. It allows you to access media from your iTunes library, rent movies and TV shows from the iTunes Store, and access a variety of Internet services such as Netflix, and includes two iCloud services. It gives you access to your Photo Stream and to music available in iCloud using iTunes Match (see Chapter 6 for more about that).

To view your Photo Stream on your television, you'll first need to make sure the Apple TV software is updated to version 4.4 or later (the Apple TV uses a modified version of iOS with a very different user interface). Then a new item, Photo Stream, appears in the Internet menu of the Apple TV. Naturally, if you hadn't already set up the Apple TV with your Apple ID (as you would have needed to do to purchase rentals from the device), you'll need to enter it before you can view your Photo Stream. Of course, if you have more than one Apple ID, you'll need to use the one associated with your iCloud account. If you like, you can set the Photo Stream as the source for your screen saver. Or you still have the option of using one of your iPhoto albums.

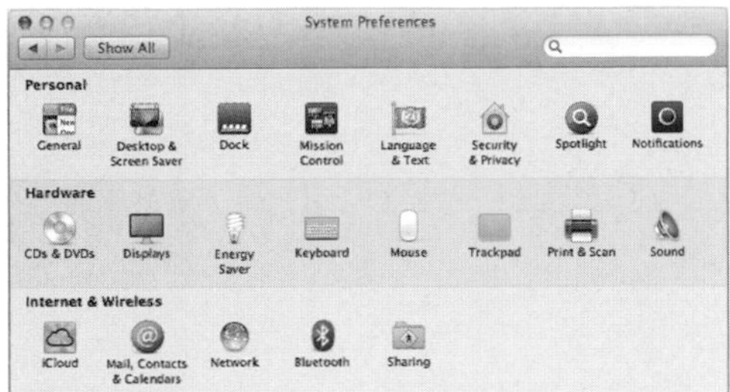

A Begin the iCloud setup process by opening System Preferences.

B In the iCloud preference pane, enter the Apple ID you wish to use with iCloud, as well as its password.

Configuring iCloud on Your Mac

To activate iCloud on your Mac, you have to make sure that you have first upgraded to OS X Lion 10.7.2 or later. That update added the iCloud preference pane in System Preferences.

To set up and configure iCloud on your Mac:

1. From the Apple menu, choose System Preferences **A**.
2. Click the iCloud icon.

   The ICloud preference pane appears **B**.
3. Enter your Apple ID and password, then click Sign In.

continues on next page

4. In the iCloud preference pane, select the checkboxes next to the services you want to enable **C**.

C Choose the iCloud services you want to use from the preference pane.

iCloud Is Master of Your Data

In any situation where you're synchronizing data between different devices, there needs to be one master data set (also sometimes known as the *canonical* data). With the old MobileMe service, if there was a conflict between the local copy of the data and the copy on the online service, sometimes you would get a dialog that would ask you which version of the data (on your Mac or on MobileMe) was correct, and you could choose which one to use. Not so with iCloud, which considers itself to always be the canonical data. You can even have situations (for example, if you have some duplicated calendar events) where you can delete all the events on your local machine, yet when you sync with iCloud, all those events will reappear. Sometimes, the solution is to turn off iCloud syncing on all your devices, then turn them on one by one until you get a clean set of data on all devices.

Configuring iCloud on Your PC

If your main computer is a Windows PC, as opposed to a Mac, you can still use iCloud with it, though you only have access to a subset of the services that you would have on a Mac. On the PC, you can use iCloud for email (with a **`icloud.com`** or **`me.com`** address), contacts, calendars, and tasks (called Reminders on the iOS device), all synchronizing with Microsoft Outlook 2007 or 2010. The bookmark synchronization service works with Internet Explorer 9 or later, or Safari for Windows 5.1.7 or later. Your Photo Stream can also be pushed to and from your Windows PC, using folders you designate as the source and destination for iCloud photos (usually your Pictures library).

Before you can use iCloud on Windows, you'll need to download the iCloud control panel from Apple's website at **`http://support.apple.com/kb/DL1455`**. This download will be a standard **`.exe`** file, which you open and install like any other Windows program.

To set up and configure iCloud on your PC:

1. On a Windows Vista or Windows 7 PC, choose Start Menu > Control Panel > Network and Internet **A**.

   or

   On a Windows 8 PC, begin on the Start screen and click the Desktop tile, which switches you to Desktop mode. Move your mouse to the upper or lower right corner of the screen to reveal the Charms bar, and then click the Settings charm. In the resulting settings bar, click the Control Panel link.

   The Control Panel appears.

2. Click iCloud.
3. In the resulting iCloud control panel **B**, select the checkboxes for the services you wish to enable.

TIP The system requirement for iCloud for Windows is Microsoft Windows Vista SP2, Windows 7, or Windows 8.

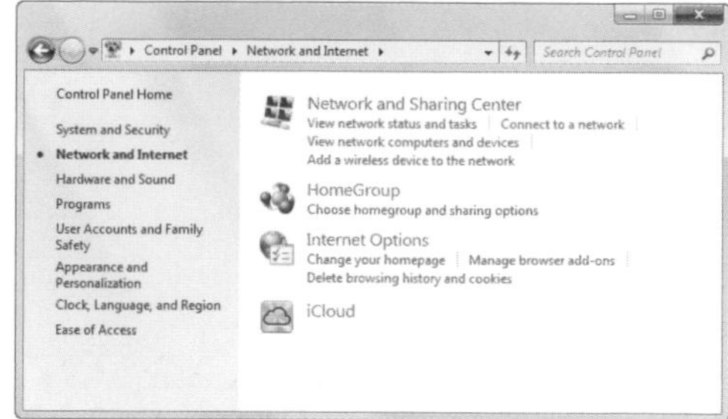

A Open the Network and Internet section of the Windows Control Panel to start working with the iCloud Control Panel.

B Click the checkboxes for the iCloud services you want to use.

Working with Mail, Notes, and iMessages

Like its MobileMe predecessor, iCloud provides a full set of email services. There are changes (some for the better, some not so much) from MobileMe mail, but for the most part I think that iCloud email is a better product. And you can't beat the price; it's free with your iCloud account. In this chapter, we'll see how to set up your iCloud email account on both the Mac and on an iOS device, and manage that mail on the iCloud website.

As part of the Mac and iOS Notes app, you also have the ability to create notes that will sync between your devices via iCloud. You'll see how to deal with notes on both platforms.

One of the great features in iCloud is iMessages, which allows you to send text messages to other people on iOS devices with iCloud accounts, and without incurring phone carrier messaging charges. iMessage is integrated into the Messages Mac and iOS apps, and we'll see how it works and its limitations.

In This Chapter

Setting up iCloud Mail Accounts on Your Mac 18

Setting up Mail Accounts on Your iOS Device 22

Working with Mail on the iCloud Website 25

Working with Notes 40

Sending iMessages 46

Setting up iCloud Mail Accounts on Your Mac

One of the benefits of every iCloud account is a free `@icloud.com` email address (if you previously had a `me.com` or `mac.com` address, that serves as an alias to the `icloud.com` address). All iCloud email accounts use the IMAP email protocol, so messages are saved on the server, and you can read, reply to, and mark your email as read from any device. Because IMAP is a standard mail protocol, you can use many different email programs, on many different computing platforms, to work with your mail. You're certainly not locked into just using Apple devices or email programs.

Because messages are saved on the server, the amount of space your `icloud.com` email takes up counts against the free 5 GB of storage space you get with your iCloud account.

When email arrives in your iCloud email account, the email is also automatically pushed to your iOS devices, so your mail picture is the same whether you're on a Mac or on a mobile device.

Dealing with how to use the Apple Mail program on the Mac (to send and receive mail, for example) is outside the scope of this book; instead, in this chapter I'm going to focus on showing you how to set up Mail with your iCloud account, depending on if you were a previous Mail user or not. Again, since your iCloud email account is just like any other IMAP account, you can set it up on almost any email program: Just follow the maker's instructions for setting up an account. I will go into working with many aspects of mail using the iCloud website, which can be accessed from any web browser; see "Working with Mail on the iCloud Website" later in this chapter.

MobileMe Mail Features Missing from iCloud Mail

There are a few things you could do with MobileMe mail that you can't do with iCloud mail. First of all, iCloud uses the more modern IMAP email protocol exclusively, so you can't retrieve your messages with the POP email protocol. In my opinion, that's not necessarily a bad thing, but it does limit flexibility for some people.

MobileMe email allowed you to use Apple's mail servers, but you could change the From address of your messages, so if you had previously had a long-standing email address (on, for example, your own domain), you could use MobileMe as your mail provider and still send email that apparently came from your other address. For example, I could previously send mail from `tn@negrino.com` via the MobileMe servers. That's no longer possible; you must now use your `.icloud` account (or legacy `.me` or `.mac` account) as the From address. If this ability is important to you, it is available from other free email providers, such as Google's Gmail.

One minor change is that MobileMe allowed up to five email aliases, and iCloud only allows three aliases. An alias is an email address that points to another address; for example, you could have a `workmail@icloud.com` alias that you pick up on your main `.icloud` account. You can also use an alias address to help filter your mail using mail rules.

A If you've never used Mail on your Mac before, setting up your first account welcomes you to the program.

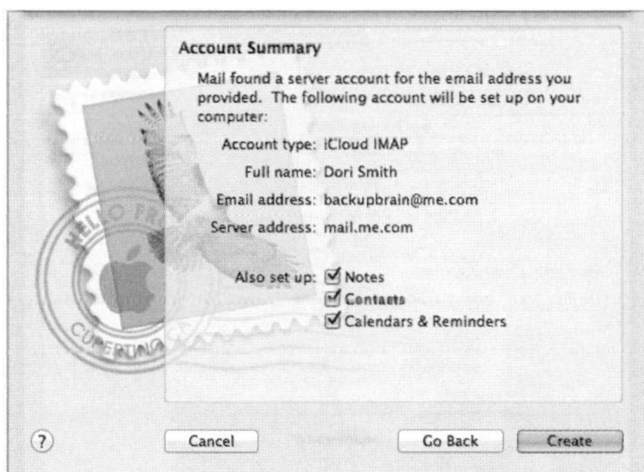

B Mail checks to make sure that the email address and password you entered were valid.

To set up your iCloud email account in Apple Mail (if you haven't used Mail before):

1. On your Mac, choose Applications > Mail.

   The Welcome to Mail Screen appears **A**.

2. You'll be prompted for the Full Name, the Email Address, and the Password. Enter these, then click Create.

   Mail checks to see if the email account exists, and if so signs you in and the Account Summary screen appears **B**.

3. (Optional) If you also want to set up your Notes, Contacts, Calendars, and Reminders to work with iCloud, select those checkboxes next to Also set up. I recommend that you do this.

4. Click Create.

   Mail opens, displaying the mail window **C**.

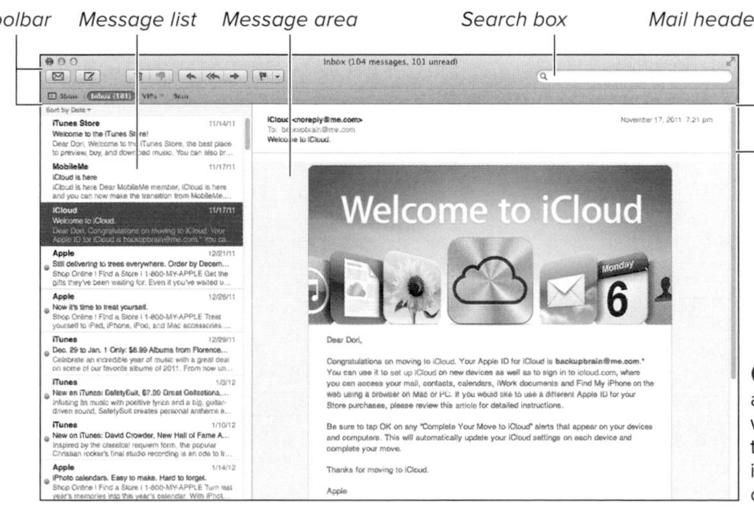

C The Mail application window on the Mac, in its default configuration.

To set up your iCloud email account in Apple Mail (if you've used Mail before):

1. On your Mac, choose Applications > Mail.
2. In Mail, choose Mail > Preferences > Accounts.

   The Accounts pane appears **D**.
3. At the lower left corner of the pane, click the plus button.

   The Add Account pane appears **E**.
4. Enter the Full Name, the Email Address, and the Password, then click Create.

   Mail checks to see if the email account exists, and if so signs you in and the Account Summary screen appears **B**.
5. (Optional) If you also want to set up your Notes, Contacts, Calendars, and Reminders to work with iCloud, select those checkboxes next to Also set up. I recommend that you do this.
6. Click Create.
7. Close the Mail Preferences window.

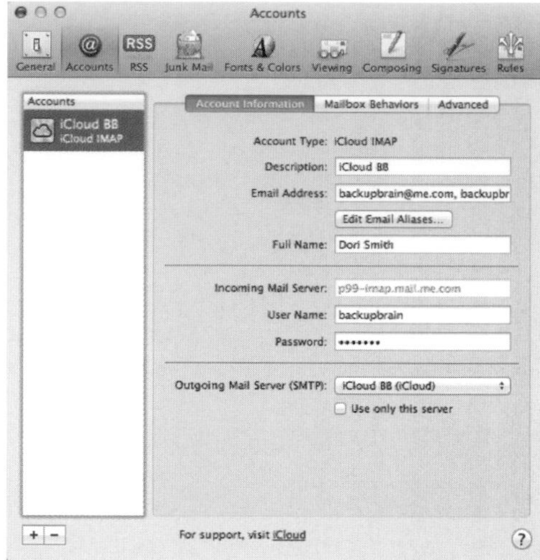

D If you already have an email address in Mail, you begin adding a new one in the Accounts pane of Mail's Preferences.

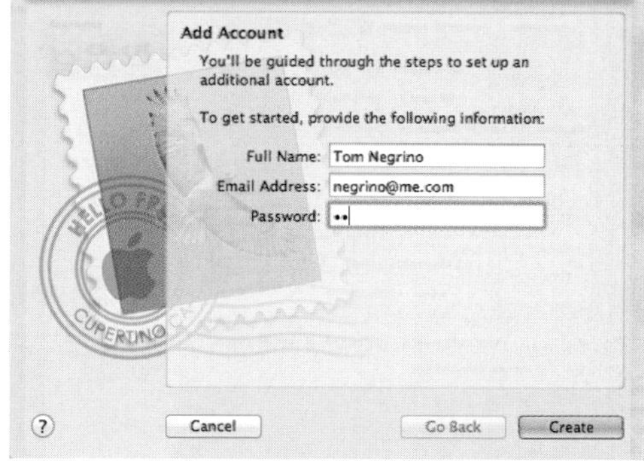

E Enter your name, email address, and password on the Add Account screen.

The Great App Alignment

Beginning with OS X 10.8 Mountain Lion, several apps were added or changed their names to make them the same as their equivalents on iOS. Sometimes, that meant changes (pretty much in name only) to long-standing Mac apps, and in other cases, Apple introduced entirely new apps, moving the functionality away from older apps. The idea is a good one: If you are working with the Notes app on your iPhone, it makes more sense (especially for users new to the Mac) to look for a companion Notes app on the Mac, certainly more sense than to look in Mail, which was the repository of Notes prior to Mountain Lion. I've listed the new app equivalents in **Table 2.1**.

In this book, I've decided to refer to all apps in their latest incarnations, which as I write this is iOS 6 and OS X 10.8 Mountain Lion. I've updated the book accordingly. If you are still using iOS 5 or OS X 10.7 Lion, I strongly recommend you upgrade; the new and improved features in the newer operating systems are well worth it.

TABLE 2.1 App Names and Equivalents

iOS App Name	10.7 Lion App Name	10.8 Mountain Lion App Name
Calendar	iCal (events)	Calendar
Contacts	Address Book	Contacts
Game Center	Did not exist	Game Center
Messages	iChat	Messages
Notes	Mail (part of Mail)	Notes
Reminders	iCal (reminders)	Reminders

Setting up Mail Accounts on Your iOS Device

On the Mac, you set up new email accounts in the Mail program, but that's not the case on iOS. Instead, you use the Settings app. You can have more than one mail account on your iOS device, and you can even have more than one iCloud account (if, for example, you have separate iCloud accounts for personal and school, or home and work). In this example, we'll focus on setting up an iCloud account, but the steps you take are much the same for any email provider.

To set up a mail account on an iOS device:

1. Tap Settings, then scroll down to Mail, Contacts, Calendars **A**, then tap that.

   The Mail, Contacts, Calendars screen appears **B**.
2. Tap Add Account.
3. On the resulting Add Account screen **C**, tap iCloud from the list of email providers.

   If you choose a different provider, you may have to enter a bit more information. For example, if you choose Gmail, you'll be asked for your name, email address, password, and a description of the account.

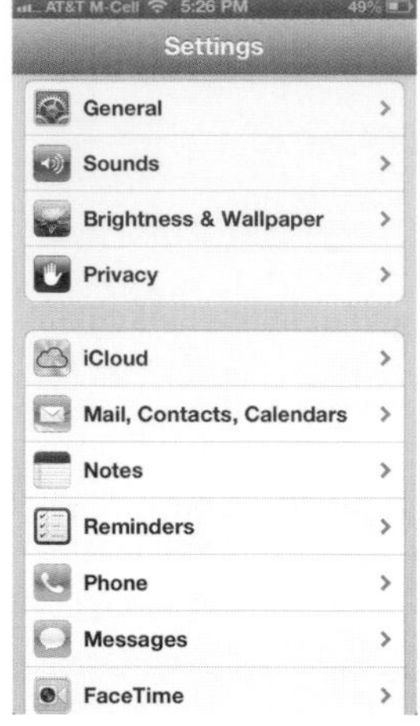

A Begin setting up a new email account in the Settings app.

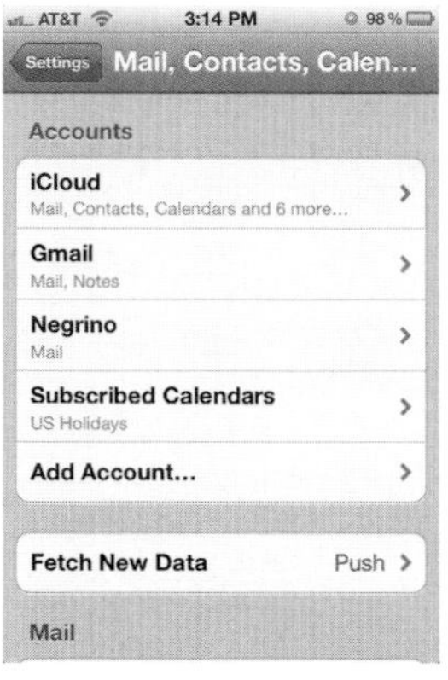

B Tap Add Account to start the new account process.

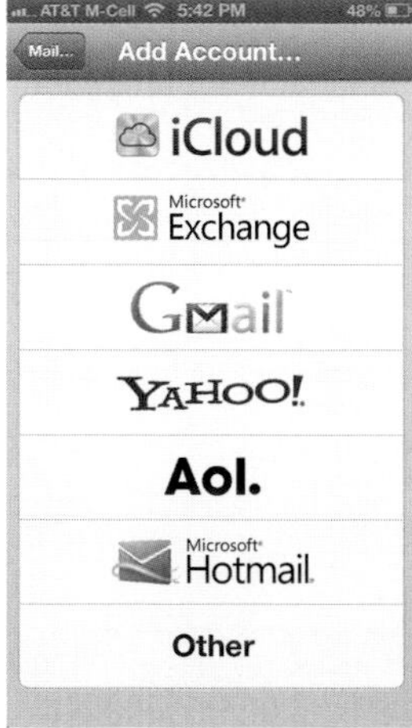

C In iOS, there are a variety of preset email providers. In this case, we want iCloud.

4. Enter your Apple ID and password, then tap the Next button **D**.

   On this screen, if you don't already have an Apple ID, you have the opportunity to get one by tapping the Get a Free Apple ID button at the bottom of the screen. That takes you through creating an Apple ID process.

5. The device verifies your Apple ID and password, then brings you to the iCloud settings screen **E**, which allows you to turn iCloud services on or off for your device. As you can see, most settings are turned on by default. Choose the settings you wish to enable on that particular device, then tap Save.

   The device will return to the Mail, Contacts, Calendars screen, showing the new account **F**. If you have more than one iCloud account, the second one will appear showing the email address associated with that account as the name of the account.

continues on next page

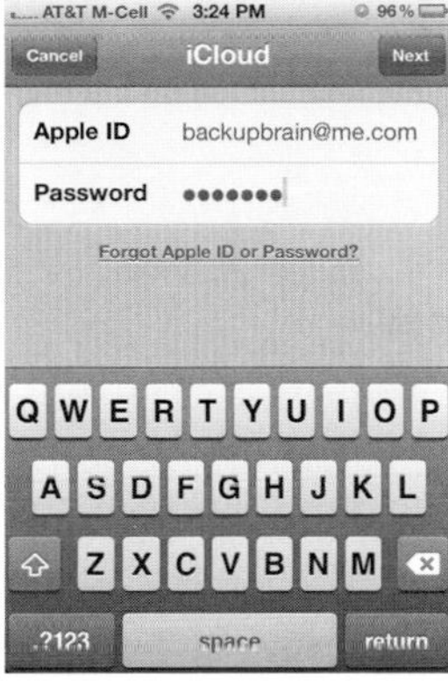

D Enter your Apple ID and password, then tap the Next button.

E Because we're setting up an iCloud account, you can choose which iCloud services to enable.

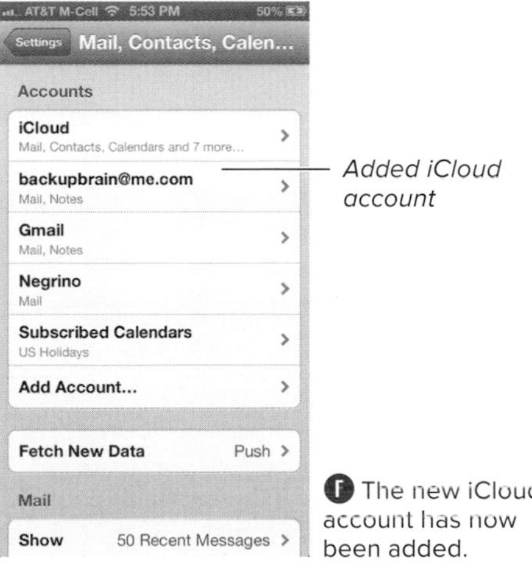

F The new iCloud account has now been added.

6. (Optional) If you want to rename the additional account to something other than the email address, tap the account name on the Mail, Contacts, Calendars screen, tap the Account field **G**, and in the resulting Account screen, change the Description **H**. Tap the Done button. When you are returned to the Mail, Contacts, Calendars screen, things may not appear to have initially changed, but leaving that screen and returning shows the change was made **I**.

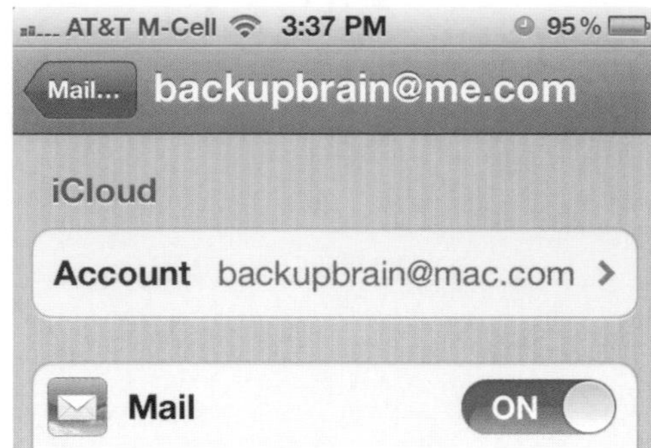

G Tapping the Account name allows you to change its description.

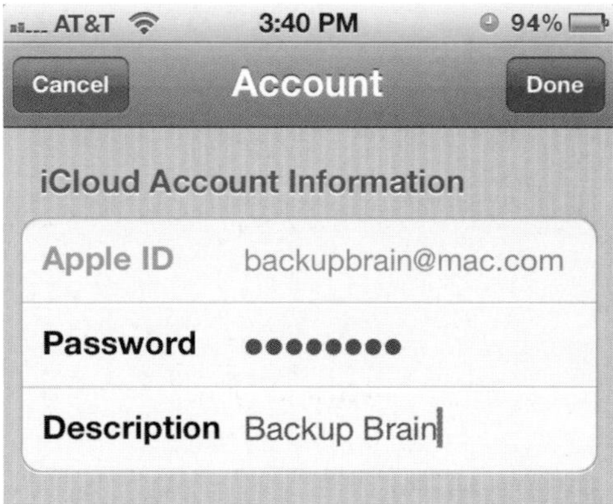

H Type the new description for the account.

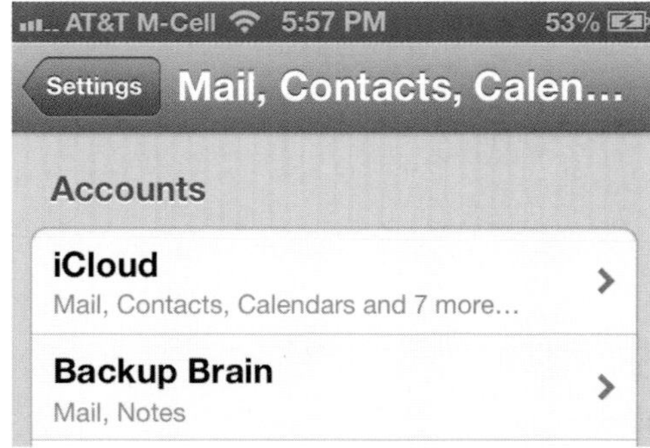

I Back in the Mail, Contacts, Calendars screen, the updated description appears.

Working with Mail on the iCloud Website

If you are familiar with Mail on the Mac, you'll immediately feel at home in the Mail application on the iCloud website. It's designed to resemble the desktop application fairly closely **A**.

Like the desktop application, you'll find a Mailboxes and Folders list; a message list; a message area; a search box; and a toolbar that allows you to create and work with messages. The Actions icon, which looks like a gear in the upper right corner of the window, allows you to customize the behavior of the web application and apply actions to individual messages.

If you're wondering about spam, I'm happy to report that Apple has generally got a pretty good set of spam filters. On my iCloud account (and before that on my MobileMe account) spam rarely gets through to my Inbox. And from a security standpoint, iCloud Mail uses the HTTPS protocol, which encrypts all traffic to and from the website; it's the same level of security used for online shopping.

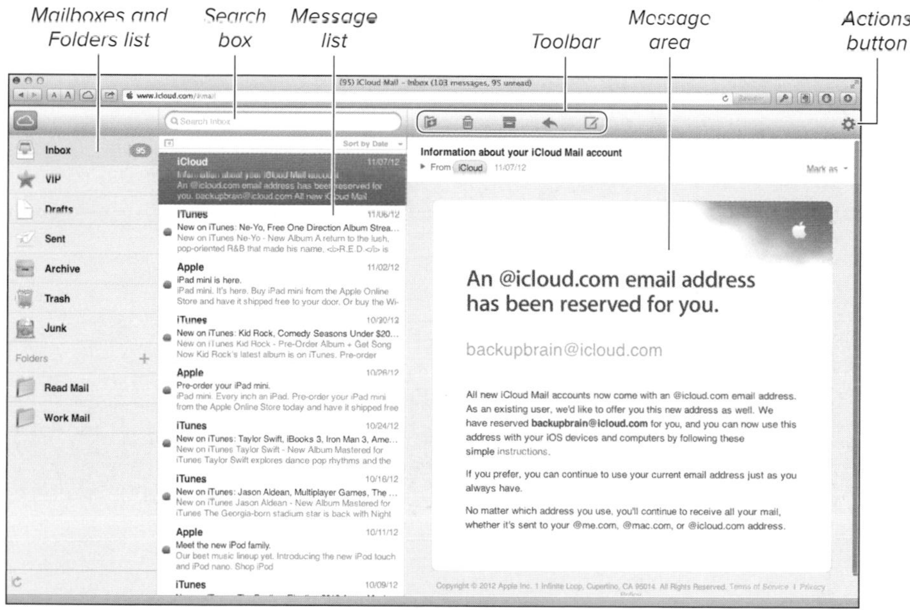

A Mail on the iCloud website looks a good bit like Mail on the Mac.

Using the Mail Application

Besides working with messages, mailboxes, and folders, Mail lets you customize it so that it works the way you want it to.

To resize or hide the Mailboxes and Folders list or message list:

To resize the width of the Mailboxes and Folders list, point to the bar between that list and the message list. The cursor will change to a double-headed arrow **B**. Click and drag to the right or left to resize.

or

To resize the width of the message area, point to the bar between the message list and the message area. The cursor will change to a double-headed arrow. Click and drag to the right or left to resize.

or

To hide the Mailboxes and Folders list altogether, click the Hide/Show mailboxes toggle button. Click it again to display the list again.

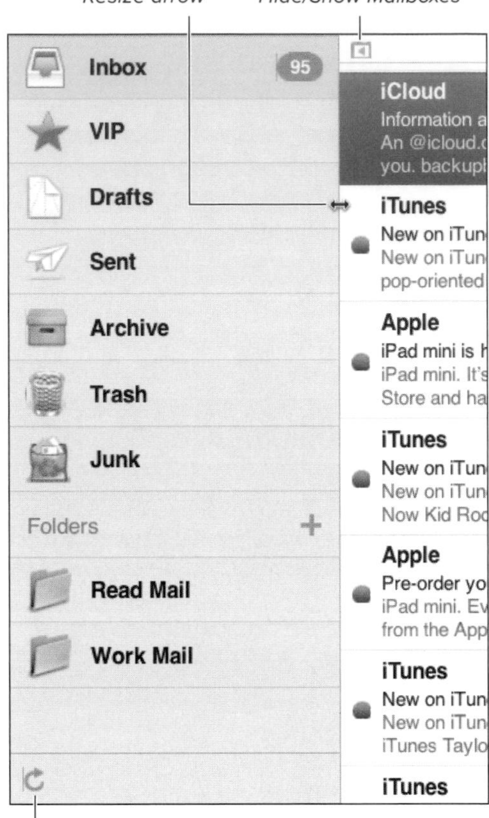

B Drag the double-headed arrow right or left to change the width of the Mailboxes and Folders list.

To view messages:

1. In the Mailboxes and Folders list, click the mailbox or folder whose contents you wish to view.

   The contents of the message list will change to display the contents of the selected mailbox or folder.

2. In the message list, click the message you wish to view to show its contents in the message area **C**.

   or

   In the message list, double-click the message you wish to view to open the message in a new window.

C Clicking a message in the message list shows its contents in the message area.

Working with Email

When working with email, you want to receive it, file it, write replies to emails you get, sort it so that you can see your message list in some comprehensible fashion, and search your email to find mail that matches a particular keyword. The iCloud Mail application handles all these needs with aplomb.

Many of these features use the toolbar at the top of the message list **D**. Let's take a closer look at the functions of each of the toolbar icons.

- **Move to Folder** takes a selected message and moves it to one of the other folders in the Mailboxes and Folders list.
- **Delete** moves the selected message to the Trash mailbox. Messages in the Trash are automatically deleted after 30 days. You can also immediately delete the contents of the Trash mailbox by clicking the Actions icon in the upper right corner of the window and choosing Empty Trash from the pop-up menu.
- **Archive** moves the selected message to the Archive mailbox. Each account you have has its own Archive mailbox. Use Archive when you want to move something out of the Inbox—to get it out of your way—but you still want to be able to easily search for that item.
- **Reply, Reply All, Forward** allows you to reply to an incoming message, reply to all addressees for that message, or forward that message to a new recipient.
- **Compose** allows you to create a new message.

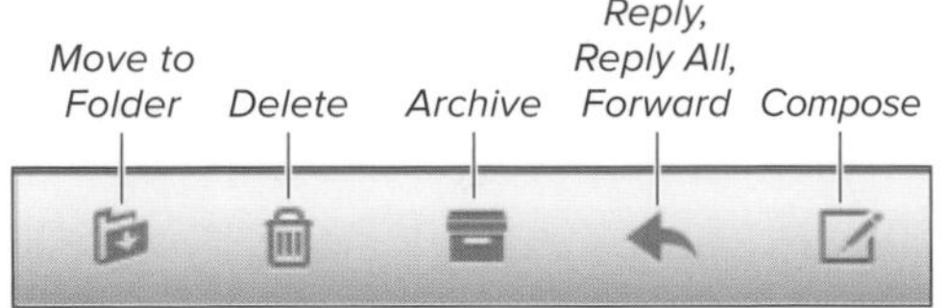

D You'll use the toolbar to do a lot of your work with email messages.

To get new messages:

When you first sign in, iCloud checks for new messages automatically, but if you're working in the application for a while and you want to recheck manually, click the refresh icon at the bottom of the Mailboxes and Folders list B. You can tell a message is unread because it has a blue dot next to it.

To compose new mail:

1. In the toolbar, click the Compose button.

   A new message window opens E.

2. Begin typing the recipient's name in the To field. If the recipient is in your Contact list, a pop-up menu with matching addresses will appear. Choose the recipient you want from the pop-up menu, then press the Return key.
3. (Optional) To add additional recipients to the To field, click the blue plus in a circle icon at the right edge of the To field, then choose additional recipients.
4. (Optional) To add CC recipients, add them to the CC field.
5. Enter the email subject in the Subject field.
6. Type the message body.
7. (Optional) You can use the Style toolbar to style text in your message by changing the font, font size, font color, adding bold, italic, or underlined text, changing the justification, adding a bulleted or numbered list, changing the text indent, adding hyperlinks, or adding file attachments.

   By default, iCloud mail is HTML mail, which supports this sort of text styling.

8. When you are done composing your message, click the Send button.

TIP If you click the Save button at the right edge of the Style toolbar, it saves the message as a draft, and files a copy of the message in the Drafts mailbox. You can then close the message window without sending the message and return to it later to finish it up.

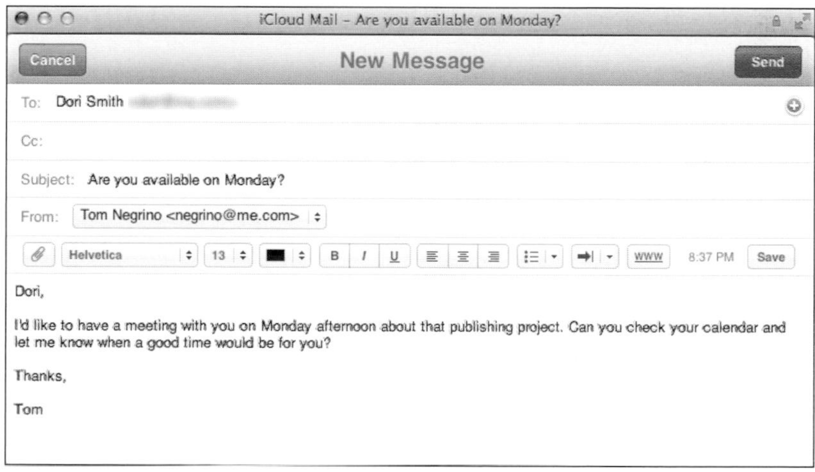

E You'll compose new messages in the New Message window.

To reply to or forward mail:

1. Click to select a message in the message list.
2. In the toolbar, click the Reply, Reply All, Forward button.

   A pop-up menu appears with the various choices **F**.
3. Pick the choice you want from the pop-up menu, and a new message window appears, by default with the contents of the message you're replying to already in the message body as a quotation.
4. (Optional) If you are forwarding the message, enter the new recipient in the To field.
5. Enter your reply, or a message you want to add if you are forwarding the original mail, then click the Send button.

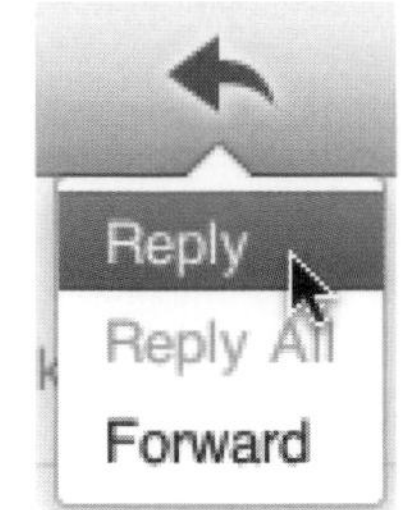

F The pop-up menu in the toolbar gives you your choices of Reply, Reply All, or Forward.

G When you click the plus button, the new folder appears, ready to be named.

To file mail:

1. In the message list, click to select the message you want to file.
2. Do one of the following:
   - Click the Move to Folder button in the toolbar, then choose one of the folders from the resulting pop-up menu.
   - Drag the message from the message list to one of the folders in the Mailboxes and Folders list.
   - Click the Archive button in the toolbar to move the selected message to the Archive mailbox.

TIP You can move multiple contiguous messages in the message list by clicking the first message, holding down the Shift key, then clicking the last message. All messages in between will be selected. Then you can drag them or use one of the toolbar buttons to move them as a group. If you want to move noncontiguous messages in the message list, hold down the Command key and click the messages you wish to move before dragging or using the toolbar buttons.

To add a new folder:

1. At the top of the Folders section of the Mailboxes and Folders list, click the plus button.

   A new folder will appear in the Folder list, ready to be named G.
2. Type the name of the new folder, then click anywhere else in the window.

TIP You can drag one folder into another to make it a subfolder. To move a folder out of another folder, drag it to the Folders header in the list.

TIP If you change your mind about creating the new folder, click the red Delete icon (the line in a circle) next to the new folder name.

To delete a folder:

1. Click to select the folder in the Mailboxes and Folders list.
2. Click the Actions button at the upper right corner of the window, then from the resulting pop-up menu, choose Delete Folder.

   or

   Double-click the folder, then click the red Delete icon next to the folder.

   iCloud will ask you if you're sure you want to delete the folder and its contents.
3. Click Delete.

TIP Remember that because your iCloud email account is synchronized across all your devices, folders that you create or delete on the website will also appear or disappear on the rest of your devices.

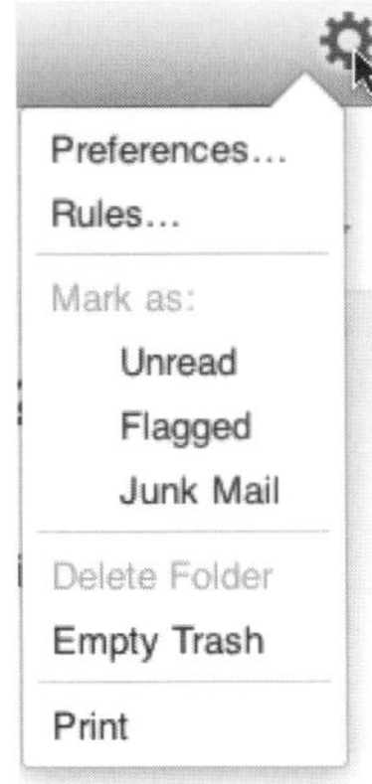

H You mark messages from the Actions pop-up menu.

To mark messages:

1. Click to select one or more messages from the message list.
2. Click the Actions button in the upper right corner of the window.
3. From the resulting pop-up menu H, choose Unread, Flagged, or Junk Mail in the Mark as section.

   Choosing Unread returns a message's state to unread if you've already looked at it. Choosing Flagged adds a flag icon to the message, which you can later use for sorting purposes. And choosing Junk Mail moves the message to the Junk folder.

TIP If you've accidentally moved mail to the Junk mailbox, you can click a message in the message list for that mailbox and the menu choice in the Actions pop-up menu will change to Not Junk Mail. Choosing that moves the message back to your Inbox.

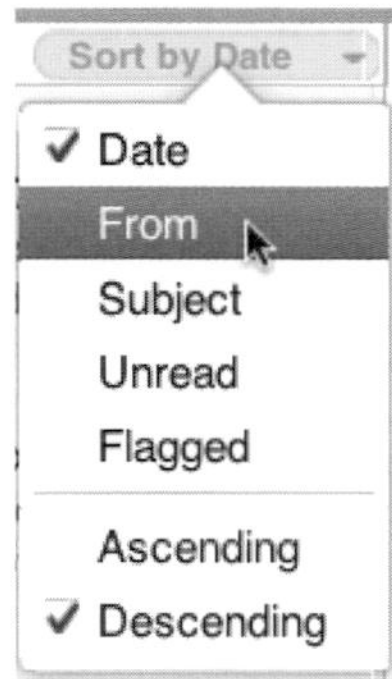

I Choose your Sort by criteria.

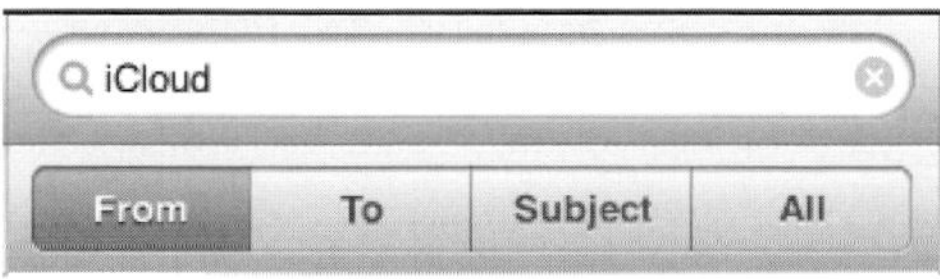

J When you click in the Search box, you have the option of narrowing your search by one of four criteria.

To sort messages:

At the top of the message list, click the Sort by button. From the resulting pop-up menu I, choose how you want to sort the contents of the message list. Your choices are by Date, From, Subject, Unread, or Flagged. You can also choose Ascending or Descending order.

The message display in the Message list changes according to the sort order you picked.

To search for messages:

1. In the Mailboxes and Folders list, click the mailbox or folder that you wish to search.

   Unfortunately, you can't search your entire mail system at once.

2. Click in the Search box, and enter your search term.
3. (Optional) When you click in the Search box, an additional toolbar appears allowing you to narrow your search to the From, To, Subject, or All fields in the messages J. Click one of these toolbar buttons to narrow your search.
4. Press the Return key.

   iCloud displays the matching messages in the message list.

TIP Although you can't search all of your Mailboxes and Folders simultaneously, iCloud does allow you to search in the contents of the messages.

To add contacts from incoming mail:

1. In a message list, click to select the message with a contact you wish to add to your iCloud Contacts list.
2. In the message, click the sender's email address, and then click Save in the resulting popover **K**.
3. (Optional) If you want to mark the contact as a VIP (which makes all messages from them appear in the special VIP mailbox), click the VIP checkbox in the popover.

To print a message:

1. Click to select a message from the message list.
2. From the Actions pop-up menu, choose Print.

   The message will open in a new window and the Print dialog for the system you're working on will appear. Choose the printing options, then click Print.

Working with Mail Preferences

The Actions menu has a Preferences choice, which leads you to a window with five tabs: General, Accounts, Composing, Rules, and Vacation **L**. In the sections below, we'll go through each of these Preferences tabs.

To set General preferences:

1. Click the Actions button, then choose Preferences.
2. Click the General tab to show the general preferences **M**.

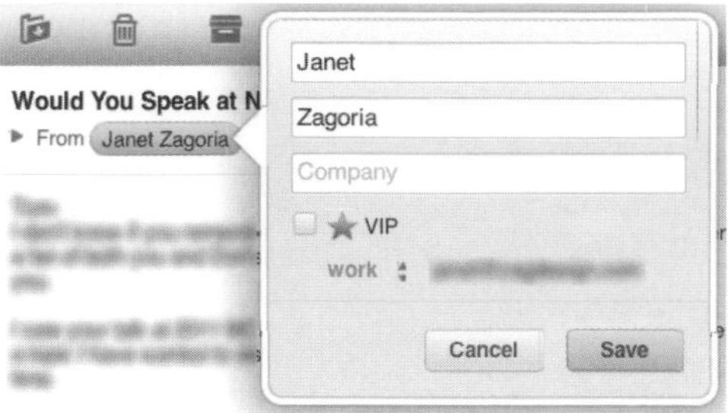

K Click an email address in an incoming message to add that person to your iCloud Contacts list.

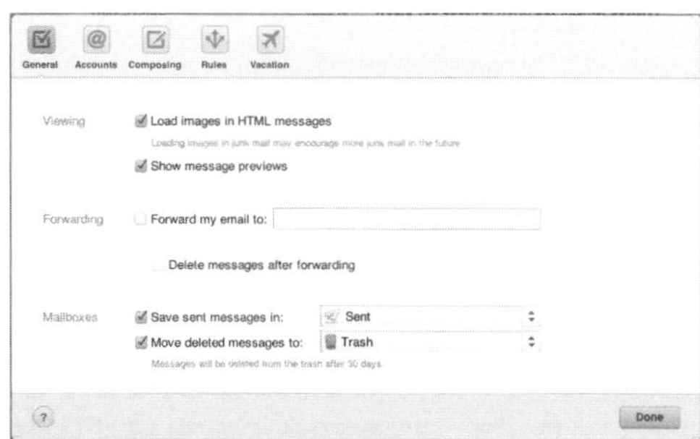

L The iCloud Mail application has many useful preferences.

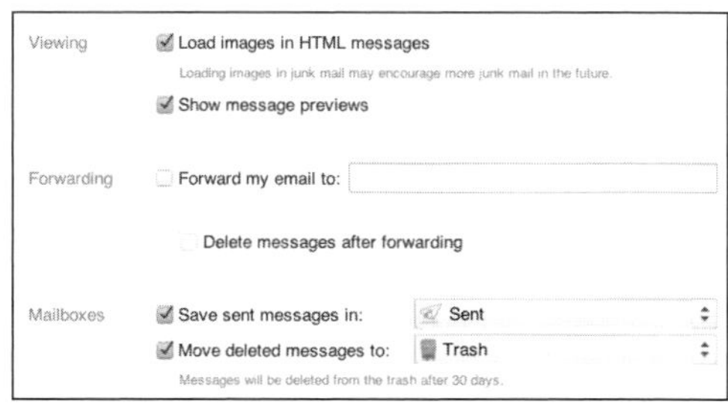

M Choose the preferences you want from the General tab.

3. Choose one or more of the following:
   - **Load images in HTML messages** shows you all images in messages. If this is unchecked, you won't see images in HTML mail unless you click a Load Images button in the message.
   - **Show message previews** tells the iCloud mail application to show the first couple of lines of each message in the message list. This is one of the default choices, and I find it extremely useful.
   - **Forward my email to** allows you to send all of your incoming email to another address. If you have an assistant who also monitors your mail, you might want to use this option. You'll need to select the checkbox and enter the forwarding email address.
   - **Delete messages after forwarding** erases your incoming messages after they have been forwarded to the alternate email address.
   - **Save sent messages in** allows you to pick the folder where sent messages are automatically filed from the pop-up menu. This is off by default, which makes no sense to me. Why wouldn't you want copies of message that you send? The only reason I can think of is that outgoing messages count against your iCloud storage quota.
   - **Move deleted messages to** allows you to choose the folder where deleted messages are sent, usually the Trash folder. A message moved to the Trash is automatically and permanently deleted after 30 days.

To set Accounts preferences:

1. Click the Actions button, then choose Preferences.
2. Click the Accounts tab **N**.
3. Click the **Add an alias** link to add an email alias (iCloud allows you to have up to three aliases), which is a secondary `icloud.com` address that points to your main `icloud.com` address. Email sent to one of the aliases is delivered to your main account. Here's how it might work in practice: my main iCloud account address is `negrino@me.com` (because my main account happens to be a legacy `me.com` address). But I might also create an alias of `tomnegrino`, which would work for both `tomnegrino@icloud.com` and my legacy `tomnegrino@me.com`.
4. In the Alias field, add the alias you want to you (you don't need to enter the `icloud.com` part).
5. Click OK. The site checks to see if the alias is already in use; if it is, the alias you asked for will be rejected, and you'll be prompted for a new one.
6. Click Done.

   The new alias appears in the Accounts Preferences pane.

TIP **You can use an alias as the From address in outgoing mail, if you want to keep a particular email address private. Replies will go to the alias.**

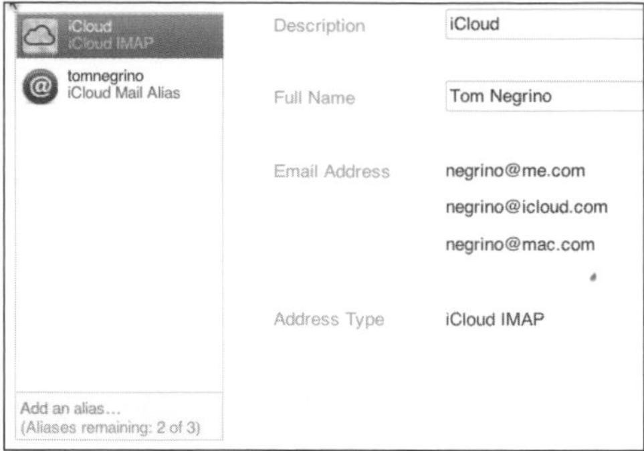

N You can add new email addresses in the Accounts tab.

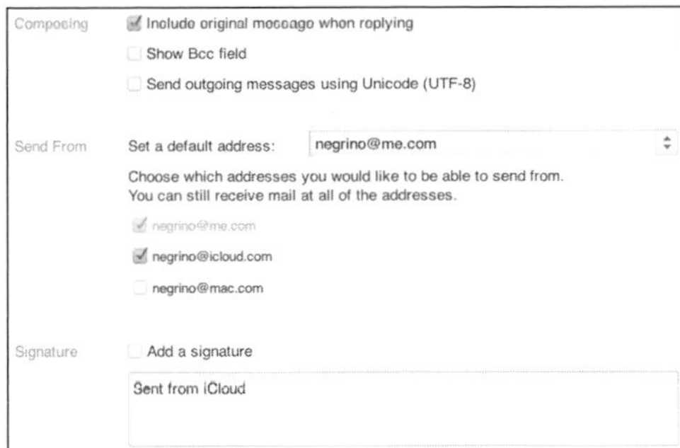

O You can fine-tune the way you send email in the Composing section of Preferences.

To set Composing preferences:

1. Click the Actions button, then choose Preferences.
2. Click the Composing tab **O**.
3. Choose one or more of the following:
   - **Include original message when replying** includes the entire message that you're replying to as a quote. I usually prefer to edit the quote down to just the essentials, because I think that it makes email conversations easier to read.
   - **Show Bcc field** makes the blind carbon copy field always appear in the Add Message window.
   - **Send outgoing messages using Unicode (UTF-8)** tells Mail to allow your messages to contain non-Latin characters, such as Hebrew, Arabic, or Chinese.
   - **Send new messages from** sets Mail to automatically use the email address or email alias you choose from the pop-up menu for new messages. The checkboxes below this choice allow you to choose the addresses you can send from.
   - **Add a signature** to your outbound mail allows you to append a message to the end of every mail that you create. For example, you might want to include your contact information.

TIP Signatures that you set up on the iCloud website don't synchronize with email signatures from Mail on the Mac or on your iOS devices, and vice versa.

To set Rules:

1. Click the Actions button, then choose Preferences.
2. Click the Rules tab **P**.

   Mail rules run on the server and can automatically run actions on incoming messages. You set some criteria, and then an action to automatically occur when that criterion is met. Let's say that I have a mail folder called Family. I can set up a rule so that all incoming email from my wife automatically gets routed to the Family folder.
3. Click the **Add a Rule** button.
4. In the resulting popover, set the If criterion and the Then action to be taken **Q**. You don't have a lot of choices here; in the If section, you can trigger an action on the From, To, CC, or Subject fields. In the Then section, your choices are Move to Folder, Move to Trash, or Forward to a different email address.
5. Click Done.

   The rule that you created appears in the Rules tab of Preferences.

TIP The Rules ability of the iCloud website is fairly rudimentary; although you can set up multiple rules, you can't set up multiple criteria or actions for a single rule, which makes it much less powerful than the Rules ability in Apple Mail, Gmail, and other systems.

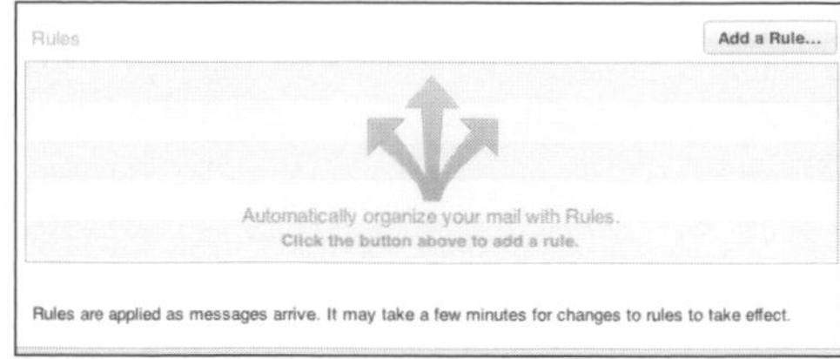

P iCloud doesn't start with any Rules. You must add them.

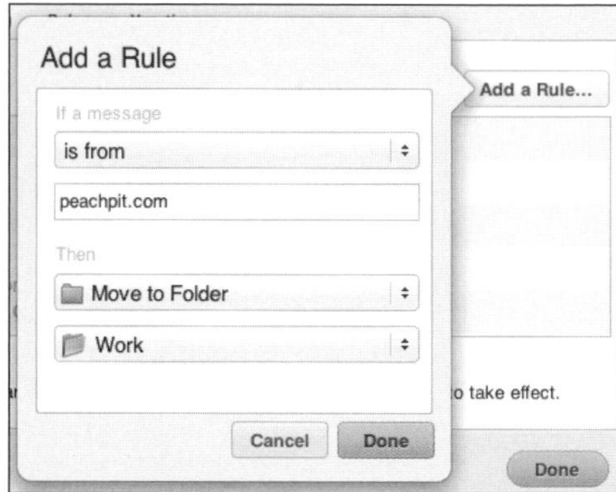

Q Choose the criteria you want for your Rule in the popover.

To set Vacation preferences:

1. Click the Actions button, then choose Preferences.
2. Click the Vacation tab **R**.
3. If you want to send out a vacation message, select the **Automatically reply to messages when they are received** checkbox.
4. Enter a vacation message in the text field, then click Done.

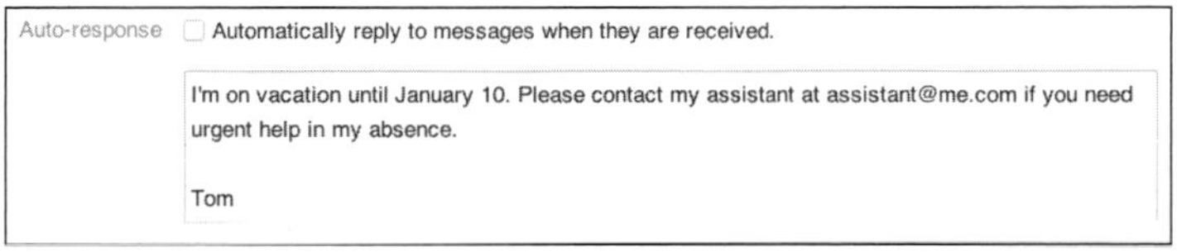

Auto-response ☐ Automatically reply to messages when they are received.

I'm on vacation until January 10. Please contact my assistant at assistant@me.com if you need urgent help in my absence.

Tom

R Enter your Vacation message.

Working with Notes

Notes on an iOS device (in the Notes app) or in the Notes app on the Mac are like a notepad in the real world. You can use them for reminders, general notes, pretty much whatever you want in terms of small snippets of text. Notes that you create or edit on one iOS device will, if you have it set up, automatically synchronize to your other iOS devices, and to Notes on the Mac.

On the Mac, synchronized iCloud notes appear in the Notes app **A**. You can create folders for Notes, and those folders also appear in the Accounts screen of the iOS Notes app **B**.

On an iOS device, you create Notes by typing in the Notes app, or if you're using a Siri-enabled device, you can dictate notes to Siri, and they will appear in the Notes app. On your mobile device, you need to first set the default account destination for your notes.

On the iCloud website, you can view, edit and create new Notes.

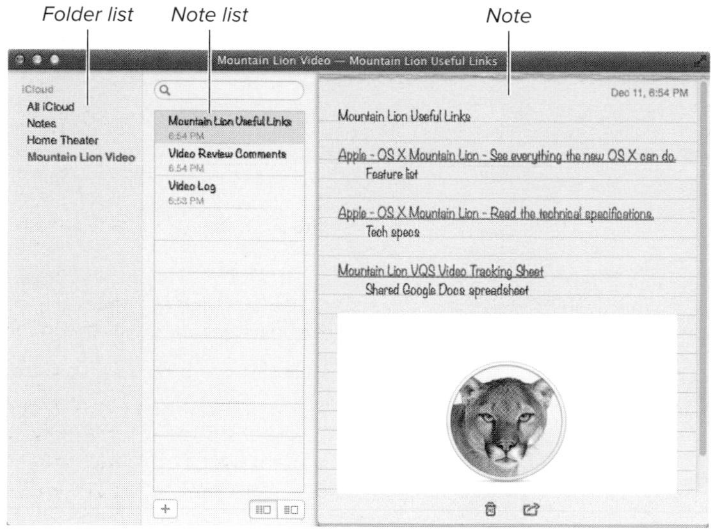

A Notes synchronized from iCloud have their own app on the Mac.

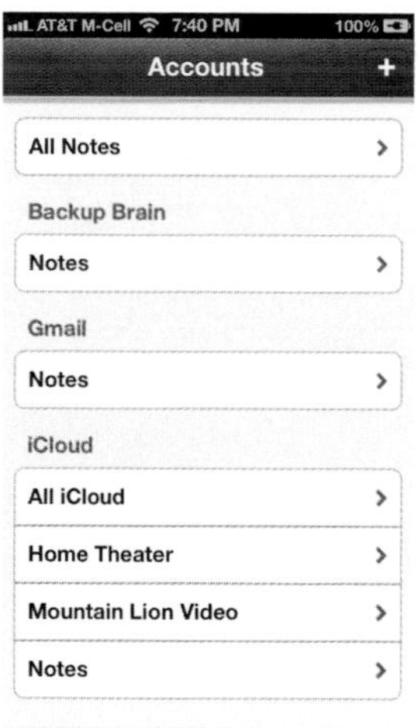

B The Accounts screen of Notes on iOS gives you access to the contents of folders you see on the Mac.

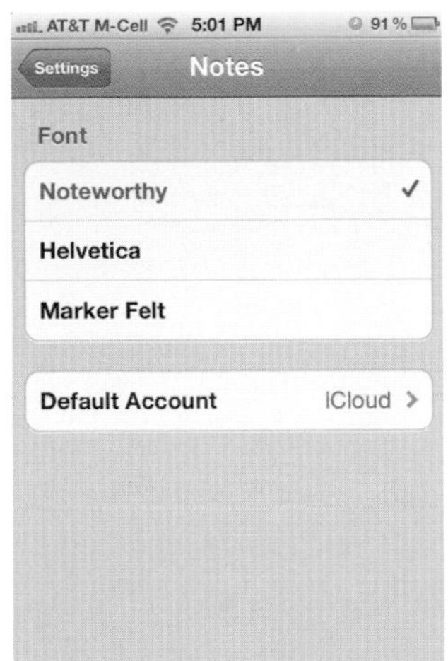

C Choose the font and default account you want to use in the Notes app on your iOS device.

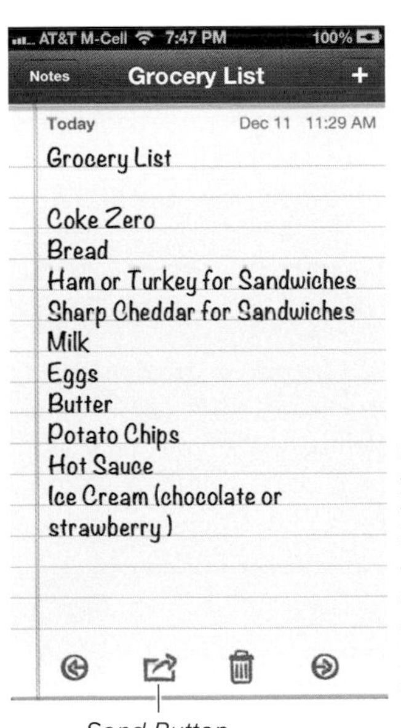

D A note that you enter on your iOS device will synchronize to the iCloud website, to your other iOS devices, and to your Macs.

To configure Notes on an iOS device:

1. Tap Settings > Notes.
2. On the Notes settings screen **C**, choose the font you want to use for your notes, then tap Default Account.

   The screen changes to show the different accounts that can accept Notes.
3. Tap the account you want to use as your default Notes account. A checkmark will appear next to that account name.
4. Press the iOS device's Home button to save your choice.

To create Notes on an iOS device:

1. Tap Notes.
2. Tap the plus button at the upper right of the screen.

   A new Note form appears. Type the note **D**.

TIP **To delete the note, tap the Trash icon at the bottom of the note.**

TIP **To get to different notes folders, tap Accounts at the top of the screen, then choose the folder you want, as seen in B.**

TIP **You can also email or print a note by tapping the Send icon at the bottom of the note. In order to print, you must have an AirPrint-capable printer available. AirPrint allows an iOS device to print wirelessly over Wi-Fi.**

continues on next page

TIP **Though AirPrint is normally a hardware feature in a printer, some clever software, Ecamm Network's (`www.ecamm.com`) $20 Printopia 2, installs as a preference pane on a Mac E and then allows any printer your Mac can use to be accessed by AirPrint on your iOS devices. This doesn't just work with Notes; it works with any app on your iOS device that can print, such as Pages or Keynote. You can also use Printopia to "print" a PDF to your Mac, Dropbox's Dropbox, or Evernote's Evernote (if you subscribe to those services).**

E You can use Printopia to AirPrint-enable any printer on your local network.

A Notable Alternative

When it comes to taking notes, the best that can be said for Apple's Notes app, on either Mac or iOS, is that it is serviceable. But that doesn't mean that it's *good;* its limitations far outweigh its benefits. Sure, it syncs via iCloud. But it's only good for text notes (you can add images to notes in the Mac app, but they don't transfer across to the note when viewed in iOS), with only three fonts, one size, and no styles, not even bold or italic. Plus, you have to put up with that ridiculous (for a computer) lined yellow pad look. Once you get past the simplest kind of notes, you're going to be looking for a better note-taking app.

There are many other note-taking apps for iOS (the App Store is thick with them in the Productivity section), and many of them synchronize to your Mac via Dropbox (**`www.dropbox.com`**), a cross-platform, automatically synchronized storage solution. The note-taking app I use is the hugely popular Evernote (**`www.evernote.com`**), which stores notes in plain text, styled text, images, many different file types including PDF, and even voice memos. Evernote is free (with a paid Premium tier providing extra features), available on Mac, Windows, as a Web app, and has native iOS and Android apps F. Evernote automatically uploads everything you put into it to the company's servers, making it available for syncing to all your devices.

You can collect similar notes in a notebook, creating as many notebooks as you need, or throw everything in one main notebook. You can add tags to notes to help categorize them further, and when you search for a tag, it finds notes with that tag in all notebooks. If your new item is a picture with words in it (say, something you snapped with your iPhone), Evernote will run optical character recognition on its servers to make the picture's text searchable (even if the text is handwriting); the text then gets synced down to your Evernote clients with the rest of the note.

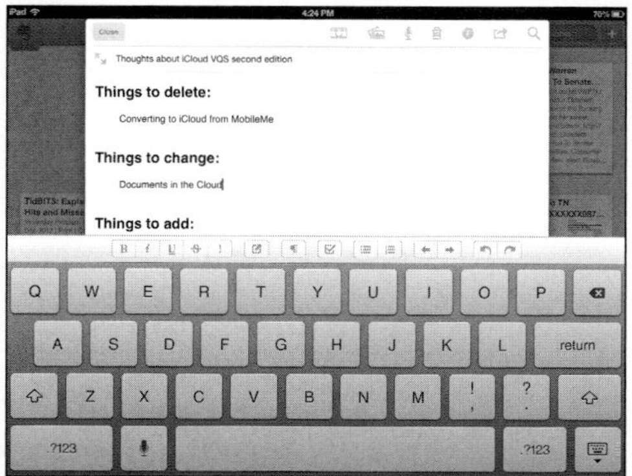

F This note in Evernote on my iPad will automatically be synchronized to my desktop and notebook computers, and to my other mobile devices.

To work with Notes on the Mac:

1. In the Notes app (which you'll find in your Applications folder), click the folder that contains the note, then select the note in the note list.

   The contents of the note appear in the note area **G**.

continues on next page

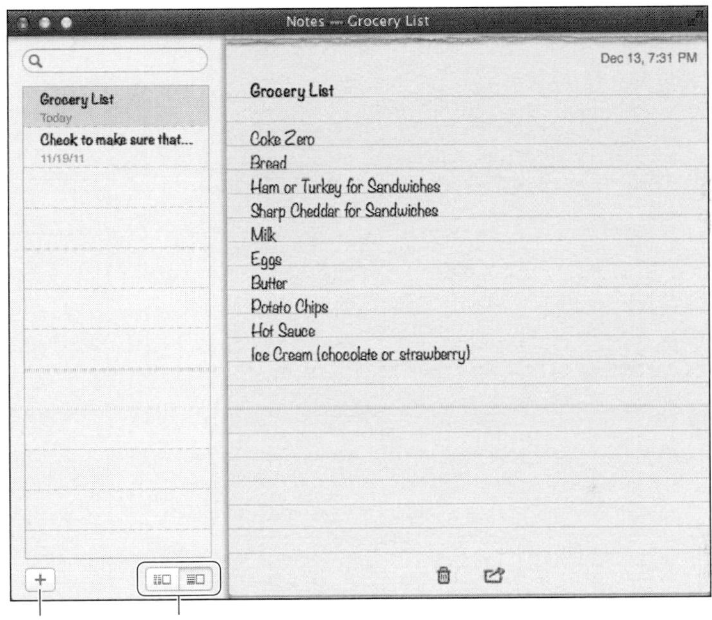

G On the Mac, an iOS Note appears much the same as it does on the mobile device. I've hidden the folder list in this shot.

2. You can edit the note in the note area, or you can double-click an existing note in the message list to open it in a new window for editing **H**.

or

To create a new note, choose File> New Note, or click the New note button at the bottom of the window.

or

To delete a note, select it in the message list and then press the Delete key or choose Edit > Delete. You can also click the Trash icon at the bottom of the note.

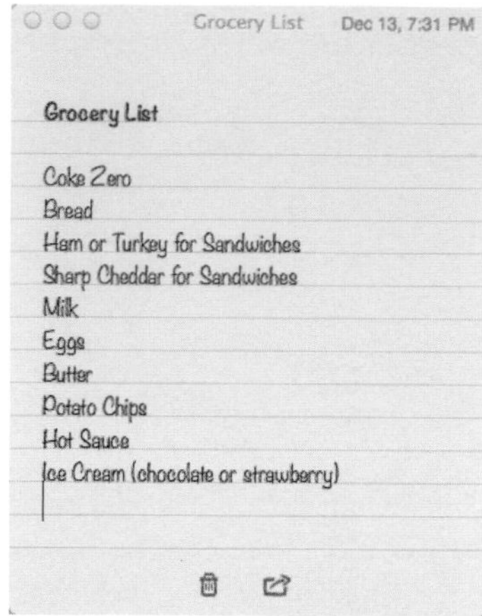

H If you want to edit the Note, you can do so in the Notes window, or open it in a new window.

I Log on to the iCloud website to view and edit your Notes online.

To work with Notes on the iCloud website:

1. Log in to the iCloud website **I**.
2. If necessary, from the homepage, click the Notes icon. If you are in another application, click the iCloud icon in the upper left corner of the window, then click the Notes icon.
3. Click the note you wish to view.

   On the iCloud website, you can view, create, and Notes in almost the same way as you do with the Mac, or in ways that are self-evident. **J**

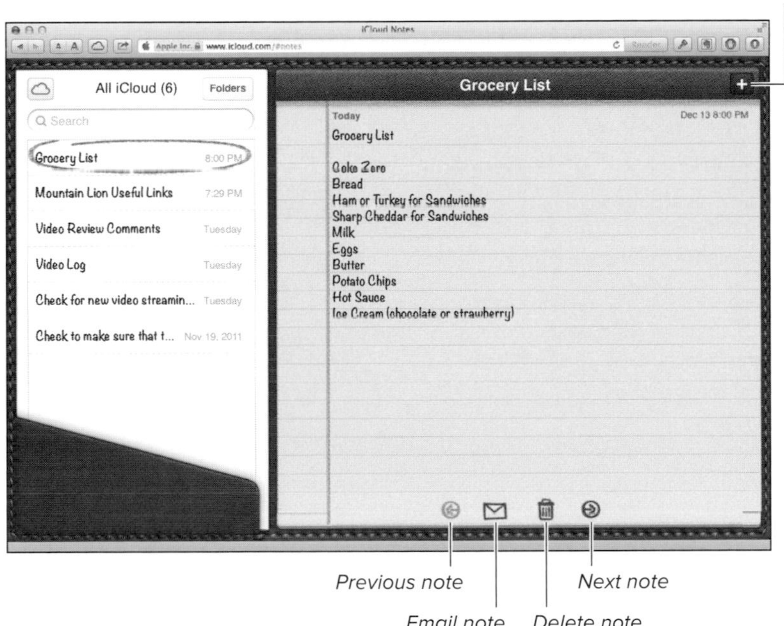

J To work with Notes on the iCloud website you work with them in much the same way as on the Mac.

Sending iMessages

SMS text messaging has been around for a long time, and for just as long, the cellular carriers have been making money hand over fist on the feature. It's widely reported that text messaging costs carriers virtually nothing, since the texts are sent over control channels used for network maintenance. At best, carrier costs have been estimated as 1/1000th of a cent per text message. But they cost *you* a *lot:* in October 2011, *Macworld* magazine compared unlimited text messaging plans for the U.S. carriers (AT&T, Verizon, and Sprint) and found that carriers were charging $20 for unlimited text messaging, or you can pay-as-you-go for $.20 per text message. Anyway you look at it, that's not a good deal. If you look at MMS (text messages that include pictures or video), the pay-as-you-go rate is $.25 or $.30, depending on the carrier. It's safe to say that there is an obscene amount of profit in the text messaging business.

iCloud and iOS 5 or later include a free service called iMessage that allow you to send unlimited messages between you and anyone else who is also using a device with a compatible version of iOS (an iPhone, iPad, iPad mini, or iPod touch) and an iCloud account. You can send photos, videos, locations, and contacts, as well as texts. If you have more than one iOS device, you can start a conversation on one device and continue it on another.

With iMessage, you can send a message to more than one person at a time, and if you do, a reply from one person is seen by everyone on the list. Unlike regular text messages, when your message appears on the recipient's iOS device, you get a delivery confirmation, and you can tell with a text balloon when the other person is typing a reply.

Of course, if you are signed up for a text plan with your carrier, you can still send text messages over the cellular network. From your standpoint, there's almost no difference between the two (except for cost, convenience, and better performance), because both standard texting and iMessage are integrated into the iOS Messages app. On the Mac, beginning with OS X Mountain Lion, iMessages are built into the Messages app, which replaces iChat.

A You can tell you're in an iMessage conversation because it says iMessage in the text field, and because of the text balloons with the blue background.

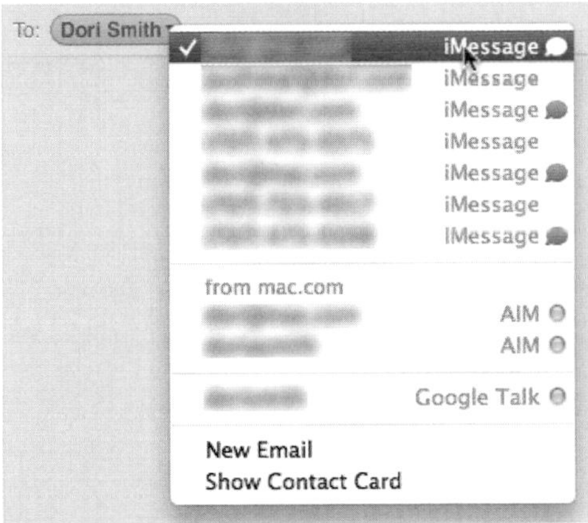

B Many recipients will have multiple possible destination addresses for their iMessage; pick the one you want from the Messages list.

To send an iMessage on an iOS device:

1. On an iOS device, tap Messages.
2. In the Messages app, either choose a previous recipient, or tap the New Message button in the upper right-hand corner of the screen.
3. (Optional) If you're sending to a new recipient, enter their name in the To field.
4. If your recipient is eligible for an iMessage, the text entry field will faintly show iMessage **A**.
5. Enter your iMessage, then tap the Send button.

To send an iMessage on a Mac:

1. Launch the Messages app.
2. Double-click the recipient in the Buddies list.
3. In the Messages window, click the down arrow on the recipient's name to display their different addresses and messaging services, then choose the iMessage address you want to send to (usually their main iCloud address) **B**.

   Addresses that have been registered with the iMessage service will have the blue message balloon next to them. It's likely that people will show multiple iMessage destinations, because you can use the person's Apple ID, their iPhone telephone number, or any other email address they have set up in the Accounts preferences pane of the Messages app on the Mac. Addresses on other services will show their green (available), yellow (idle), or red (away) status lights next to them.

continues on next page

When you choose an active iMessage address, iMessage will appear in the text field at the bottom of the Messages window.

4. Enter your iMessage in the text field, then press the Return key.

TIP You can tell the difference between an iMessage and regular text messaging in the iOS Messages app easily, because your outgoing text balloons will have a blue background for people who can accept iMessages. For people with whom you are doing regular text messaging, your outgoing text balloon will have a green background. (The color of U.S. money, Apple? Real subtle.)

TIP Besides the delivery confirmation you get when the recipient gets your iMessage, you can also get a receipt when they actually *read* the message. This seems just a bit creepy, until you think about it; it can be nice to know that not only did you send that text to your spouse about picking up some milk on the way home but that the message isn't just waiting forlornly in their pocket or purse. To turn on this receipt feature, choose Settings > Messages, then turn on Send Read Receipts.

TIP iMessage is tied not just to mobile phone numbers, as regular SMS messages are; it's also attached to email addresses. So any email address that iCloud knows about can receive an iMessage. That's how you can use iMessage with the iPad or iPod touch, which don't have mobile phone numbers. In the Receive At section of Settings > Messages, you can specify what email addresses can be used for iMessages. These addresses don't have to be the ones associated with your Apple ID; if you want, you can use any valid email address, not just a `.icloud`, `.me` or `.mac` address.

3

Working with Contacts

The people and companies that you deal with are stored in the Contacts app on your Mac, in iOS, and in iCloud. Using iCloud, changes that you make on any of your devices get synchronized immediately to the rest of your devices. So, for example, if you change a contact's address, phone number, email address, or other information in Contacts on your Mac, those changes will be pushed automatically and effortlessly to your mobile devices, and to any other Macs that share your iCloud account. The reverse is also true; changes made on a mobile device are synchronized back to your Macs over the air, whether it be via Wi-Fi or the cellular network.

In addition to the changes you can make to contacts on your Macs and mobile devices, you can also manage contacts using the Contacts application on the iCloud website. In this chapter, we'll focus mainly on using the website for contact management.

In This Chapter

Searching, Adding, and Editing Contacts in iCloud 50

Working with Contact Groups 54

Using the Action Menu 56

Setting iCloud Contact Preferences 57

Searching, Adding, and Editing Contacts in iCloud

To begin working with your contacts, go to the iCloud website **A**, sign in if necessary, and click the Contacts application **B**, which closely resembles the Contacts application on the Mac.

You can view any contact by scrolling through the All Contacts list, or by clicking one of the letter tabs at the left side of the window to jump you to that part of the alphabet (when you focus the list like this, the letter tabs disappear). Clicking to select a contact in the list gives you that contact's details on the right side of the window.

Besides simply finding things manually, you can also search your Contacts, add new ones, and edit existing contacts through the website application.

A Choose the Contacts application from the iCloud website.

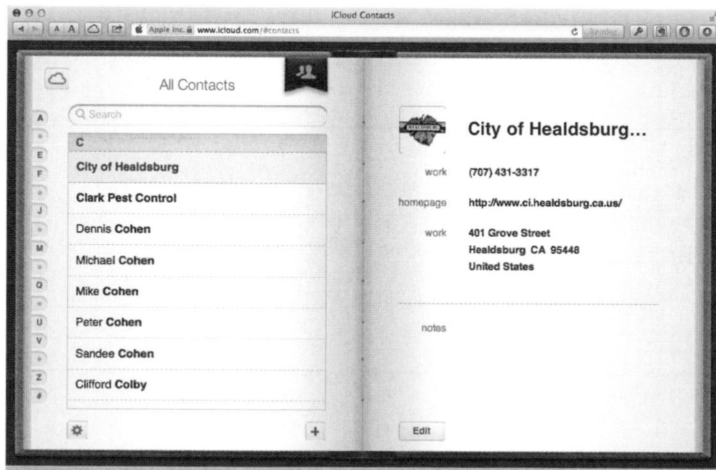

B The iCloud Contacts web application closely resembles the Mac Contacts application.

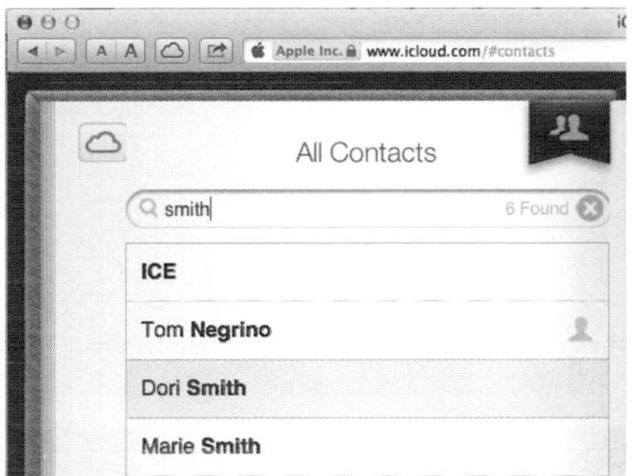

C Typing in the Search field immediately narrows the list of found contacts.

To search contacts:

In the Search field at the upper left part of the Contacts application, type all or part of any item in the contact's information. The Contacts List immediately shrinks to show the search results **C**. To clear the Search field, click the round button with an X in it.

The search term will be highlighted in each found contact's entry.

TIP Note that iCloud searches through all of the information in your Contacts data, not just names. So you can do useful things like search for all of the people with Gmail addresses, or search through your contact's Notes field. In C, my name appears because Dori Smith is listed in my contact card as my spouse.

TIP Some of the information in the contact record is clickable. To send the contact an email message, click an email address. Similarly, URLs are clickable, opening a new browser window. To display a map of the contact's address, click a real-world address, which opens another window showing you the address in Google Maps D.

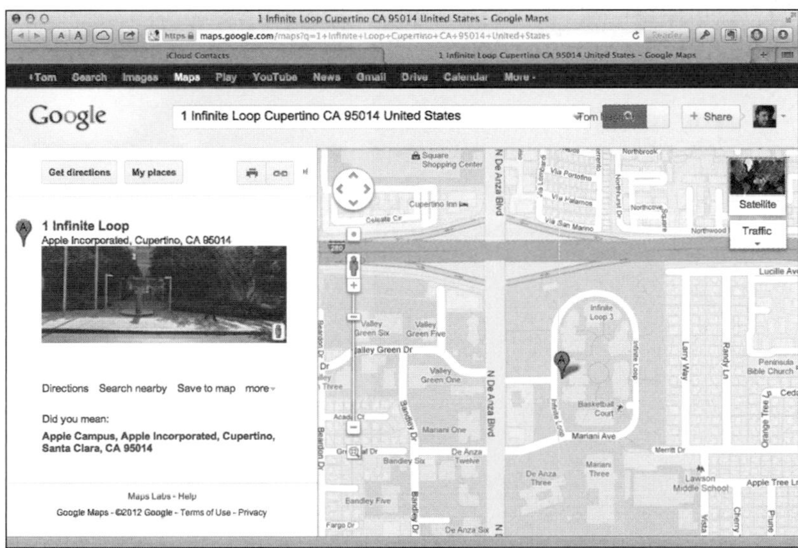

D Clicking a physical address in the Contacts application opens another browser window, displaying that location in Google Maps.

To add a new contact:

1. On the iCloud website, click the Plus button at the bottom of the Contacts list.

   or

   From the Action menu (the gear icon at the bottom of the Contacts list), choose New Contact **E**.

2. In the resulting Edit Contact screen **F**, enter the information for your new contact.

3. Click Done.

   iCloud saves your work, and will shortly synchronize it to the rest of your iCloud-enabled devices.

To edit contacts:

1. Find the contact you wish to change in the Contacts List, then click it to select it.

2. Click Edit.

3. Make the changes you need, then click Done.

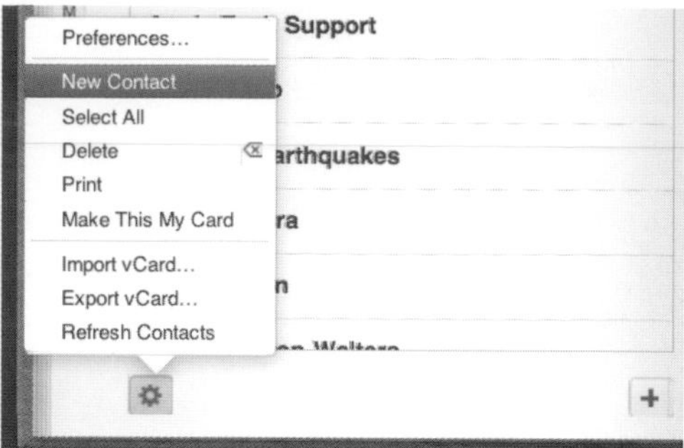

E The Action pop-up menu at the bottom of the Contacts list gives you a variety of choices.

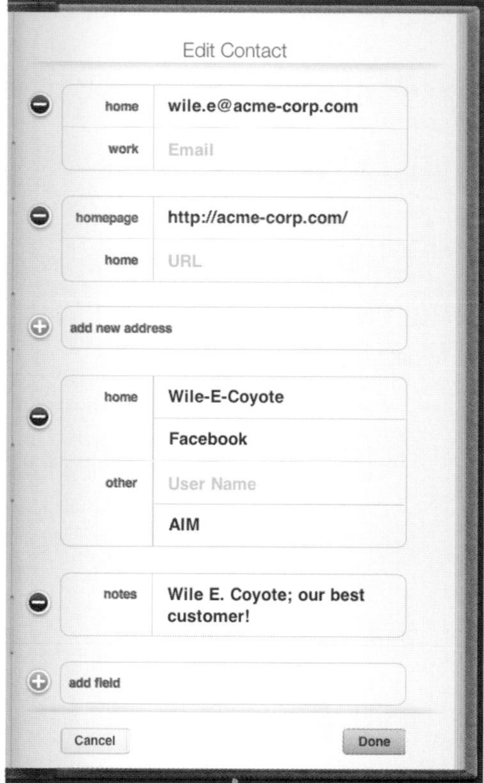

F A new contact has a variety of fields already laid out for you, but you can also add custom fields by clicking the Add Field button at the bottom of the contact record.

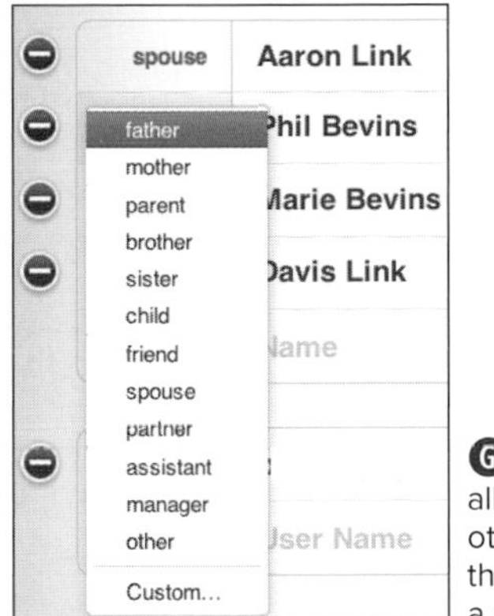

G Related People allow you to connect other people and their relationship to a particular contact.

TIP When you're editing contacts, you can add a new optional field called Related People. This new field lets you specify other people who are related to the person whose contact record you are editing. For example, if you choose to add a Related People field, you can choose the relationship (Father, Mother, Spouse, Child, and so on) from a pop-up menu, then enter the name of the related person in the field G. If you have an iOS device that uses Siri, make sure to add one or more of these fields to your own contact card, so Siri knows what you mean when you say things like "Text my wife that I'll be late."

To delete a contact:

1. Find the contact you wish to delete in the Contacts List, then click it to select it.
2. Press Delete or Backspace.

   You'll get a confirmation dialog asking if you really want to delete that record. Click Delete.

TIP You can use the Shift or Command keys to select multiple contacts in the list before you delete them.

Working with Contact Groups

A contact group is a list of one or more contacts. You can create them on the Mac or iCloud Contacts application. These are handy for things like grouping similar people together. For example, I have a Friends group in my Mac Contacts, with the names of five friends to whom I often share interesting email. In Mail on the Mac, all I have to do to address a message to all five people is to enter the name of the group in the email's To field.

While you can create and work with contact groups on the Mac's Contacts, and those groups synchronize to iOS devices, oddly, the Mail app in iOS 5 and 6 doesn't allow you to use Groups to address mail. You also can't add, edit, or delete groups on a mobile device. It's as though the feature is there as the foundation for a future revision of iOS.

You can work with groups on the iCloud website, however. Let's take a look at how to do that.

A Click the Groups ribbon at the right of the window to change to Groups mode.

B The Groups list appears on the left side of the window.

To work in Groups mode:

1. At the top of the Contacts List, click the Groups ribbon **A**.

   The display will switch to showing just your groups on the left **B**. The All Contacts group is always at the top of the list, which displays your entire Contacts list on the right side of the window.

2. Click a Group name to display its members on the right side of the window **C**.
3. Do one or more of the following:
   - Add a group by clicking the Plus button at the bottom of the Groups pane.
   - Remove a group by clicking the Edit button at the bottom of the Groups pane, then click the minus icon next to the group you want to delete. As usual, you'll get a confirmation dialog. Click Delete.
   - Rename a group by clicking the Edit button at the bottom of the Groups pane, then change the group's name. Click Done to save your changes.
   - Add a member to a group by clicking the All Contacts group, then drag a contact into another group to add it to that group. It's okay if a contact is in more than one group, so you can drag names from one group to another.
   - Remove a member from a group by first selecting the group and then the contact you want to remove. Press the Backspace or Delete key. Interestingly, you won't get a confirmation dialog when you delete a contact from any group other than All Contacts.
4. When you're done working with groups, click the individual ribbon at the top of the window.

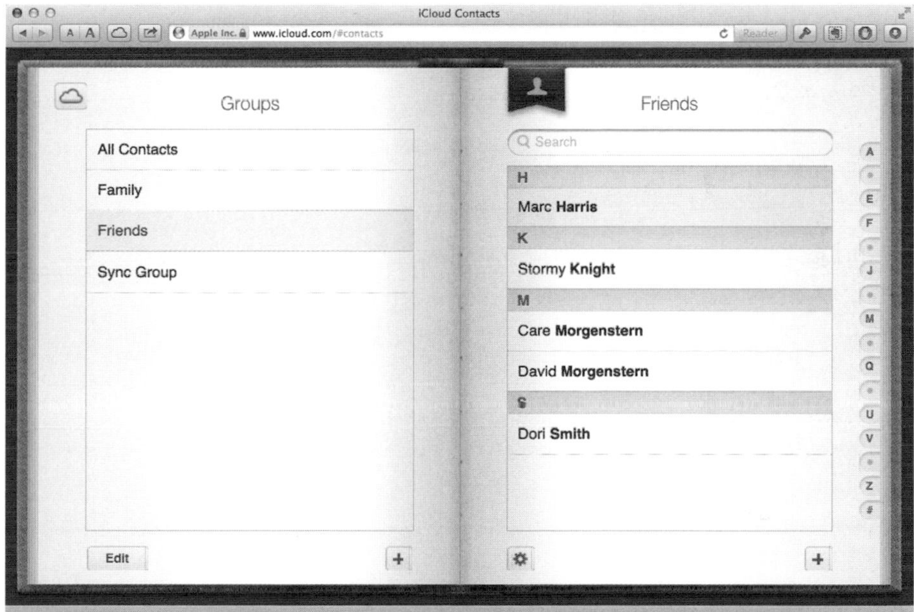

C Clicking the name of the group displays its members on the right side of the window.

Using the Action Menu

The Action menu at the bottom of the iCloud Contacts application's window gives you a variety of additional commands **A**.

- **Preferences** will be covered in the next section.
- Choose **New Contact** to add a contact to the Contacts list. This is the equivalent of clicking the Plus button at the bottom of the Contacts list.
- **Select All** lets you easily select all of your contacts at once.
- **Delete** allows you to remove one or more selected contacts. It's the equivalent of selecting a contact and pressing Backspace or Delete.
- **Print** allows you to print the selected contact cards. You will get the usual system printing dialog, so you can adjust the print settings to your liking.
- **Make This My Card** allows you to specify your own contact card. When you do this, Contacts marks it with the silhouette icon **B**. OS X and iOS use this information to identify you for mail, contacts, and more.
- **Import vCard** opens a dialog allowing you to upload a contact in the common vCard format.
- **Export vCard** downloads the selected contacts to your Mac's Contacts app.
- **Refresh Contacts** forces the website to reload your contact data if you've updated contacts on another device, and those changes haven't yet appeared on the iCloud website.

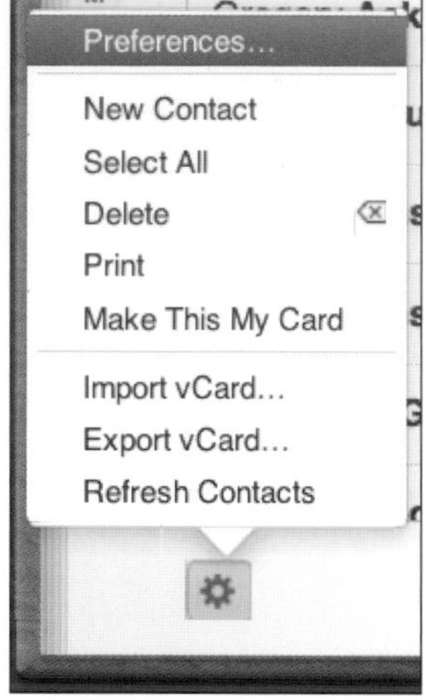

A The Action menu allows you to work further with your contacts.

B The silhouette icon denotes your own contact card.

Ⓐ The Preferences dialog allows you to choose how the iCloud Contacts application sorts and displays your contacts.

Setting iCloud Contact Preferences

Choosing Preferences from the Action menu allows you to set some general behavior of the iCloud Contacts application.

To set Contact preferences:

1. Choose Preferences from the Action menu.

   The preferences dialog appears Ⓐ.

2. Choose one or more of the following:

   - In the **Sort Order** pop-up menu, choose either First Name or Last Name to tell iCloud how you want contacts sorted.
   - In the **Display Order** pop-up menu, choose either First Name, Last Name or Last Name, First Name to tell iCloud how you want names to appear in the list.
   - In the **Address Layout** pop-up menu, choose a country name to determine how addresses are shown.
   - Choose **Automatically Format Phone Numbers** to tell iCloud to automatically format telephone numbers in the format appropriate for the country you chose in the Address Layout pop-up menu.

Working with Calendars and Reminders

One of the best—and incredibly useful—features of iCloud is its ability to keep your calendar events and reminders in the cloud, automatically synchronizing them among all your devices. Imagine you've just finished an appointment at the dentist, and the receptionist asks to set up your next date. Whipping out your iPhone, you enter the next appointment into the Calendar app, and in a moment, that appointment appears on the rest of your devices.

Similarly, iCloud can create synchronized reminders for things you need to do. With the iOS Reminders app, you can even set a reminder to appear only when you arrive at a particular geographical location.

But probably the most useful feature of iCloud calendaring is that you can share your calendars with family, friends, and colleagues. So when your daughter adds her soccer practice to the family shared calendar, it appears on the rest of the family's schedule as well.

In This Chapter

Setting up Calendars	60
Working with Calendars on the iCloud Website	67
Working with Events	73
Sharing Your Calendars with Others	77
Subscribing to Public Calendars	80
Setting iCloud Calendar Preferences	83
Adding Reminders	85
Working with Reminders on Your iOS Device	90
Managing Notifications on Mac and iOS	94

Setting up Calendars

You begin with calendars in iCloud by creating them, in either the Mac or iOS Calendar app (beginning in OS X 10.8 Mountain Lion, iCal's name was changed to Calendar to bring it in line with the iOS equivalent). You can also create calendars on the iCloud website **A**, which I'll discuss later in this chapter.

There's one important concept to get when you start managing your schedule and to-dos with iCloud. There are two kinds of items that iCloud deals with:

- **Events** are items that appear in the body of your calendar views. They will appear in the Day, Week, Month, and List views. They always have dates and times associated with them (though sometimes the associated time is "all-day").

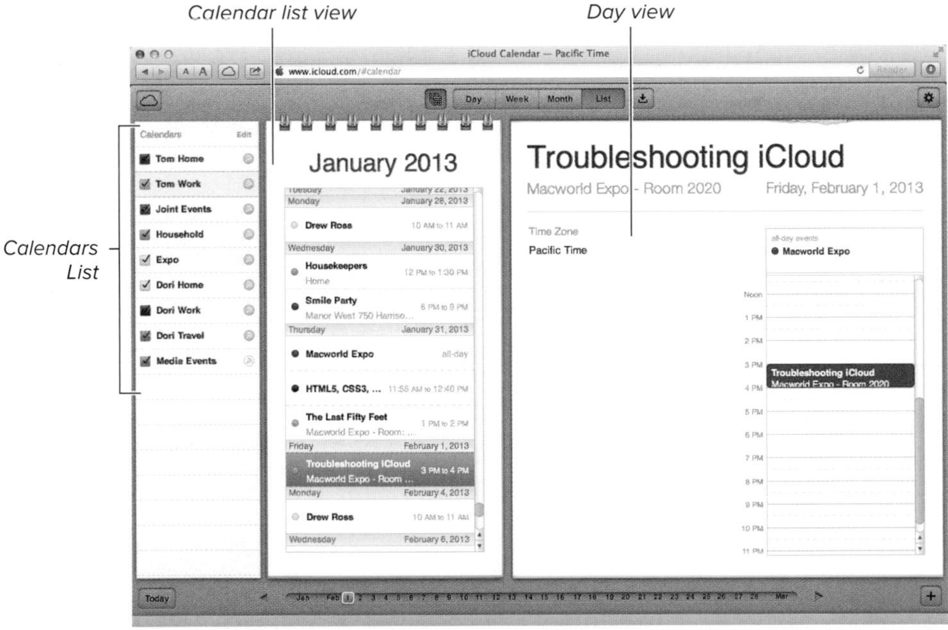

A The Calendar application on the iCloud website has a variety of calendar views.

- **Reminders** are to-do items. They work differently than they did with MobileMe and the former iCal, in that you work with them in the Mac and iOS Reminders apps, rather than with the Calendar app. Reminders don't appear in the calendar views. Reminders may have a date and time associated with them, but don't have to. Unlike Events, you can also set a Priority (None, Low, Medium, High) for a Reminder. Using a feature called "geofencing," they can also be set to trigger on your iOS device when the device is physically near a location, using your device's GPS and Location Services. Even cooler, geofencing can be set to trigger the reminder when you arrive at or leave a particular location. So that's how the Siri personal assistant built into the iPhone 4S and later can deal with commands like "Text my wife when I leave the office."

In this book, I'm focusing on iCloud, rather than working with the Mac or iOS Calendar app, so I'll deal mostly with working with events on the iCloud website, rather than in the Mac or iOS programs. However, because Reminders are so intimately connected with iCloud, I'll be going into detail with the iOS Reminders app in the "Working with Reminders on Your iOS Device" section, later in this chapter, and there's a similar section about working with the Mac Reminders app, in the "Working with Reminders on the Mac" section. Mountain Lion brought changes to how notifications work, so I've also added the "Managing Notifications on Mac and iOS" section in this edition of the book.

The Only Good Calendar... Is Online?

Beginning with the introduction of Mountain Lion, the default (and apparently only) choice when it comes to creating calendars is to share them with an online service. This is a change from previous versions of iCal on the Mac; before, you could easily have both shared online calendars and private calendars that only existed on your Mac. It's as though Apple has decided that unshared, private calendars are something to be avoided. I don't quite understand why; I can easily imagine many scenarios in which you might have calendars you only want to appear on your office machine, for events that only occur in the office, and that don't need to be shared with your iOS devices.

Besides iCloud, Calendar on the Mac makes it easy to create shared calendars with Google, Yahoo, Exchange, and any server that uses the CalDAV protocol. To create a new calendar on any of these services, you must first create the service in Calendar's Preferences, in the Accounts pane **B**. Once there, click the Plus button at the bottom of the Accounts list, then pick the kind of account you want from the Add an Account sheet **C**. Enter the email address and password for the service, then click Create.

It's actually possible to create a new calendar that is only on your Mac, but it needs a little work around to set up. To do so, you need to open the Accounts pane of Calendar's Preferences, and select your iCloud account in the list **B**. If you uncheck the Enable this account checkbox, all of your iCloud calendars and events will disappear from Calendar on your Mac (don't worry, all the information is still safe on iCloud). Then choose File > New Calendar, and give it a name that isn't the same as any of your iCloud calendars. The new calendar will be created in a section of the calendar list that says On My Mac. Then reenable your iCloud account, and the iCloud calendar and your private calendar will happily coexist on your computer.

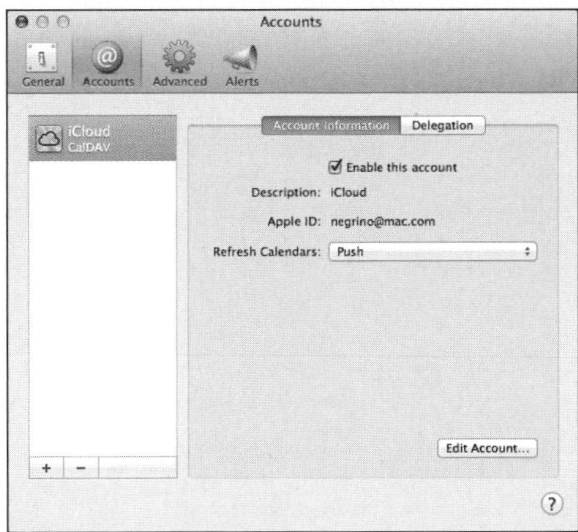

B You create new shared calendar accounts in the Accounts pane of Calendar's Preferences.

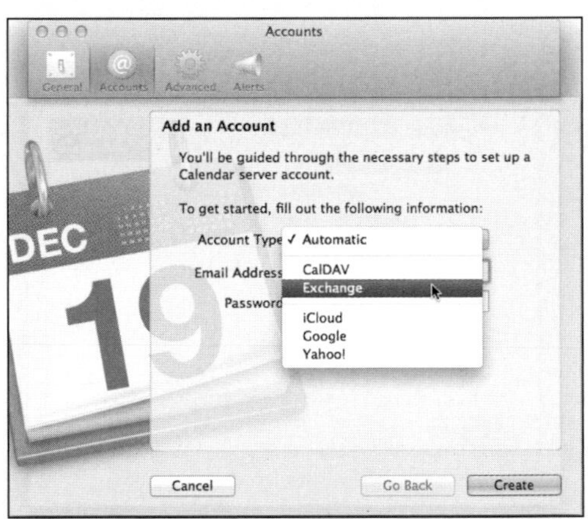

C Pick the service you want from the Account Type pop-up menu.

To create a calendar on a Mac:

1. Launch Calendar **D**.
2. Choose File > New Calendar > then either iCloud or the name of another shared calendar service, or On My Mac.

   Choosing iCloud will place the calendar on iCloud, where it can be shared by your other devices and by other people. Calendars on other services are share-able according to the particular rules of those services (check with your system administrator). If the calendar is on your Mac, it will be private and will only exist on the Mac where you created the calendar.
3. The new calendar appears in the Calendars List as Untitled, allowing you to name it **E**. Enter the name, then click anywhere else to save it.

D On the Mac, Calendar for OS X has a faux-leather look that people either love or hate.

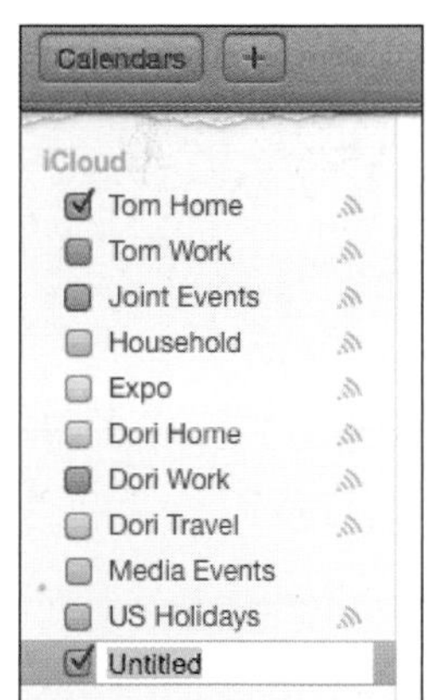

E Begin creating your new calendar in the Calendars list.

To create a calendar on an iOS device:

1. On your iPhone or iPad, start the Calendar app.
2. Tap the Calendars button.

   The Calendars (iPhone) or Show Calendars (iPad) popover appears F.
3. Tap the Edit button.

   The screen name changes to Edit Calendars.
4. At the bottom of the iCloud section, tap Add Calendar.
5. In the resulting Add Calendar popover G, type the name you want for the new calendar.
6. Tap next to the color you want the calendar events to appear as.

   You may be able to see additional colors by scrolling.
7. Tap Done.

   The popover will go back to the Edit Calendars screen, and the new calendar you created appears in the list.
8. Tap Done.

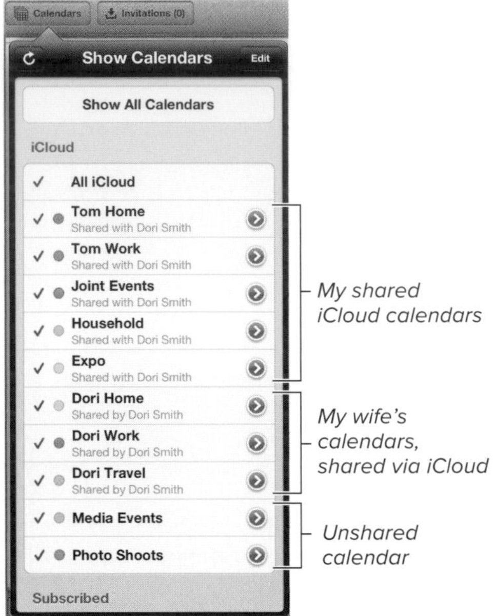

F On the iPad, the Show Calendars popover tells you the status of all your iCloud calendars.

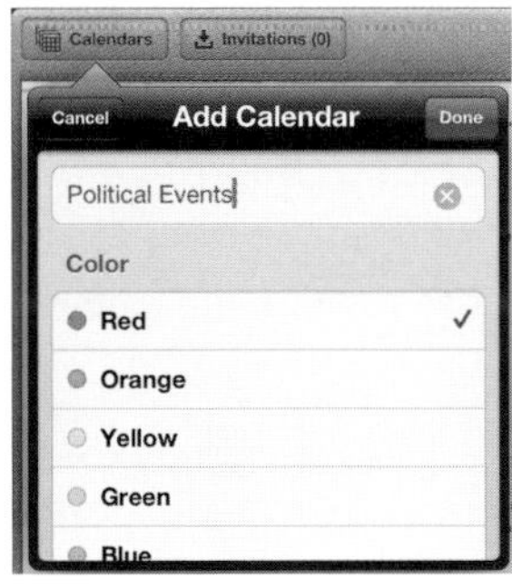

G Type the name you want for your new calendar.

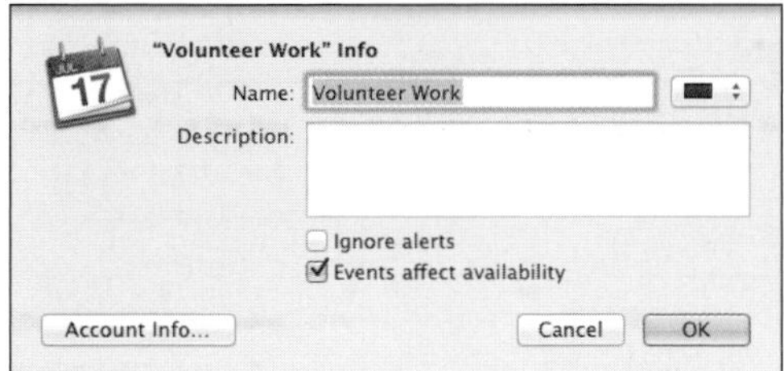

H In Calendar on the Mac, each calendar has an info dialog.

To edit a calendar on a Mac:

1. In Calendar, in the Calendars List at the upper left corner of the window, right-click the calendar you want to change, and choose Get Info.

   The info dialog appears for that calendar **H**.

3. Do one or more of the following:

   - Change the name of the calendar.
   - From the color pop-up menu next to the Name field, choose the color in which you want the calendar's events to appear. One difference in Calendar versus the Calendar app on iOS is that one of the color choices is Other, which when chosen brings up a color picker that allows you to choose any color you want, rather than a preset color.

4. Click OK.

To edit a calendar on an iOS device:

1. On your iPhone or iPad, start the Calendar app.
2. Tap the Calendars button.

   The Calendars (iPhone) or Show Calendars (iPad) popover appears **F**.

3. Tap the Edit button.

   The screen name changes to Edit Calendars.

4. In the Calendar list, tap the name of an existing calendar.
5. In the Edit Calendar screen, change the name or the associated color of the calendar, then tap Done.

Using Alternative Calendar Programs with iCloud

Just because Calendar comes with OS X, that doesn't mean that it's universally beloved, or even especially liked, by people who are heavy calendar users. For those people (like me) who have been using calendars on a computer for a very long time, and have used excellent calendar programs over the years, Calendar is too limited, too lowest-common-denominator, for our comfort. The trouble is that all of the really useful calendar features (event synchronization between devices, calendar sharing between people) use Calendar (or at least its data file) and iCloud as a conduit.

Happily, if Calendar isn't feature-rich enough for your needs, a variety of alternative calendar programs still use the Calendar events and reminders data and provide a superior calendaring experience. My favorite for Mac is BusyMac's BusyCal **I**, which allows you to share events and to-dos over iCloud or Google Calendar; gives you much more flexibility in calendar views; has easier event entry than Calendar; has a wide variety of event types, such as all-day banners, sticky notes in the calendar, and graphics; and much more.

On iOS, there are many alternatives for the Calendar app, but the ones I've used are called Fantastical from Flexibits, and Calvetica **J**, from Mysterious Trousers. I like Calvetica because of its minimalist design, and because it requires just a couple of taps (and the text entry for the event name, of course) to enter an event, far fewer than Calendar. It's fast, lets you create an event quickly, and gets out of your way. One really attractive thing about Fantastical is that it understands natural-language requests, so you can simply enter "Lunch next Tuesday at 2 with Cliff" and the program correctly parses the sentence creates the calendar event. This is terrific when combined with dictation on iOS 6.

I I prefer to use BusyCal over Calendar, because it shows me more information at a glance, such as the mini-months, the reminders list, and the detail for the selected event.

J On iOS, the faster you can enter an event the better, which is why I prefer Calvetica, rather than the stock Calendar app.

Working with Calendars on the iCloud Website

The iCloud website gives you a great deal of control over your calendar. With it, you can add, view, and change events; manage calendars; and share your calendars with others (for that last, see the “Sharing Your Calendars with Others” section, later in this chapter).

In this section, all the action will take place on the iCloud website. We’ll begin by creating, editing, and deleting calendars, then move on to working with calendar events.

To create a calendar:

1. Go to the iCloud website, and login using your iCloud Apple ID and password.
2. On the iCloud Home screen **A**, click Calendar.

   The Calendar screen appears **B**.

A On the iCloud website, click the Calendar icon to get started.

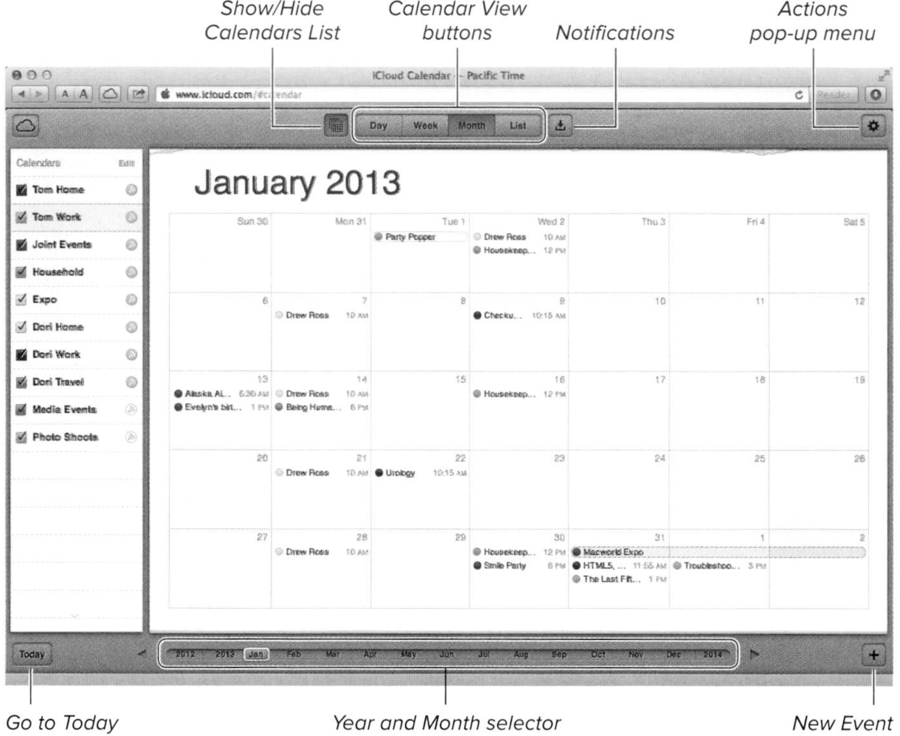

B You can do almost anything that you can do in Calendar on the iCloud website.

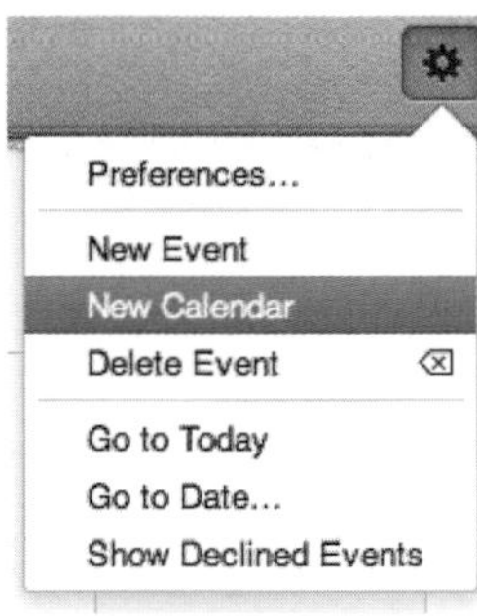

Ⓒ Choose New Calendar from the Actions pop-up menu.

Ⓓ Type the name of your new calendar.

3. Click the Actions button at the upper-right of the window.

   The Actions pop-up menu appears Ⓒ.

4. Choose New Calendar.

   A new calendar appears at the bottom of the Calendars List, ready for you to add a name Ⓓ.

5. Enter the name, then click outside the name field to save it.

   See "Working With Events" later in this chapter to add and edit calendar events.

To view (or not) a calendar or the Calendars List:

In the Calendars List, select the checkbox next to a calendar's name to see that's calendar's contents. If the checkbox is cleared, the events associated with that calendar will disappear from your calendar views. Nothing's happened to the events; you are simply choosing not to see them.

or

If you want to hide the Calendars List, click the Show/Hide Calendars List button at the top of the window. Clicking the button again will bring the list back.

To edit or delete a calendar:

1. In the iCloud website's Calendar screen, click the Edit link at the top of the Calendars list at the upper-left corner of the window **E**.

   The Calendars list changes into edit mode **F**.

2. Do one or more of the following:
   - To change the color associated with the calendar, click the color button next to the name of the calendar, then choose a different color from the popover **G**. You can also click the Custom color link to pop up a more full-featured color picker, if you don't like the six standard choices.
   - Click in the name field of the calendar, and change it to rename the calendar.
   - To delete a calendar, click the red button with a minus sign in it. As usual when you're potentially about to destroy data, iCloud warns you and asks if you're sure **H**. If you are, click Delete Calendar.

3. When you're done changing your calendars, Click the Done link.

TIP **That dialog isn't joking; remember that iCloud is the master repository for all your data. So if you delete that calendar, it and all of its events will disappear not just from the iCloud website but from all your Macs and iOS devices as well. Be careful!**

TIP **Note that a Plus button also appears when you're editing calendars F. Yes, that means that it's another way to add a calendar.**

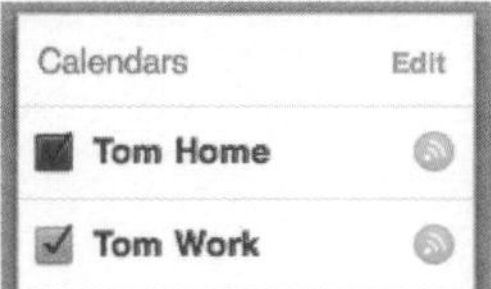

E To enter calendar Edit mode, click the Edit link.

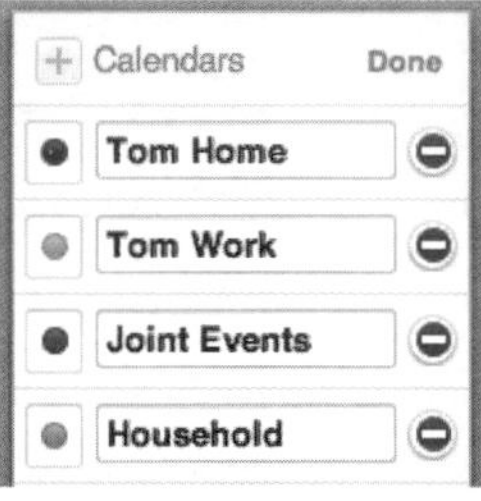

F In Edit mode, you can change the calendar color, the calendar name, or delete the calendar.

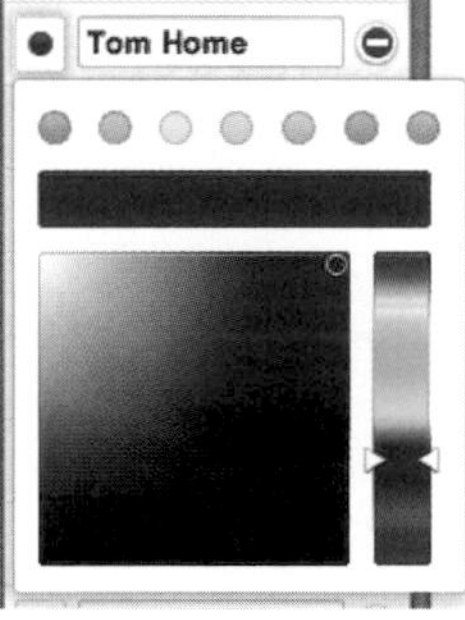

G Clicking the color button brings up a color picker.

H Make sure you really want to delete that calendar!

To change calendar views:

On the iCloud website, you have a choice of Day, Week, Month, or List calendar views. Click one of the Calendar View buttons in the toolbar B to view the calendar as you wish.

To change date views:

At the bottom of the window, you'll find the Date selector I. This selector changes depending on the calendar view. For example, if the Month view is set, you'll see years and months in the Date selector. If the Day or List view is set, you'll see individual days in the selector. Do one or more of the following (assuming the Month view is active; the other views are similar in operation):

- Click one of the months to view its contents.

continues on next page

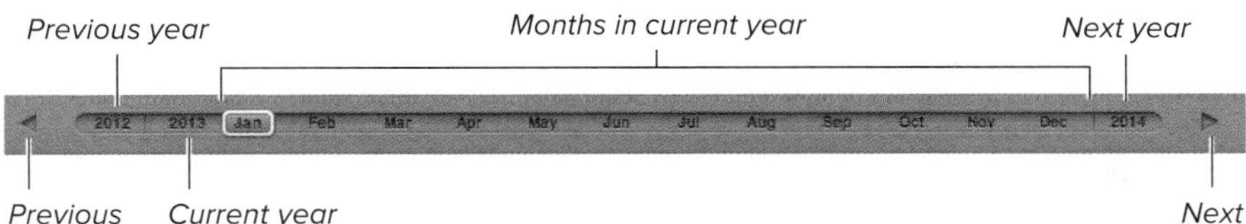

I The Date selector changes, depending on the calendar view.

- Click the Previous or Next buttons to move to the previous or next month. If you're already viewing January or December, your view will change to the previous or next year.
- Click the Previous Year or Next Year buttons to change the calendar view by an entire year.
- Click the Today button at the lower left corner of the window to jump to today's date.
- If you need to view a date that's more than a few clicks away, click the Actions menu C and choose Go to Date. The resulting date picker J allows you to type or navigate to the date you want. Choose that date, then click OK.

J You can jump to dates many months or years away with this date picker.

Working with Events

The Calendar application on the iCloud website makes it easy to create or change events. Its abilities are very similar to Calendar on the Mac or the iOS Calendar app, but there are a couple of differences. With the website, you can't mark an event as one that shows that you are Busy or Free.

To create an event:

1. In the Calendars List, click to select the calendar in which you want to create the event.
2. Do one or more of the following, and the New Event popover appears:
   - In Month view, double-click in the day in which you want the event.
   - In Day, Week, or List view, drag the mouse cursor across a time range to create an event that covers that range.
   - In any view, click the New Event button (it looks like a plus) in the lower-right corner of the window. When you do this, the event is created on the date you last selected in the calendar.
   - From the Actions pop-up menu, choose New Event.

continues on next page

3. In the New Event popover Ⓚ, do one or more of the following:

   ▸ Enter the title of the event.

   ▸ (Optional) Enter the event's location.

   ▸ (Optional) If the event is going to last all day, click the all-day checkbox.

   ▸ In the From section, set the event's starting date and time.

   ▸ In the To section, set the event's ending date and time.

   ▸ (Optional) If this will be a recurring event, choose the recurring schedule from the pop-up menu next to Repeat. You can choose Every Day, Every Week, Every Month, Every Year, or Custom. If you choose Custom, you get a pop-up dialog that allows you to choose dates with any flexibility you want on a Daily, Weekly, Monthly, or Yearly basis. The Monthly or Yearly Custom choices also allow you to choose intervals such as the first, second, third, fourth, or last days of a month.

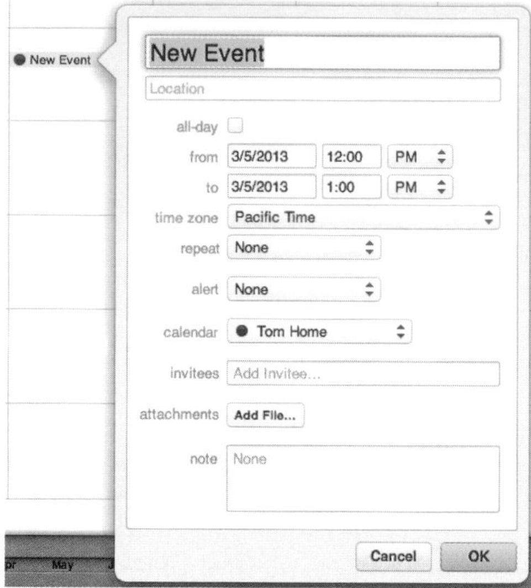

Ⓚ Get to know the New Event popover well, because you'll be seeing it a lot.

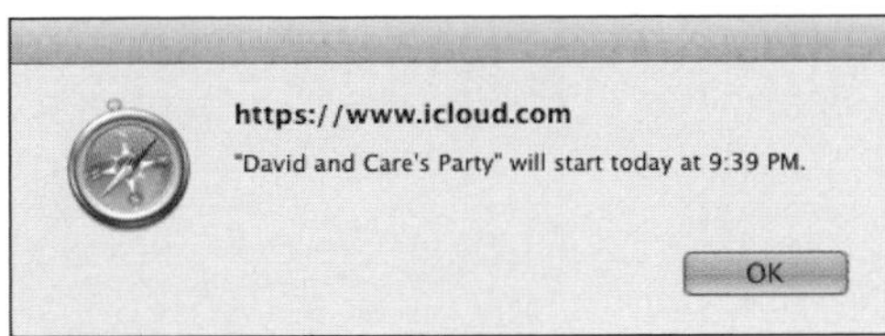
https://www.icloud.com
"David and Care's Party" will start today at 9:39 PM.
OK

Ⓛ One of the places that alerts can appear is on the iCloud website.

- (Optional) If you want to be reminded before the event starts, choose from the Alert pop-up menu, and select the interval before the event. If you set an alert, a 2nd Alert pop-up menu appears, allowing you to set an interval for a second reminder. Alerts appear as notifications on your iOS devices, and also in Calendar on your Mac, and as a dialog on the iCloud website in your browser Ⓛ.
- (Optional) If you want, you can change the calendar for the event with a pop-up menu in the Calendar section.
- (Optional) If you want to invite friends or colleagues to the event, enter their name or email address into the Invitees field. As you type, iCloud looks up a matching contact in your iCloud contacts list, providing a pop-up menu with possible matches. Select a contact from the menu to accept it. You can add multiple invitees to an event. If your invitees use iCloud, the invitation will appear in the Notifications button on the iCloud website, in Calendar, and in the Calendar app on their iOS devices. Invitees have the option to Accept, Decline, or mark the event as Maybe.
- (Optional) You can also add a note to the event, perhaps with details about the meeting.

4. Click OK to save the event.

   The event appears on your calendar.

To edit an event:

Double-click an event in your calendar to bring up the popover with the event details, change the details you desire, then click OK.

or

In the Date or Week views, drag the top or bottom border of an event on the calendar to change its duration.

To move an event:

Do one or more of the following:

- On the calendar, drag the event from one location to where you want it. For example, you might want to move the meeting that is been rescheduled from one day to the next.
- Double-click the event to open its pop-up window, then change the event details. You might need to use both these techniques if an event is moved both in day and time.

To delete an event:

In any calendar view, click an event to select it, then press the Delete or Backspace keys.

or

Double-click the event to bring up the popover with the event details, then click the Delete button.

TIP If I'm going to be making a lot of changes to my calendar events or reminders, I'll often choose to do them on my Mac, rather than on an iOS device, because I still find it easier to use a separate hardware keyboard and mouse, rather than tapping and swiping on a touchscreen. Perhaps I'm a dinosaur.

Sharing Your Calendars with Others

Perhaps the most useful thing about iCloud's calendar is its ability to share your calendars and events with family, colleagues, and friends who are also using iCloud. You can allow other people to share any of your calendars, and they can ask you to share theirs. Of course, you can still have calendars that are private to you; iCloud will synchronize those private calendars among all your devices, but nobody else will be able to see them. You can have any mix of shared and private calendars you want.

There's a difference between *sharing* and *inviting*. When you share, you're sharing a whole calendar and *all* its events with another iCloud user. When you invite, you are offering to share a particular event with another person, whether or not they are using iCloud. Keep this difference in mind when you decide which of the kinds of collaboration you want. For example, I'm comfortable in sharing most of my calendars with my wife. But there might be a particular meeting on my Work calendar that I have with an editor; rather than share the whole calendar, I'd be likely to simply invite that editor to only that one meeting; the invitation will be sent via email. When the editor accepts the invitation, the event appears for both of us.

iCloud's calendar sharing uses the industry-standard CalDAV protocol, so you can share calendars with people running Calendar or variety of other calendar programs on the Mac, and Microsoft Outlook 2007 or later on Windows.

To turn on calendar sharing:

1. On the calendar application of the iCloud website, the Calendars List will show a Share icon next to each calendar **A**. A gray icon indicates the calendar isn't being shared, and a green icon indicates that it is.
2. Click a gray icon to begin the sharing process.

   The Calendar Sharing popover appears **B**.
3. In most cases, you're going to want to share the calendar privately with one or more people. Click the Private Calendar checkbox, then in the Add Person field underneath, begin typing the person's name or email address. iCloud will do a lookup of your Contacts list and provide a pop-up menu with possible matches. Click a contact with the mouse to select it.
4. Click the person's name to display the pop-up menu with permissions. Decide whether you want the person to be able to View & Edit the calendar (that's the default choice) or to just be able to View the calendar.

   You might want to make a calendar read-only (the View choice) if the events of the calendar are ones that you merely want to have the other person informed about, but not to be able to change, such as your business travel plans.
5. (Optional) Repeat steps 3 and 4 for anyone else you want to share the calendar with.

A The icons next to the calendars tell you the calendar's sharing status.

B Enter the name and the sharing privileges for each person with which you want to share the calendar.

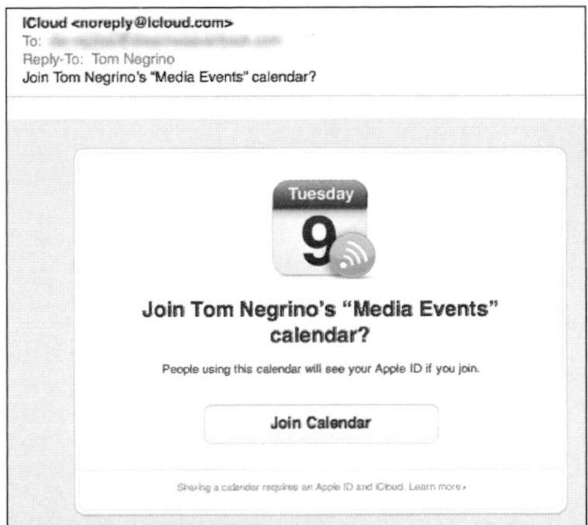

C Invitees get an email invitation to your calendars. Accepting the invitation is as easy as clicking the Join Calendar button.

D You can see who is sharing calendars that you don't own.

6. Click Share.

   iCloud sends email invitations to the people you chose **C**. If they accept the invitation by clicking the Join Calendar button in the email, they'll be added to the calendar.

7. Click OK.

TIP **If you share one of your calendars, you are considered to be the calendar's owner. Only you have the right to allow other people to view or edit the calendar. Conversely, if you are sharing someone else's calendar you only have the privileges they have allowed you. And you can't change those privileges for yourself or anyone else.**

TIP **To check the status of a calendar you don't own, click the green Share icon next to it. iCloud will show you the Shared Calendar Info popover D.**

TIP **To remove someone from calendar sharing of the calendar you own, click the Share icon, which brings up the Share Calendar popover. The popover will show you the people who are currently sharing the calendar. Click the person whom you would like to remove from sharing, then click the red minus icon next to their name.**

TIP **You can stop sharing a calendar altogether by clicking the Share icon, which brings up the Share Calendar popover, and clicking the Stop Sharing button at the bottom. You'll get the usual iCloud confirmation dialog; click Stop Sharing again.**

Subscribing to Public Calendars

Besides the calendar events of yourself, family, friends, and colleagues, you might be interested in importing other kinds of calendars. For example, you might want to subscribe to an automatically updated calendar for holidays in your country. Or if you're a sports fan, you might want the playing schedule for your favorite team to appear in your calendar. Maybe you want the local weather, or the phases of the moon. All of these, and many more, are available as public calendars to which you can subscribe. You'll typically use Calendar on the Mac to subscribe to one of these calendars, but once you do, you can choose to either keep that calendar local to your Mac, or to share it with the rest of your devices via iCloud.

In this section, I'm going to show you how to find a public calendar using Calendar, subscribe to it, and then view it in your calendar.

To subscribe to a public calendar:

1. Open Calendar on your Mac.
2. Choose Help > Find Calendar Subscriptions.

   Your default web browser will open and bring you to Apple's list of available public calendars **A**. At the top of the list, you can choose to view the calendar feeds by Most recent, Most popular, or Alphabetical.

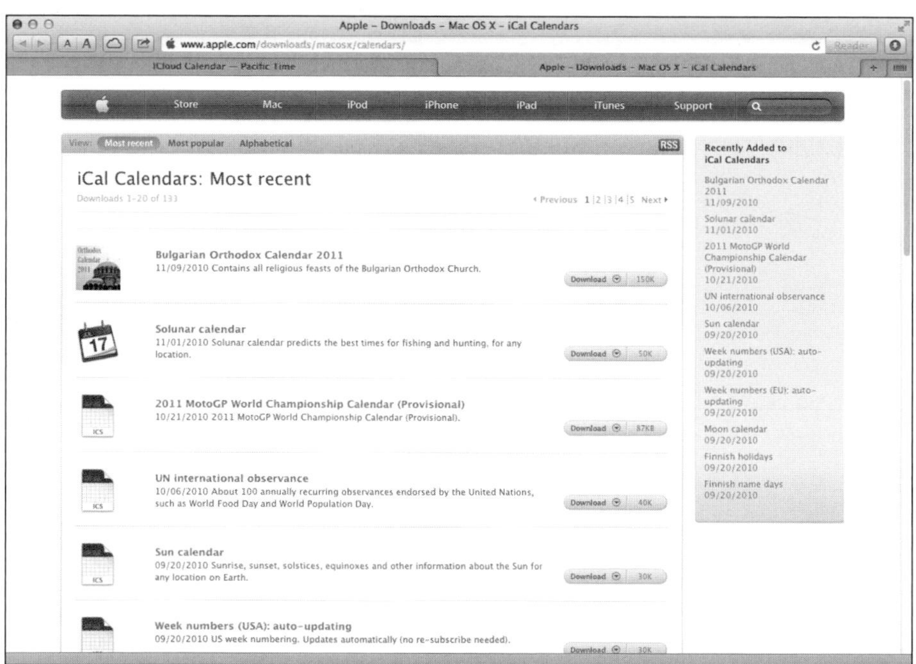

A Apple maintains a list of public calendars.

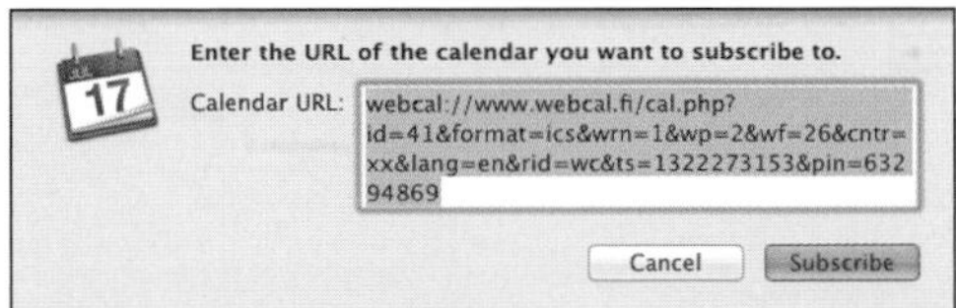

B When you subscribe to a calendar in Calendar, it shows you the calendar's URL

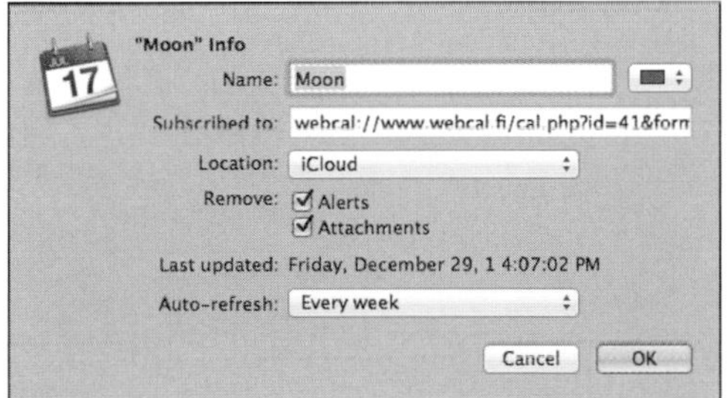

C Subscribing to the calendar gives you its information, and the Location pop-up menu allows you to choose whether you want to subscribe to it only on your local Mac, or via iCloud, to share it with all your devices.

3. Find the calendar to which you wish to subscribe, then click the Download button for that calendar.

   Depending on the source of the calendar, you may be taken to a different website where you can choose from a number of calendars. If so, find the calendar feed you want from that website, then click to subscribe to it.

   When you subscribe to a public calendar, Calendar shows you a dialog with the URL of the calendar **B**.

4. Click Subscribe.

   Calendar shows you a detail screen about the calendar **C**.

5. Do one or more of the following:

   - Change the name of the calendar.
   - From the color pop-up menu next to the Name field, choose the color in which you want the calendar's events to appear.
   - Using the Location pop-up menu, choose either iCloud or On My Mac. This is probably your most important choice in this dialog; choosing iCloud will make the subscribed calendar appear on all your devices.
   - By default, most subscribed calendars have Alerts, Attachments, and Reminders removed. In most cases, I recommend you keep it that way.
   - From the Auto-refresh pop-up menu, choose how often you want the calendar to refresh its data from the original URL.

continues on next page

6. Click OK.

   The subscribed calendar appears in Calendar. Double-click one of the calendar events to see its details **D**.

TIP You can find public calendars in many more places than just Apple's directory. For example, in the U.S., all the Major League Baseball clubs offer calendars that you can download into Calendar. Many of them will still refer to their calendars as working with iCal, rather than Calendar; that's fine, as only the app name changed; the subscribed calendar format didn't.

To delete a subscribed calendar:

1. In Calendar, click the Calendars button in the upper left corner of the window to display the Calendars list, if it isn't already visible.
2. Right-click the calendar you want to delete, then choose Delete from the shortcut menu **E**.

   Calendar asks you if you're sure you want to delete the calendar.
3. Click Delete.

   The calendar and its events and reminders are deleted. If you had the calendar shared on iCloud, the events and reminders will disappear from all your devices.

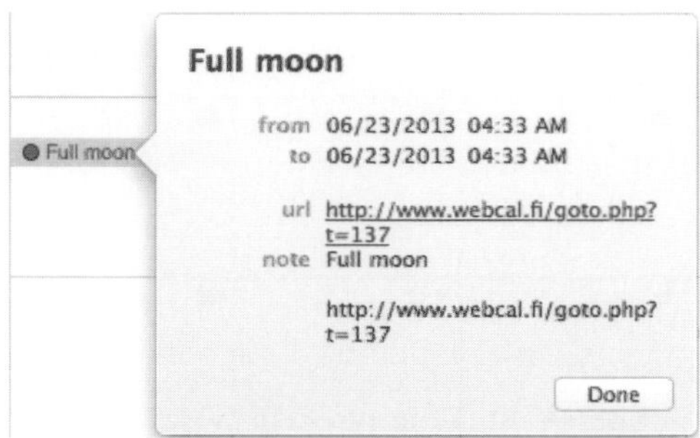

D You can't change the details of the events in a subscribed calendar, but you can view them.

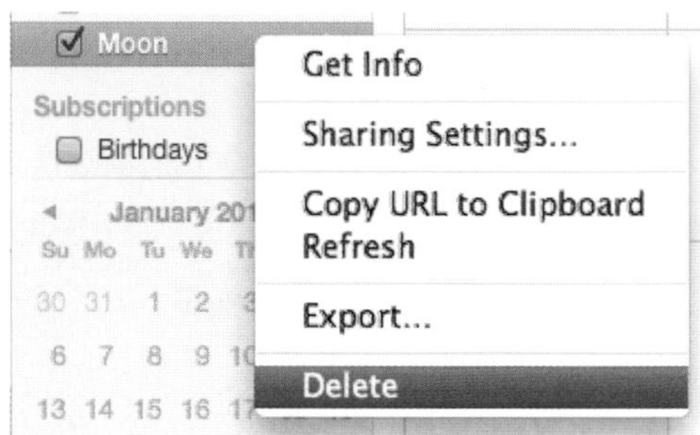

E Right-click the calendar you want to delete, then choose Delete from the shortcut menu.

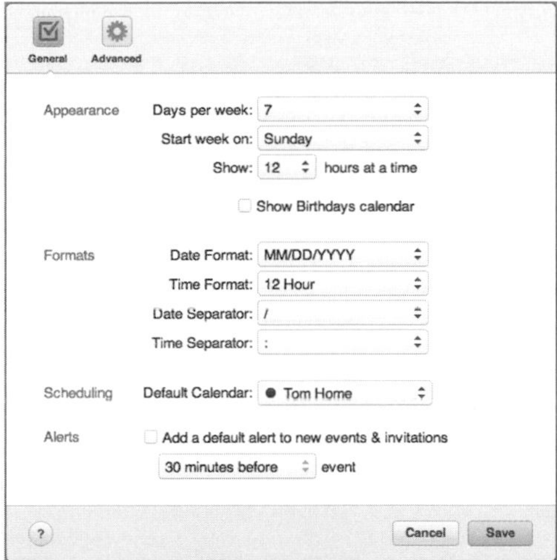

Ⓐ The General Preferences screen lets you set the calendar's appearance, formats, and alerts.

Setting iCloud Calendar Preferences

The iCloud Calendar application has two preference panes, General and Advanced. They closely mirror the preferences in Calendar.

To set General preferences:

1. Click the Actions button, then choose Preferences from the pop-up menu.

   The General preferences appear Ⓐ.

2. Choose one or more the following:

   - In the Appearance section, choose whether you want to display 5 or 7 days per week, on which day of the week you want the displayed week to start, and how many hours at a time you want to display in the Day and Week views. If you select the Show Birthdays calendar checkbox, the Calendar application will show a new Birthdays calendar, with information taken from the Birthday field of the people in your iCloud Contacts list.
   - In the Formats section, choose the Date format (your choices are MM/DD/YYYY, DD/MM/YYYY, and YYYY/MM/DD) and the Time format (12 hour or 24 hour). You can also choose the Date Separator (/, -, or .) and the Time Separator (: or .).
   - In the Scheduling section, pick the default calendar you want to use for new events.
   - In the Alerts section, if you select Add a default alert to new events and invitations, you can choose from the pop-up menu the amount of time before which the event is scheduled that you'll get an alert on your iCloud-enabled devices.

To set Advanced preferences:

1. Click the Actions button, then choose Preferences from the pop-up menu.
2. Click the Advanced button in the toolbar.

   The Advanced preferences appear **B**.
3. Choose one or more the following:
   - In the Time Zone section, if you select Enable time zone support, you can change the time zone for the whole calendar, or just for individual events that are different from the time zone you're in. If you choose this, a new Time Zone pop-up menu will appear in the New Event and Edit Event popovers. Choosing a new time zone from the pop-up menu will make Calendar automatically change the time of the event as shown on your calendar to match the chosen time zone. For example, if you're on the West Coast of the United States, you have time zone support enabled, and you set an event to occur at 3 p.m. Eastern time, the event will automatically be translated to noon Pacific time.
   - In the Old Events section, select the checkbox to hide events, and choose the number of days after the event is over you want the hiding to occur.
   - In the Event Updates section, if you select Ask before sending changes to events (it's on by default), iCloud will check with you before it sends out emails alerting people to changes in events. This keeps changes in your calendar from cluttering other people's mailboxes. Choosing Email me shared calendar updates is self-explanatory.
   - In the Invitations section, choose to get iCloud invitations as either in-app notifications (they will appear in the Notifications box in the toolbar) or as emails.

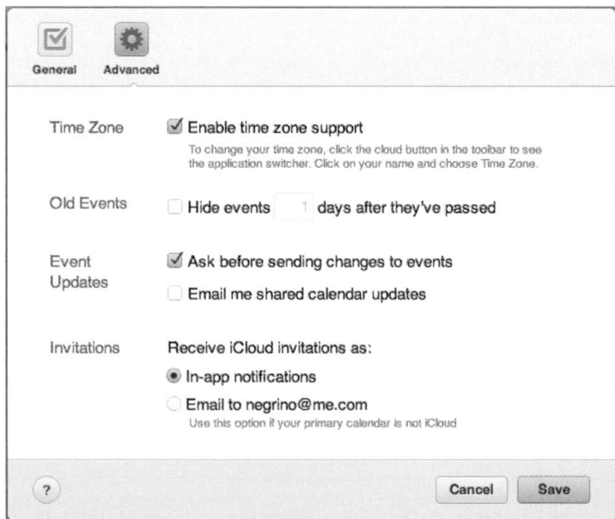

B The Advanced Preferences screen is a potpourri of settings.

Ⓐ On iOS, you use two separate applications to handle events and reminders.

Adding Reminders

What some of us call to-do items, Apple refers to as *reminders*. In a major change from the way reminders were handled previously, events and reminders have now been completely separated, with dedicated Reminders apps for reminders, and with events being handled by the Calendar apps.

The iCloud website, iOS devices, and the Mac now all have you work with calendar events and reminders in two entirely separate apps, the Calendar and Reminders apps, respectively Ⓐ. On Windows you can use Microsoft Outlook 2007 or later (which calls reminders *Tasks*).

Reminders are different from calendar events, in that they can be checked off as completed; you can assign a priority to them; and you can give them a due date (but you don't have to). Reminders with due dates not yet marked as completed automatically remain in your Reminders list. All of the Reminders apps allow you to maintain multiple reminder lists (for example, Home, Work, and the like).

In this section, you'll learn how to use the iCloud website to work with reminders and reminder lists. Remember that as you use the iCloud website, changes you make there will automatically propagate to the rest of your iCloud-enabled devices.

To add and edit Reminders on the iCloud website:

1. In your web browser, open the Reminders app on the iCloud website **B**.

   The Reminders app appears **C**.

B You'll find the Reminders app on the iCloud web site.

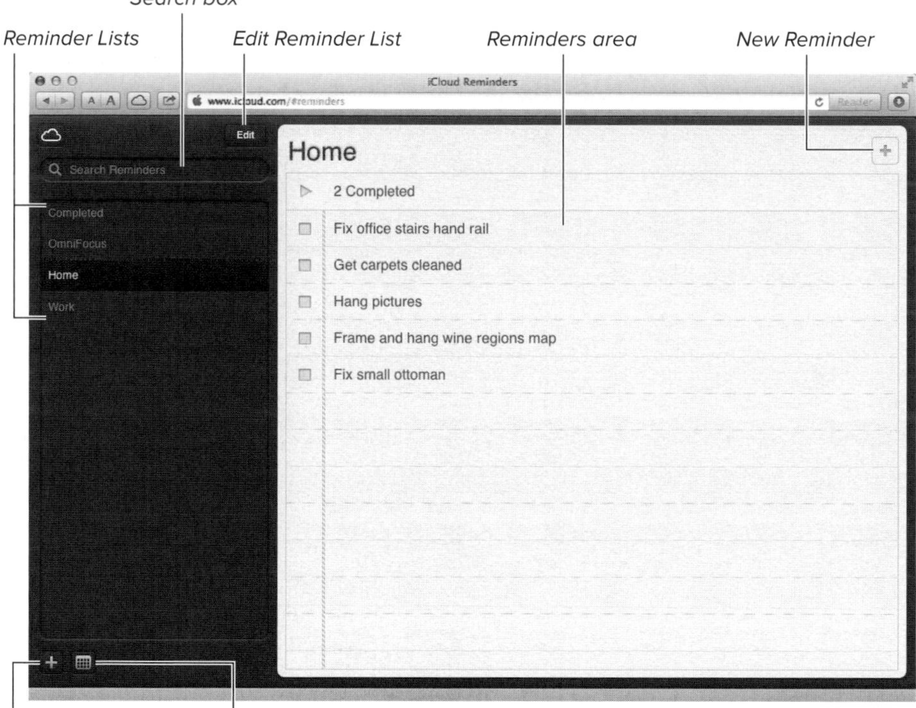

C The Reminders app works very much like the similar apps for iOS and Mac.

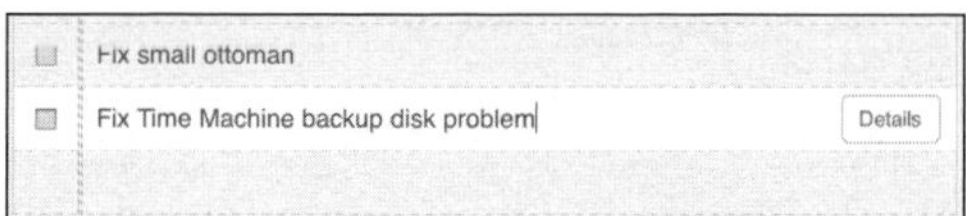

D Type your new reminder.

E The Details popover allows you to make changes to your reminders.

2. Click to select the reminder list you want your new reminder to appear in and then double-click in an empty area of the Reminders pane.

   or

   Click the New Reminder button.

   The insertion point appears in the line below the last reminder D.

3. Enter the reminder, then press Return.
4. (Optional) Click the Details button to bring up the Details popover E, then do one or more of the following:
   - If you want to assign a due date to the reminder, in the Remind me section, select On a day, then enter a date and time in the fields that appear. You can also choose if and how often you want the reminder to repeat from the pop up menu.
   - If you like, you can change the Reminder List for the reminder.
   - From the Priority pop-up menu, assign the reminder's priority level (None, Low, Medium, or High). If you assign a priority, the reminder will show the priority as an icon of one or more exclamation points in the Reminders pane.
   - If you want, add a Note to the reminder.
   - You can delete the reminder by clicking the Trash button.

continues on next page

5. Click Done.

   The changed reminder appears in the Reminders pane, with information letting you tell the details at a glance **F**.

TIP **A faster way to delete a reminder is to select it in the Reminders pane, then press Delete or Backspace.**

TIP **You can mark a reminder as completed by clicking the checkbox next to it in the Reminders pane. Completed reminders appear in a Completed section at the top of each list, and are aggregated in a separate Completed Reminder List.**

TIP **Entering a search term in the search box and pressing Return or Enter does a search across all your lists.**

F When you've edited the details of a reminder, those details appear with the reminder name. In this case, the reminder's Medium priority is shown with the two exclamation marks.

G Type the name of your new reminder list.

H The Edit mode allows you to delete, edit, or reorder your reminder lists.

I Like calendars, you can share your reminder lists.

To add or edit a Reminder List on the iCloud website:

1. In the Reminder application on the iCloud website, click the New Reminder List button.

   A new Untitled reminder list appears, ready for you to name it G.

2. Enter the new reminder list name, then press Return or Enter.

3. (Optional) To edit a reminder list, click the list name to select it, then click the Edit button at the top of the Reminder Lists column H. Do one or more of the following:

   - To delete the list, click the icon with the red circle with a line through it.
   - To rename the list, select the name and type over it.
   - To reorder the lists, click and drag the handle at the right side of the list.

   When you are done editing, click the Done button at the top of the Reminder Lists column.

TIP You can share your Reminder Lists with other iCloud users. Click the Edit sharing settings button next to a list I, then enter their name in the Sharing Reminders popover that appears.

TIP I was thinking of adding a section to this book called "Working with Your Reminders on a Mac," but using the Reminders app on the Mac is so similar to using the iCloud website Reminders app that I decided there was no need to take up the space.

Working with Reminders on Your iOS Device

As mentioned before, you work with iCloud reminders on an iOS device in the Reminders app, which was introduced with iOS 5. In this section, you'll see how to use the Reminders app to set up a to-do. Adding or editing a task in Reminders makes it automatically synchronize with the rest of your iCloud-enabled devices.

To set a reminder:

1. Start the Reminders app.

   The app appears, set to its default list **A**.

   On the iPhone or iPod touch, you can move between your different reminders lists by swiping right or left in the list name at the top of the screen, or by tapping the Show/Hide Reminders Lists button. On the iPad, with its larger screen, you can see more information at one time, including a handy mini-calendar **B**. Tapping on a date in the calendar shows you any reminders set for that date **C**.

2. Tap the plus button to add a reminder.

   In the list that you're on, on the first blank line, an insertion point appears.

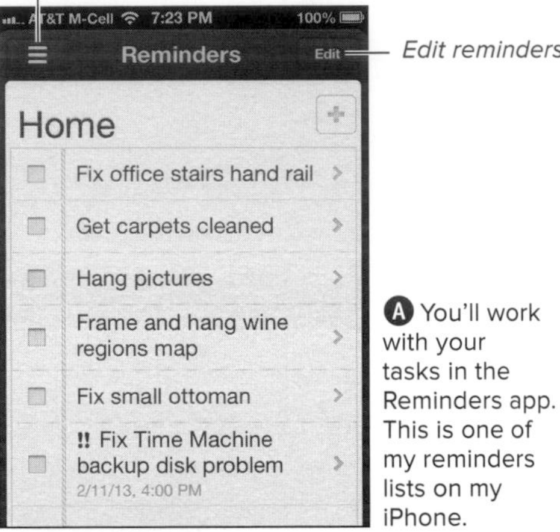

A You'll work with your tasks in the Reminders app. This is one of my reminders lists on my iPhone.

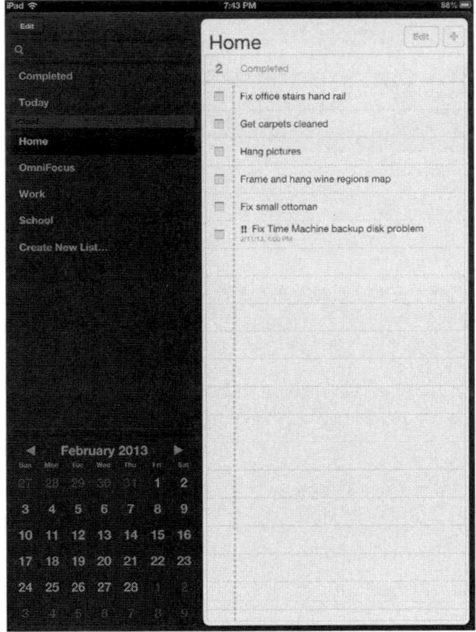

B The Reminders app on the iPad gives you a nice mini-month calendar, making it easier to jump to future dates.

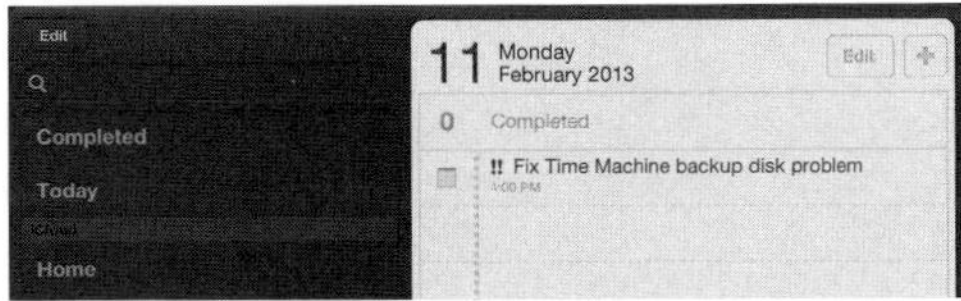

C On the iPad, when you tap on a date in the mini-calendar, tasks associated with that date appear.

Ⓓ Enter the title for your reminder.

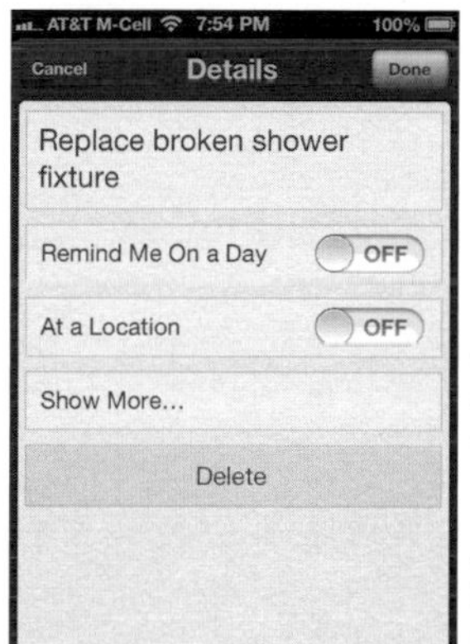

Ⓔ On the Details screen, you can choose to set a reminder date or location, or you can add other information to the reminder.

Ⓕ If you choose to be reminded at a location, you can also choose whether that reminder triggers when you leave or arrive at the location.

3. Type the reminder title Ⓓ.
4. (Optional) You can tap the Return key and enter more tasks.
5. On an iPhone or iPod touch, tap the Done button. On an iPad, tap somewhere other than the line you're typing in, or tap the Hide Keyboard key.

   The new reminder appears in the list.
6. To adjust the reminder's details, tap it in the list. A Details screen or popover (on the iPad) appears Ⓔ.

   If you tap Show More, you have the opportunity to set the reminder's Priority, change its assigned reminders list, or add Notes.
7. To set a due date or geographical reminder, you can turn on either (or both) Remind Me On a Day and At a Location.

   If you choose On a Day, Reminders will show you the standard date and time picker. Choose when you want to be reminded, then tap Done.

   If you choose At a Location, the Location screen will appear, showing your current location, your Home and Work locations from your iCloud Contacts list, and an Enter an Address field. Tapping that field allow you to either type an address, or you get the standard blue plus button that opens your Contacts list, from which you can choose the location where you want to be reminded. Pick a contact with an address, and you'll be returned to the Details screen, which now shows the contact name and address Ⓕ. You'll also get two new options, When I Leave and When I Arrive. Choose one of these.
8. Tap Done.

continues on next page

TIP **Location-based reminders are associated with the iPhone 4 and later. They don't work on earlier iPhones, the iPad, or iPod touch. Reminders with location information still appear on those other devices, but the location-specific information doesn't appear.**

TIP **You can delete, edit, or reorder your reminders by tapping the Edit button at the top of the screen.**

Reminders Versus the World

Reminders is a free app from Apple that enters an already very crowded field of iOS task managers, many of which also have Mac application counterparts that they sync with. Examples of apps with Mac versions include The Omni Group's OmniFocus, Appigo's ToDo, and Cultured Code's Things. Task managers that shine on iOS include BusyMac's BusyToDo (which works with their BusyCal desktop program); Toodledo, from the company of the same name, and WebIS' Pocket Informant Pro. Reminders also competes with iOS apps that are front ends to Web-based task management services, such as Remember the Milk's eponymous app.

So how does Reminders stack up in this crowd? Well, it's kind of the same situation as with calendaring. The Apple app does the job, but has a set of features that will leave power users wanting more, *more*, MORE! Reminders, based as it is around a simple list metaphor, doesn't have important features for hardcore task management warriors, such as the concept of grouping tasks into projects, or the ability to organize a bunch of tasks and show you the most important next action that needs doing. For devotees of the Getting Things Done or Franklin Covey organization methods, Reminders is not going to cut the mustard.

Interestingly, if you do choose to use one of these more-powerful task managers, you can leverage Reminders to make it easier to work with them. Apple is very picky about which apps can interface with Siri, the voice activated assistant, but Reminders is one of them. Other apps can use the default list created by Reminders, and can build in the ability to take information from that list into their own data. So for example, I use Siri to create reminders all the time, which make a quick stop in Reminders before being pulled into OmniFocus for iOS. Remember the Milk and Things have similar features.

But let's say that you don't have such a complicated life, you don't care about organizing tasks into projects, and you just want a decent to-do list. My advice is that you start with Reminders. If you find yourself after a while wanting more organizational control, there are plenty of apps in the App Store that can scratch that itch, starting with the ones I've listed above.

Reminders or Alarms?

With the advent of the Reminders iOS app, you now have more than one way to alert yourself when things need doing. You can use the Reminders app, as described above. But for some purposes, you might want to instead use the Alarm function of the iPhone's Clock app. Let's take a look at the differences between the two approaches.

The Reminders app is associated with your iCloud calendars and to-dos, and as a result synchronizes across all of your devices. That's great when you want that to happen, but sometimes you don't. For example, let's say that you need to take a medication each evening. You could certainly set up a Reminder for that, and it would appear on your Reminder List every day. That would tend to clutter up the Reminder List, especially if you had similar routine reminders. When the Reminder triggers, because it is associated with iCloud and synchronizes between your devices, you'll get alerts on all your devices, and you'll need to dismiss those alerts on all devices. I've certainly found it to be jarring when I had my iPhone, iPad, and Mac all in one room, and they all popped up a Reminder alert and made a noise at the same time.

On the other hand, the Clock app only runs on the iPhone, which you often carry on your person, and you can set it up to give you a recurring alarm (as well as setting as many different alarms you need in a particular day). Because it's not integrated with iCloud, there is no calendar clutter. And the Clock app's repeating function **G** has day-of-the-week options that the Reminders app does not **H**. By the way, if you need multiple reminders in the same day, there's a terrific app called HabiTimer from Sciral that's perfect for things that neither Clock nor Reminders does well, like alerting you to take medications multiple times in a day.

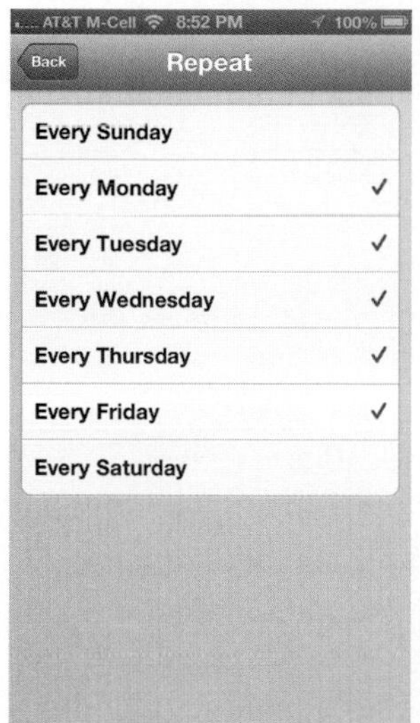

G In the Clock app, you have a bit more flexibility in terms of recurring day-of-the-week alarms.

H The Reminders app allows you to set reminders at intervals up to a year away.

Managing Notifications on Mac and iOS

Earlier in this chapter, you've seen lots of information about setting up and editing events and reminders on iOS devices, the Mac, and the iCloud website. But a large part of the power of event notifications is that they can take a proactive role in your life, actively letting you know when they come due. They do this through *notifications*, which are banners, dialogs, and sounds that appear on your devices. You set up notifications when you are creating an event or reminder, and they are pushed to your various devices via iCloud when those events and reminders are synchronized.

There are two kinds of visual notification that appear:

- *Banners* appear on the screen, hang around for a moment or two, then discreetly tuck themselves away Ⓐ.
- *Alerts* appear on the screen, but require action from the user (such as a click on a button) before they go away Ⓑ.

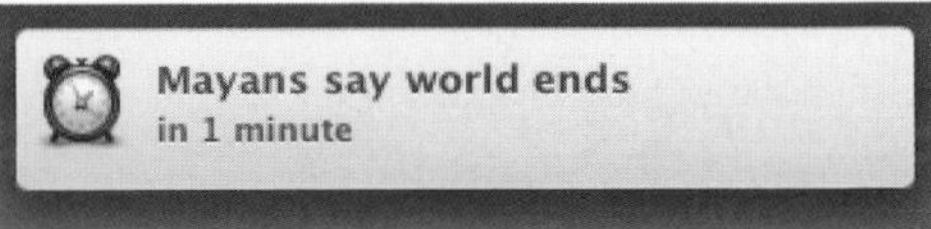

Ⓐ This is the banner notification, with a somewhat unsettling message.

Ⓑ This alert notification requires you to click one of the buttons before it leaves your screen.

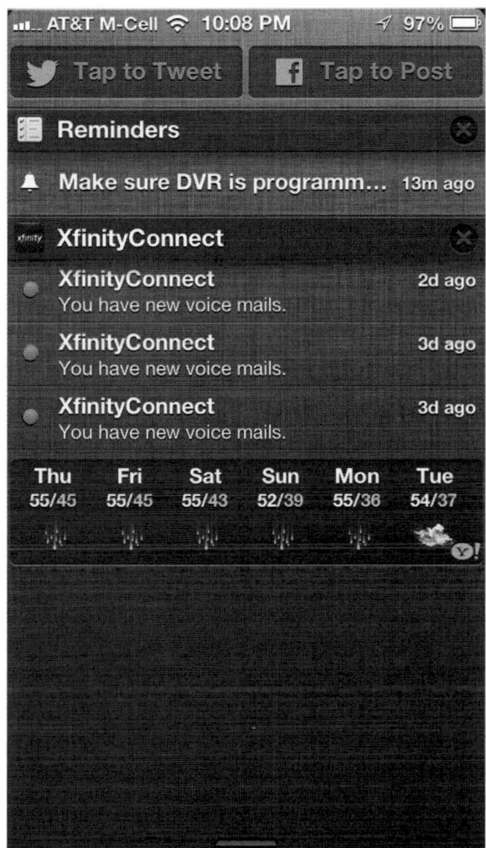

C Notification Center (shown here on an iPhone) can show you notifications from many different apps, allow you to post to Twitter and Facebook, and can even give you the weather forecast.

Beginning with Mountain Lion on the Mac and iOS 6, there is a central spot for working with notifications, cleverly called Notification Center. On the Mac, Notification Center is available from within all apps. By clicking an icon in the right edge of the menu bar, the contents of your screen slide to the left, showing you a bar with your latest notifications. On iOS, Notification Center is always available by swiping down from the top of the screen **C**. If you have your device configured to work with Twitter and Facebook on the operating system level, then Notification Center will also show widgets that allow you to quickly tweet and post to your Facebook Wall. The iPhone also has Notification Center widgets for Whether, Stocks, and Sharing.

On the Mac, Notification Center gets configured through the Notifications pane of System Preferences. On iOS, you use the Notifications section of the Settings app. On either operating system, you have the ability to configure notifications on an app-by-app basis. So, for example, on the Mac you can have your Calendar events appear as a banner, and your Reminders appear as an alert, and have the opposite setting on your iOS devices. The settings are per device, so you can even have different settings for your iPhone and iPad.

To configure notifications on a Mac:

1. From the Apple menu, choose System Preferences, then click Notifications.

   The Notifications preference pane appears **D**.

2. In the list on the left, find the app for which you want to configure notifications settings. If the app is down at the bottom of the list in the "Not in Notification Center" section, click and drag it up to the "In Notification Center" part of the list.

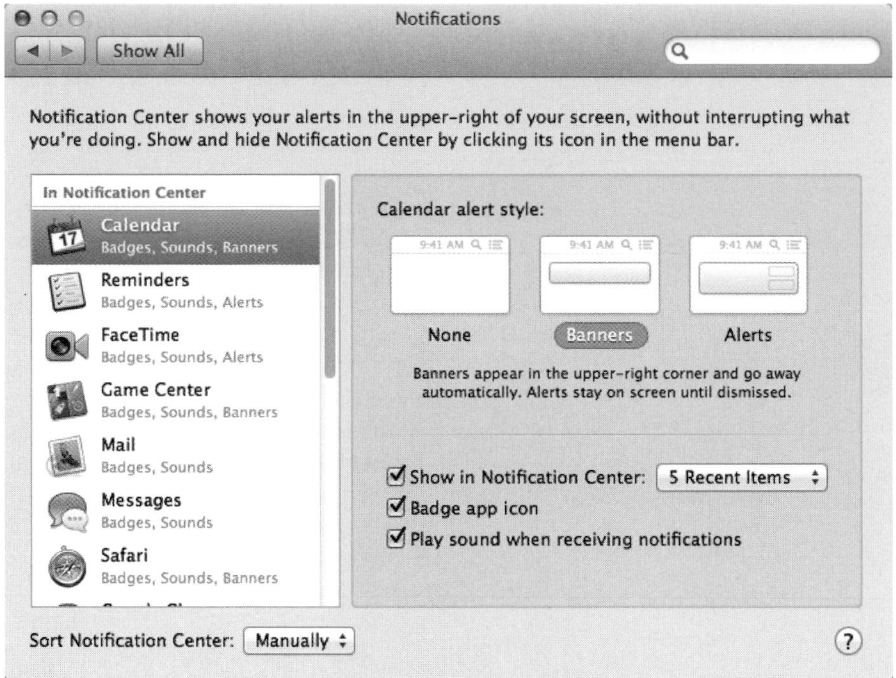

D On the Mac, set up your notification styles in System Preferences.

3. On the right side of the preference pane, do one or more of the following:
   - Pick the kind of alert style you want (None, Banners, or Alerts).
   - Choose whether or not you want the app's alerts to appear in Notification Center, and if so, how many items (1, 5, 10, or 20) you wish to appear there.
   - Select the checkbox if you want an incoming notification to put a numeric badge on the app's icon in the Dock.
   - Choose whether or not you want an alert sound to play when the notification comes in.
4. At the bottom of the preference pane, from the Sort Notification Center pop-up menu, choose Manually or By time. I prefer manually, because that keeps apps from moving around by themselves in the list.
5. Close System Preferences when you're done configuring things.

To configure notifications on an iOS device:

1. Tap the Settings app, then tap Notifications.

   The Notifications Screen appears **E**.

2. Scroll the list of apps until you find the one you want to configure, then tap it.
3. In the notification settings screen for the app **F**, first make sure that the Notification Center switch is turned on.
4. Set the number of recent items you want to show in Notification Center.
5. Set the Alert Style you want the app to use.
6. Different apps have different options available, but Badge App Icon and Sounds are two common settings. Choose whether you want them on or off.
7. Decide whether or not you want the alert notification from this app to appear in the lock screen of the iOS app; that is, the screen that appears after you wake the device but before you swipe to unlock it.

E On iOS, you'll make your decisions about Notifications in the Settings app.

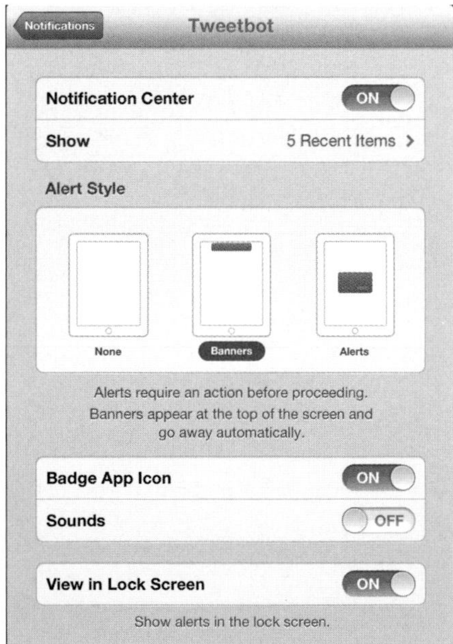

F Each app allows fine-grained choices about how its notifications appear.

Using iPhoto with iCloud

Photo Stream, part of the iCloud service, solves a familiar problem. You take a photo *here*, but you'd like to view it or work on it over *there*. For example, you might have taken a picture with your iPhone (following the hallowed adage that the best camera is the one that you have with you), then want to add it to your iPhoto library on your Mac. Or maybe you imported a bunch of pictures into iPhoto from your digital camera, and you'd like to show them off to people using your iPad. With Photo Stream, your new photos will be uploaded to the iCloud servers and will automagically be pushed to your other iCloud-enabled devices when they are connected to Wi-Fi.

You can choose to share all or part of your Photo Stream with other people, and you can delete individual photos from the Photo Stream (these two features were added to Photo Stream since iCloud's initial release.

On the Mac, Photo Stream works with Apple's iPhoto or Aperture programs. Since those programs don't exist on Windows, you can designate automatic download and upload folders on your PC's hard disk for use with Photo Stream.

In This Chapter

Setting up Photo Stream in iCloud	100
Working with Photo Stream in iPhoto	104
Sharing Your Photo Stream	109
Deleting Photos	113

Setting up Photo Stream in iCloud

Photos uploaded to Photo Stream are stored in iCloud for 30 days. Your iOS devices keep a rolling collection of the last 1,000 photos in your Photo Stream, in order to make the best use of their limited storage. Since computers generally have way more storage space than mobile devices, all of the photos that are part of your Photo Stream are kept on your Mac or PC, even if you shoot more than 1,000 photos in a month.

Photo Stream supports JPG, TIF, PNG, and most RAW photo formats. On a computer, your photos will be downloaded and stored in full resolution. iCloud delivers photos to your iOS device (iPhone, iPad, iPad mini, iPod touch, and Apple TV), in a reduced resolution to save storage space and speed up download times. And while we're on the subject of storage space, pictures in your Photo Stream don't count against the 5 GB of free storage that you get with your iCloud account.

TIP Photo Stream only works with still photos, not with video.

TIP The system requirements for Photo Stream on a Mac are the same as for iCloud in general. On a PC, you'll need to be running Microsoft 8, Windows 7, or Windows Vista with Service Pack 2. You can download the Windows iCloud control panel from `http://support.apple.com/kb/DL1455`. After downloading, double-click the iCloudSetup.exe file to install the control panel.

To enable Photo Stream on either a Mac or PC, you'll use the iCloud preference pane (Mac) or Control Panel (Windows).

A You enable Photo Stream in the iCloud preference pane on a Mac. Note the Options button.

B On a Windows PC, you use the iCloud Control Panel to enable Photo Stream. Note the Options button.

To enable Photo Stream on your Mac or PC:

1. On a Mac, choose System Preferences > iCloud **A**.

   or

   On a Windows Vista or Windows 7 PC, choose Start Menu > Control Panel > Network and Internet > iCloud **B**.

   or

   On a Windows 8 PC, begin on the Start screen and click the Desktop tile, which switches you to Desktop mode. Move your mouse to the upper or lower right corner of the screen to reveal the Charms bar, and then click the Settings charm. In the resulting settings bar, click the Control Panel link.

   The Control Panel appears.

2. On either platform, select the checkbox next to Photo Stream.

   On the Mac, close the System Preferences window. On Windows, click Apply, then close the iCloud control panel.

continues on next page

3. (Optional, but recommended) On a Mac, you should make sure your Photo Stream settings are configured for automatic downloading and to allow Photo Stream sharing. Click the Options button Ⓐ to display the Photo Stream Options dialog Ⓒ. Make sure both the My Photo Stream and Shared Photo Streams checkboxes are selected.

   or

   On a PC, you can choose to change the default folders Photo Stream uses for uploads and downloads. Click the Options button Ⓑ to display the Photo Stream Options dialog Ⓓ. The dialog shows you the default paths to the download and upload folders; click the Change buttons next to either of those folders to switch them to a different location on your PC's hard drive, navigate to the new locations, select the location, then click OK. Back in the Options dialog, click OK again.

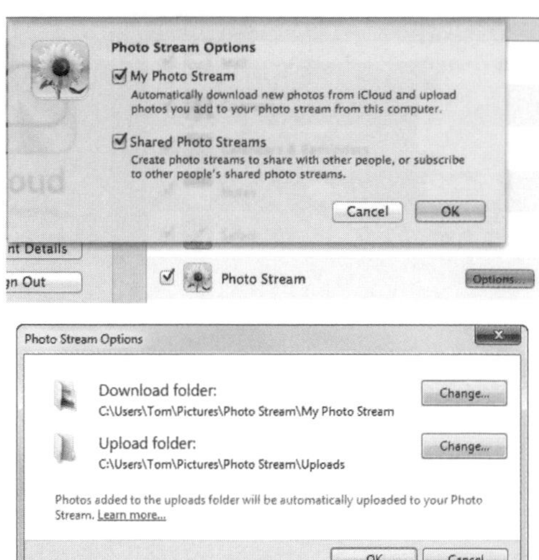

Ⓒ You can set options on both platforms. On Mac (top), you turn on automatic uploading and syncing, and enable Photo Stream sharing. On Windows (bottom), if you want to change the download and upload folders, you can do so in the Photo Stream Options dialog.

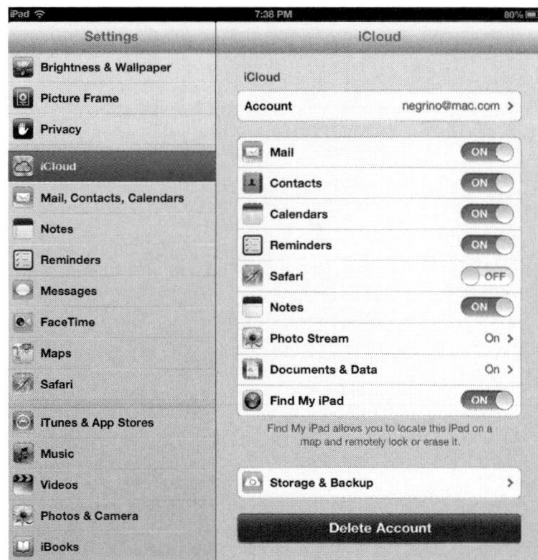

Ⓓ Begin setting up Photo Stream on an iOS device in the iCloud Settings.

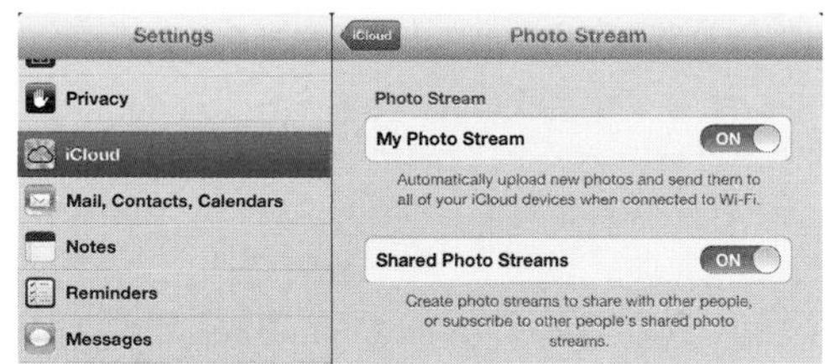

E When you turn the My Photo Stream switch to On, photos will automatically begin uploading and downloading. Turning on the Shared Photo Streams switch enables the feature for that iOS device.

Setting up Photo Stream on your iOS device:

1. Choose > Settings > iCloud.
2. Tap Photo Stream.

   The screen changes to show the Photo Stream preferences **E**.
3. Slide the My Photo Stream and Shared Photo Streams switches to On.

   If your mobile device is connected to Wi-Fi, it will immediately begin downloading photos from the iCloud servers, and uploading new photos.

TIP If you want to remove the Photo Stream from your iOS device, simply turn it Off in Settings. The Photo Stream photos will be removed from your iOS device, but will remain on the iCloud servers.

Photo Stream Drawbacks

The ability of Photo Stream to automatically make your photos appear on all of your devices is quite useful. However, iCloud is missing some functionality compared to the previous photo capabilities in MobileMe. For example, as of this writing, you can't view your Photo Stream on the iCloud website. There's no iCloud equivalent yet to the MobileMe Gallery, so you can't share Events or Albums online. And of course, because you can't view your Photo Stream online, you also can't edit or delete individual photos from the Photo Stream from the iCloud website. These features are so obvious that I expect Apple to add them sooner or later, but for now Photo Stream feels a bit unfinished.

Working with Photo Stream in iPhoto

Pictures from Photo Stream appear in iPhoto '11 (version 9.2.1 or later) in a new entry in the iPhoto sidebar **A**. Clicking this entry in the sidebar shows you the pictures in your Photo Stream **B**. It's important to understand that pictures that appear in your Photo Stream haven't yet been imported into your photo library; you'll either need to enable Automatic Import or manually import the photos in a separate step, as described later in this section.

Photo Stream works with either iPhoto or Apple's Aperture (see the "The Aperture Alternative" sidebar in this section), but not both at the same time. You have to choose which program you'll use with Photo Stream, and turning the feature on in one program automatically turns it off in the other.

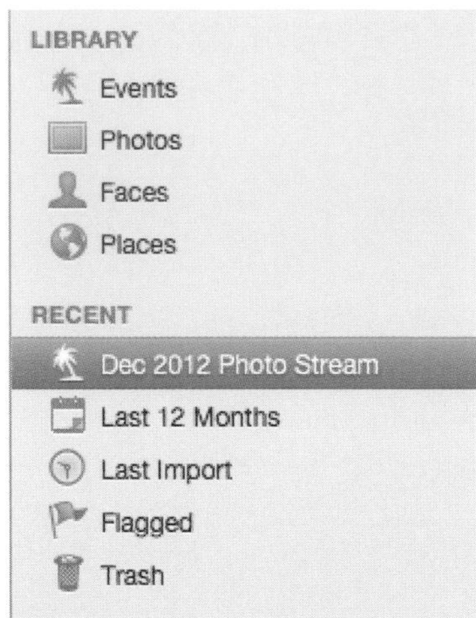

A Photo Stream appears as just another source in the iPhoto sidebar.

B Clicking Photo Stream in the sidebar displays the photos in the iPhoto document window.

In either program's preferences, you can decide whether or not you want the program to automatically import Photo Stream photos into the program's Events, Photos, Faces, and Places, and, if you want, automatically upload those imported photos to the iCloud servers.

Since automatically pushing your photos to all your devices is the whole point of Photo Stream, why wouldn't you want to automatically upload photos to iCloud? Remember that Photo Stream accepts full resolution photos from digital cameras, so if you're shooting RAW format photos with your digital SLR, then importing them on a computer, iPhoto or Aperture will automatically upload all those pictures, which could potentially be many gigabytes in size. If you happen to live in an area with slow Internet connections or metered data, uploading those pictures could get very expensive (and if your iOS devices are on your Wi-Fi network, you'll also incur bandwidth for downloading the resolution-optimized versions of those photos when they get pushed to your mobile devices). In that case, you might want to deselect the Automatic Upload checkbox in the Photo Stream preferences in your photo management application.

TIP There's also a caveat in allowing automatic upload to Photo Stream from your iOS device. If you're the kind of person (and you know who you are) who could happen to shoot a potentially embarrassing picture with your iPhone, it will automatically be pushed up to iCloud and down to your iPad and computers. So if you share the latter devices with other people, they'll immediately see the photographic evidence. See "Deleting Photos," later in this chapter, for a possible remedy for your faux pas.

To set Photo Stream preferences:

1. Choose iPhoto > Preferences > Photo Stream **C**.

   or

   Choose Aperture > Preferences > Photo Stream.

2. Select the Enable Photo Stream checkbox.

   By default, the Automatic Import and Automatic Upload checkboxes are also selected. Deselect one or both, according to your needs.

To disable Photo Stream in your photo program:

1. Open the Photo Stream preferences of your photo program.

2. Deselect the checkbox next to Enable Photo Stream.

   The photo program warns you that all the photos in the Photo Stream view will be removed **D**. You may already have imported all the photos into your photo library, but it's still usually a good idea to click the Import Photos and Turn Off button. It won't duplicate already imported pictures.

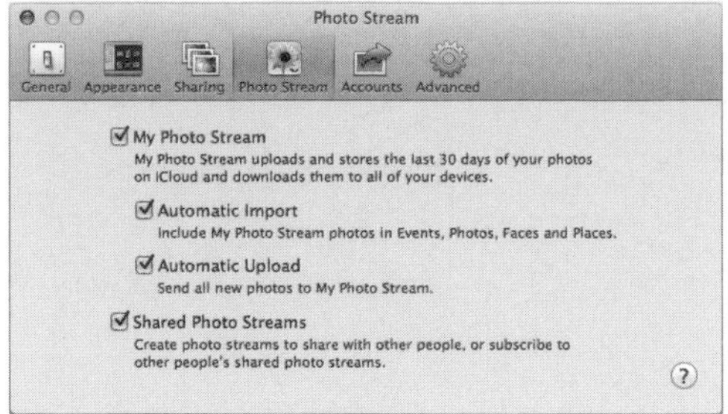

C Enable Photo Stream and Photo Stream Sharing in iPhoto's preferences.

D If you turn Photo Stream off, iPhoto warns you that you will lose photos that you have not imported into your iPhoto library.

E To import photos from your Photo Stream into the iPhoto library, select them in the document window, then drag them to Photos in the sidebar.

F iPhoto helps you deal with accidentally importing duplicate photos.

To import Photo Stream items into an iPhoto or Aperture library:

1. Click on Photo Stream in the sidebar of your photo management program.
2. Select individual photos in the Photo Stream. You can use the Shift key to select multiple contiguous photos, or use the Command key to select multiple noncontiguous photos.
3. Drag the selected photos to the Photos item in the sidebar **E**.

   If you inadvertently try to import photos that have already been imported, the program will let you know and allow you to decide what you want to do **F**.

The Aperture Alternative

Photo Stream doesn't just work in iPhoto; it also works with Apple's Aperture program (version 3.2 or later). Aperture is Apple's high-end photo application; you can think of it as (and Apple positions it as) iPhoto Pro. Compared to iPhoto, Aperture gives you many more tools for retouching, editing, adding effects, and managing your photos. Aperture is designed to work with very large photo libraries, and unlike iPhoto, you can maintain separate Aperture libraries to better segregate your different kinds of photography.

When you enable Photo Stream in Aperture, it appears as just another category in your library **G**. If you try to enable Photo Stream in Aperture and the feature is already turned on in iPhoto, Aperture gives you the opportunity to switch the Photo Stream **H**, which automatically turns off the feature in iPhoto.

G Like iPhoto, Aperture displays Photo Stream as another choice in its Library.

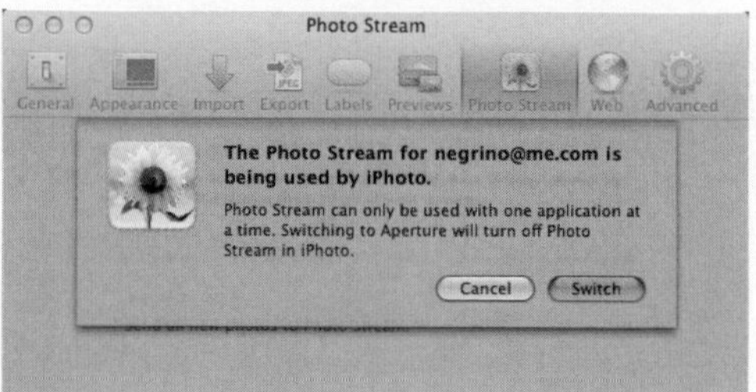

H If you already have iPhoto selected as the destination for your Photo Stream and you try to turn it on in Aperture, the program lets you know it will be switching the Photo Stream to Aperture from iPhoto.

Sharing Your Photo Stream

Beginning with iOS 6 (and companion upgrades to iPhoto 9.4 and Aperture 3.4), you can share selected photos from your Photo Stream with other people you choose. When people you invite to share your Photo Stream subscribe, they can view the photos, mark individual photos as "liked," and leave comments on a photo. You can optionally allow people to view photos on the web.

You can create a shared Photo Stream on an iOS device, in iPhoto or Aperture on a Mac, or from the iCloud control panel on a Windows PC. We'll focus in this section on working with iOS devices; see the Help files for the photo programs or Windows control panel for detailed instructions on working with shared Photo Streams using that software.

To share your Photo Stream from an iOS device:

1. On your iOS 6 or later device, tap Photos **A**.

   The Photos app appears **B**.

2. Tap the Photo Stream tab.

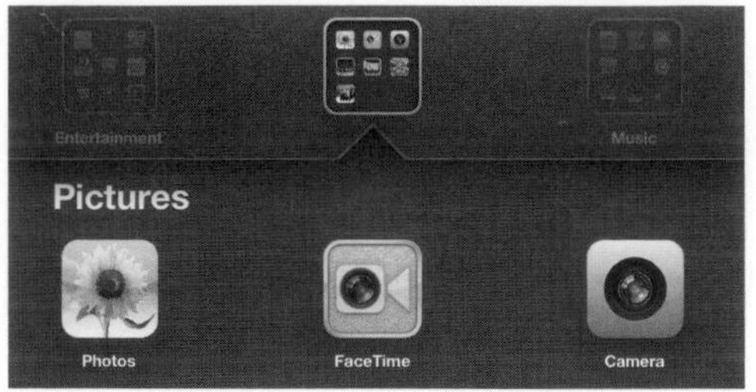

A Find the Photos app on your iOS device, then tap to launch it.

B The Photos app appears, with several tabs across the top of the screen.

Ⓒ Tap My Photo Stream to begin selecting photos to share.

Ⓓ Tap the photos you wish to share.

Ⓔ Tap the Share button, then the Photo Stream button, to begin the sharing process.

3. Tap My Photo Stream Ⓒ, then tap the Edit button at the upper-right corner of the screen.
4. On the Edit screen tap to select the photos you wish to share Ⓓ. Blue checkmarks appear on your selected photos.
5. Tap the Share button, then from the resulting popover, tap Photo Stream Ⓔ.

continues on next page

6. In the Photo Stream sheet **F**, enter the sharing recipients, give the shared Photo Stream a name, and optionally turn on viewing from a public website. Tap Next.
7. Add an optional brief comment to introduce the shared stream to your recipients, then tap the Post button **G**.

   The new shared Photo Stream appears on the Photo Stream tab of Photos **H**.

TIP Besides the Photos app, you can also create Shared Photo Streams from the Camera Roll or an album in your Camera Roll.

TIP People you invite who want to view the shared stream on an iOS device must be using iOS 6 or later.

TIP The Public Website switch allows people without an iCloud account to view the photo stream in a web browser; this might be perfect for, say, grandparents who don't have their own iOS devices. They'll get the URL of the shared stream when they accept the invitation to join the stream.

F Add the recipients for the shared stream, and give the stream a descriptive name.

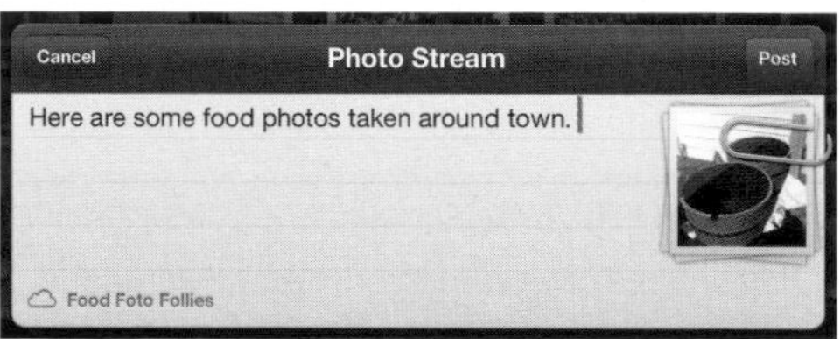

G If you like, add an additional comment explaining the shared stream, then send it off.

H The new shared stream appears on the Photo Streams tab.

Deleting Photos

Control of Photo Stream on iCloud isn't very granular. You can't view your main Photo Stream on the iCloud website, nor can you delete individual pictures from the Photo Stream on the web. What you can do is reset your entire Photo Stream, deleting all photos from the server or from individual devices.

To delete your Photo Stream photos from the iCloud server, you'll use the iCloud website. To delete all Photo Stream photos from your photo management program or your iOS devices, you simply turn off Photo Stream in the Preferences of the program or the iCloud Settings of the device. On a PC, you need to delete any photos in the Import folder.

If you want to completely delete all of the photos in your Photo Stream, you'll need to first reset your Photo Stream on the iCloud website, then turn Photo Stream off from your various devices.

Beginning with iOS 6, you can delete individual photos, but you must do that using an iOS device, from iPhoto, or with Aperture. Again, we'll focus on the iOS procedure, which begins in the same fashion as sharing photos. Refer to "Sharing your Photo Stream" for screenshots.

TIP If you leave Photo Stream enabled on any of your devices, that device will refill iCloud with all of the photos you deleted from the website (at least the last 1,000 photos that were pushed to the mobile device).

To delete your Photo Stream on the iCloud website:

1. Log in to the iCloud website.
2. Click your name on the iCloud homepage.
3. Click the Advanced button.
4. In the Advanced screen **A**, click the Reset Photo Stream button.

   A confirmation dialog will appear **B**.
5. Click Reset.

   The photos will immediately be deleted from your Photo Stream.

continues on next page

A You can delete your Photo Stream photos from the iCloud servers on the iCloud website.

B As usual when you want to do something destructive, you'll get a confirmation dialog.

TIP If you had Automatic Import enabled in your Photo Stream settings in iPhoto or Aperture, your Photo Stream photos were imported into your program's library, and will remain after you disable Photo Stream. You can, of course, manually delete any of these photos in the programs.

TIP If you turn Photo Stream off on your iOS device, you'll lose access to the Photo Stream on that device, and it will also stop uploading new pictures to the Photo Stream. If you turn Photo Stream back on, any new photos you shoot will start flowing to iCloud again, but any photos you took while Photo Stream was off won't be uploaded.

To delete individual pictures from your Photo Stream:

1. On your iOS 6 or later device, tap Photos.

   The Photos app appears.
2. Tap the Photo Stream tab.
3. Tap the photo stream from which you want to delete photos (if you have more than one stream), then tap the Edit button at the upper-right corner of the screen.
4. On the Edit screen tap to select the photos you wish to delete. Blue checkmarks appear on your selected photos.
5. Tap the Delete button. You'll get an "are you sure?" popover **C**.
6. Tap Delete Selected Photos.

C Only tap that red button if you're sure you want to delete the selected photos on all of your devices. Don't say you weren't warned.

6

Using iTunes with iCloud

Since the whole point of iCloud is that all your stuff should be on all your devices, it wouldn't make much sense if the contents of your iTunes Library didn't make it to the iCloud party. Happily, almost any music you have in one place can now appear anywhere you want.

Using a feature called iTunes in the Cloud, you can share your purchased iTunes items with up to ten of your (and perhaps your family's) iOS devices and computers. New items you purchase from the iTunes Store automatically appear on all your devices; there's no more need for manual syncing.

You can also purchase a subscription to a service called iTunes Match, which scans your iTunes Library for music tracks you didn't purchase from the iTunes Store. Matched files are replaced by streaming versions from the Store, at full quality. Any tracks that can't be matched are uploaded from your computer to iCloud and can be downloaded to all your devices.

In This Chapter

Configuring iTunes in the Cloud 116

Configuring and Using iTunes Match 122

Updating Your Music with iTunes Match 130

Configuring iTunes in the Cloud

With its iTunes in the Cloud feature, iCloud has the ability to automatically download purchases to your iOS devices, and re-download purchases that you bought in the past but aren't currently on a particular device.

First, let's talk about automatic downloading. Before iCloud, if you purchased something from the iTunes Store (apps, books, music, movies, or TV shows) you needed to use iTunes to make sure those items were on all of the devices you wanted them on. With iCloud, you can choose to push apps, books, and music automatically to all your devices, no matter on which device you buy the media, as long as you bought the item on the iTunes Store. You can choose to use just Wi-Fi for this automatic downloading, or you can also enable the ability via cellular data. The best part of all this automatic downloading is that it really is automatic: once you set it up, purchased items simply appear on all your devices without your having to worry about item management. Automatic downloading isn't available if you buy music from other online stores, say, Amazon; see the "Configuring and Using iTunes Match" section later in this chapter for a workaround.

TIP Although you can buy TV shows and movies from the iTunes Store, they can't be automatically downloaded, no doubt because they would require so much bandwidth. You can, however, copy video to your iOS device via Wi-Fi, not just USB; that's one of the features introduced with iOS 5.

You also have the ability to re-download items to your iOS device. Imagine that you had previously purchased something from the iTunes Store, and you removed it from your iOS device to free up some space. Or perhaps there was an app that you previously used only on your iPhone, but now you would also like it on your iPad. Or if you replace an iOS device with a newer model, you can choose which purchased items you would like to put on the new device.

To set up automatic downloads on a Mac or PC:

1. In iTunes, choose iTunes > Preferences > Store **A**.
2. In the Automatic Downloads section of the Store dialog, choose one or more of Music, Apps, or Books.

TIP As you would expect, iTunes does the right thing when it comes to the appropriateness of its automatic downloading. For example, an app that works only on an iPad won't be downloaded to an iPhone or iPod touch.

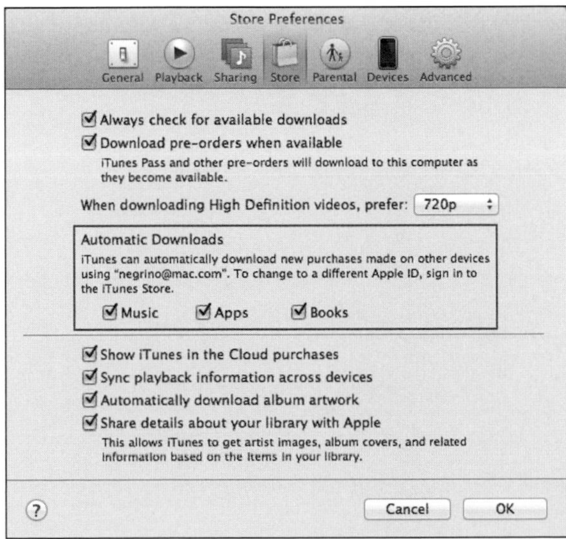

A Turn on automatic downloads in iTunes' Preferences.

To set up automatic downloads on iOS:

1. On your iOS device, tap Settings > iTunes & App Stores.
2. On the iTunes & App Stores screen **B**, choose which items (Music, Apps, or Books) you want to automatically download.
3. (Optional) Turn on Use Cellular Data. On devices with 3G and 4G support, this will use the cellular data network to download your purchases, not just Wi-Fi, though if Wi-Fi is active, it will always be preferred.

TIP The drawback of using cellular data for automatic downloads is that you may go over your cellular data limitation (in countries and with cellular carriers that impose such caps).

TIP For publications that appear in iOS's Newsstand app, you can turn automatic downloading on or off for each publication you have installed in Newsstand. Because each publication is actually a different app (even though it shows up in Newsstand, which you can really think of as a specialized folder), you'll find the publication's download settings in the long list of app settings at the bottom of the Settings app.

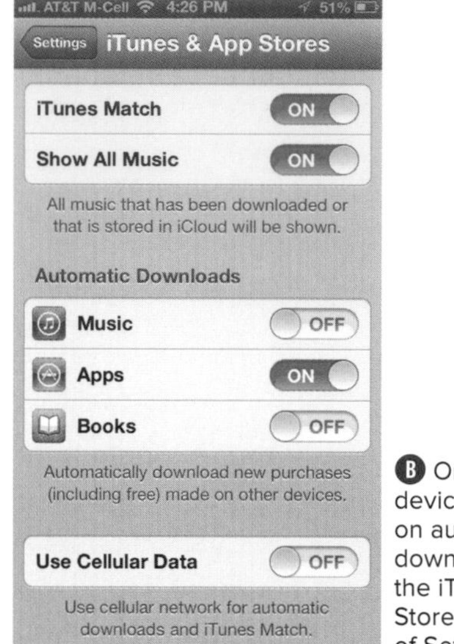

B On an iOS device, you turn on automatic downloads in the iTunes & App Stores section of Settings.

C In the App Store app, if you choose Purchased and All, you can see a list of the apps you've previously purchased.

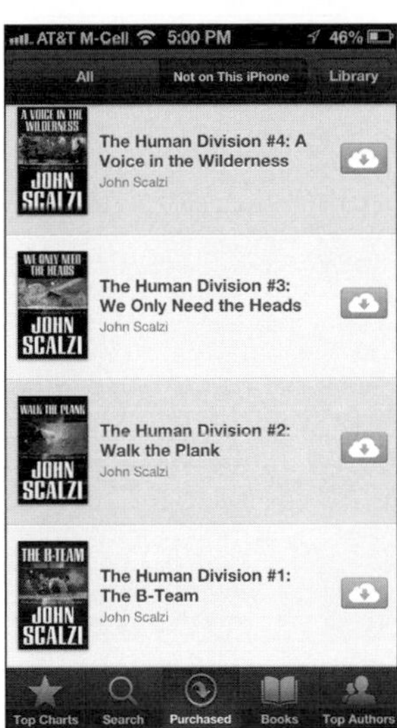

D Since you are re-downloading, you probably want to use the Not on This iPhone category.

To re-download items on iOS:

1. You re-download purchases in the iOS app that deals with the item you want to re-download. So you use the iBooks app to retrieve books from the iTunes Store; the iTunes app for Music or TV Shows; and the App Store app to re-download apps. The process is similar in all three apps. Do one or more of the following:

   In the iTunes app, tap More at the bottom of the screen, then choose Purchased, then choose from Music, Movies, or TV Shows.

   or

   In the iBooks app, tap the Library button (if you're already reading a book), which displays the Library screen. Tap the Store button, then tap Purchased at the bottom of the screen.

   or

   In the App Store app, tap Updates at the bottom of the screen, then tap Purchased **C**.

2. In all three apps, tap the Not on This (*device name*) button so that you don't inadvertently re-download an item that's already on your device **D**.

continues on next page

3. Find the item or items that you want to re-download, then tap the download from iCloud button next to the item, or the Download All button (the latter only appears in the iTunes app) **E**.

TIP It's important to note that in order to re-download items, you must be signed in to iCloud with the same Apple ID you used to purchase those items in the first place. If you want an item that was purchased under a different Apple ID (for example, my wife and I each have the other's devices authorized under our individual Apple IDs, so we can share purchases), you must sign out of iCloud on your device and sign back in using the other Apple ID.

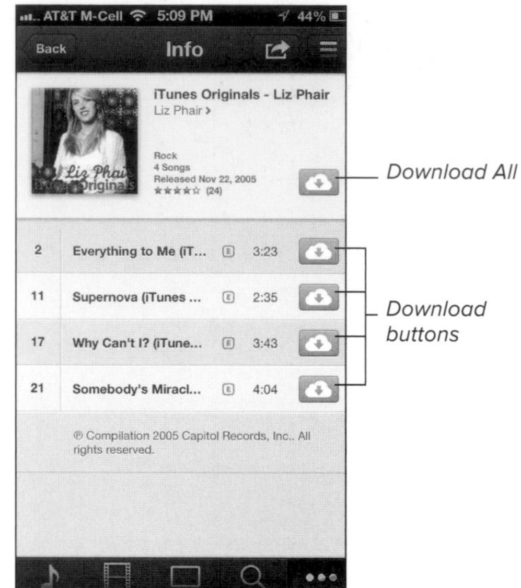

E Tap the Download button for an individual item, or Download All for all the items.

To re-download items in iTunes:

1. In iTunes 11, click on the iTunes Store button in the toolbar.

   iTunes connects to the iTunes Store.

2. Click the Purchases link in the Quick Links section of the window **F**.

   All the items that you purchased from the iTunes Store appear in the list.

F Click the Purchased link in the iTunes store to see your purchased items.

3. Click the category from which you want to re-download an item (Music, Movies, TV Shows, Apps, or Books) **G**.
4. Click the Not on This Computer button near the top of the window.
5. Find the item you wish to re-download, then click the Download button next to it. Alternatively, you can click the Download All button at the bottom of the window.

   iTunes downloads the selected items.

TIP The Download All button is not available for Movies or TV Shows.

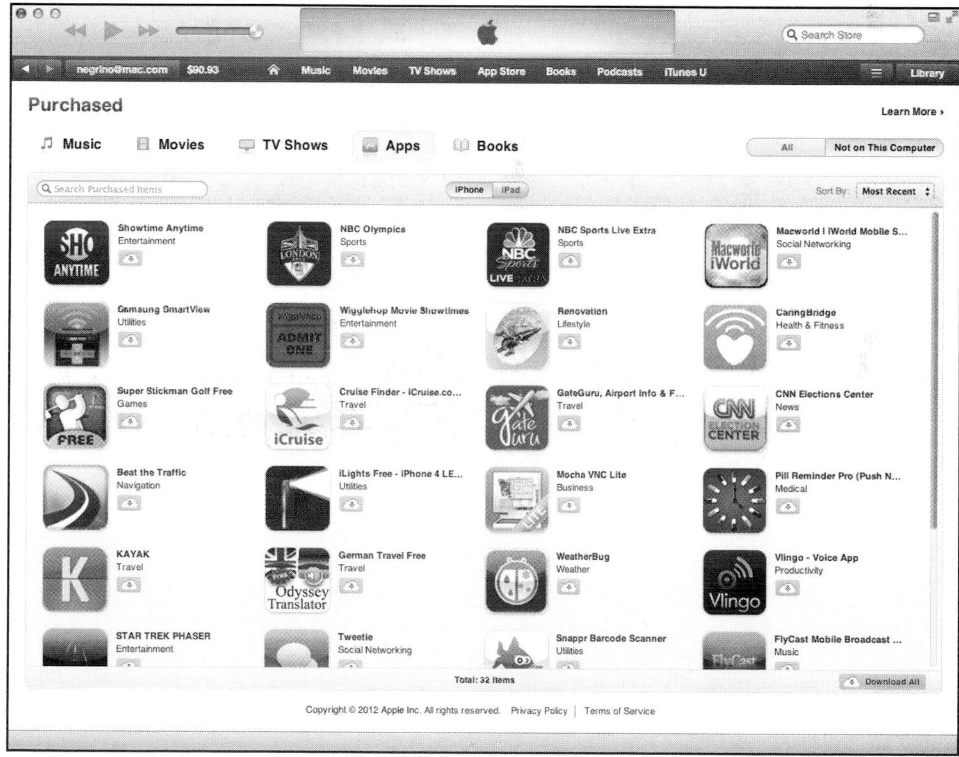

G Choose the category of the item that you wish to re-download.

Configuring and Using iTunes Match

iTunes in the Cloud works fine to distribute apps, books, individual music tracks, and albums you purchased from the iTunes Store to your different devices. But if, like many of us, much of your music collection comes from CDs you've ripped over the years into your iTunes Library, you probably want a way to get that music onto your devices as well. Of course, you've always been able to synchronize your music from iTunes to another device via a cable. But that requires that you know what it is that you want to synchronize before you leave on a trip, and move that music manually over to the mobile device. It would be better if you could simply download any part of your music collection to your mobile device according to your mood.

With a subscription service called iTunes Match, you can do exactly that Ⓐ. Launched initially only in the United States, iTunes Match costs $25 a year. What it does is clever: it scans all the tracks in your iTunes Library, and then matches them with the same files that are already on the iTunes Store (as of this writing, there are more than 26 million tracks in the iTunes Store). Once it matches your files with the Store's files, it shows your entire library and marks your files as downloadable on all your devices. When you want to listen to a track, iCloud uses the version from the Store, so you don't need to upload your entire music library (and saving Apple valuable server space; this way, it doesn't have to keep thousands of copies of popular songs on their servers, just the one copy from the Store). A real advantage of using iTunes Match is that matched music files

Ⓐ iTunes Match allows you to replicate the contents of your local iTunes Library on iCloud, without the hassle of needing to upload your entire music collection.

iTunes Match Requirements

One interesting feature of iTunes Match is that unlike most iCloud-related services, it doesn't require OS X Lion (though because it's part of iCloud, for use on iOS devices, it does need iOS 5.0.1 or later). iTunes Match works with any version of OS X that supports the needed version of iTunes (10.5.1), which means that at this writing, you can use iTunes Match on OS X 10.5 Leopard or later, and the hardware requirements are trivial: any Mac with an Intel or PowerPC G5 or G4 processor and 512MB of RAM.

that you stream or download from the Store are in the 256 Kbps AAC format, with no DRM (Digital Rights Management). If you had previously ripped a song at a lower quality, the matched version will be sonically superior. See the "Updating Your Music with iTunes Match" section, later in this chapter.

If iTunes Match can't find a match for some of your files, it will upload the unmatched files to iCloud for use on all your devices. Neither the matched tracks nor uploaded tracks count against the 5 GB of free storage you get with iCloud.

There are some significant limitations to iTunes Match. First, the service isn't available in all countries (to check if your country is included, see **support.apple.com/kb/ht5085**). Second, if you have more than 25,000 tracks in your iTunes Library, you can't use the service (there are workarounds if you split up your library). iTunes Match will only match music files that are encoded at a bit rate of 96 kbps or greater, and files that are 200 MB or smaller. Also excluded from iTunes Match: podcasts, audio books, TV shows, movies, ebooks, and ringtones. However, it does work with music videos purchased from the iTunes Store.

You'll need to enable all devices you want to use with iTunes Match. First, we'll see how to enable it in iTunes on a Mac (a PC is similar), then turn the feature on using an iOS device and download music from iCloud onto the device. Finally, we'll see how you can manage your iTunes Match devices using iTunes.

To add a computer to iTunes Match:

1. In iTunes 11 or later, choose View > Show Sidebar (it's faster to work using the sidebar), then click iTunes Match in the sidebar. If you haven't yet subscribed to iTunes Match with the Apple ID you use with the iTunes Store, the informational screen will have a Subscribe button Ⓐ. Click the Subscribe button and go through the subscription process.

   or

   If you have already signed up for iTunes Match, and simply want to add the computer as one of the iTunes Match devices, click the Add This Computer button Ⓑ.

2. In the resulting dialog Ⓒ, enter your Apple ID and password, then click the Subscribe or Add This Computer button.

3. Once you've agreed to the iTunes Match subscription, iTunes begins scanning your iTunes Library and uploading information about the tracks within it to iCloud Ⓓ.

   This process can take quite a while (up to several hours), depending on how many tracks you have in your iTunes Library. However, you can still continue using iTunes during the process.

Ⓑ If you have already signed up for iTunes Match on a different computer, click the Add This Computer button to add it as one of your iCloud devices.

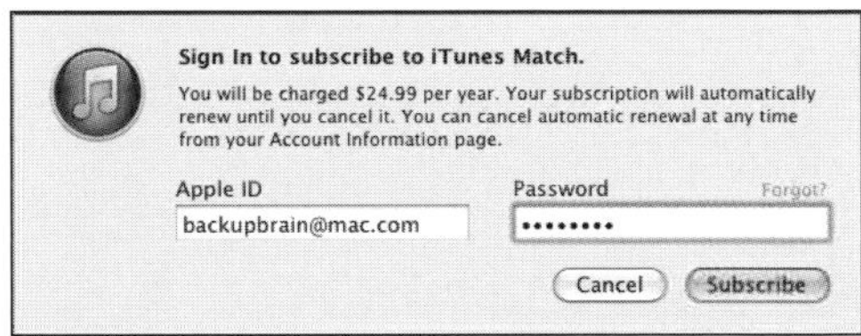

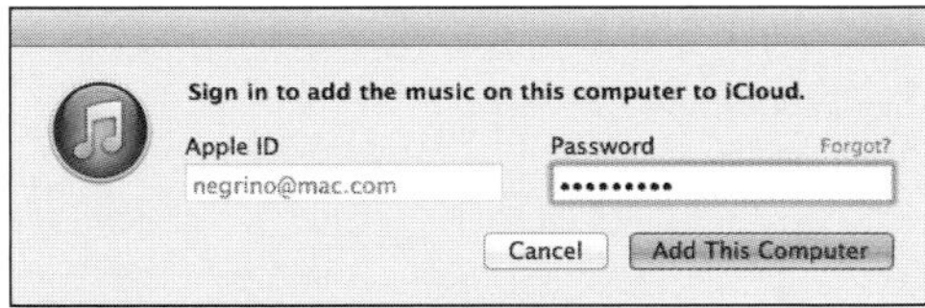

Ⓒ Enter the Apple ID and password associated with the iTunes Store to either subscribe to or add a computer to iTunes Match.

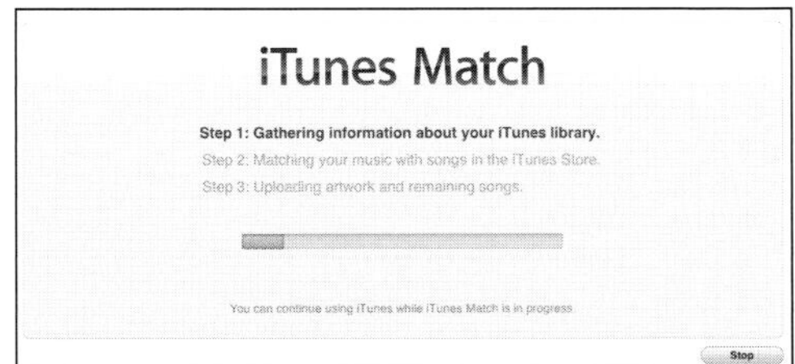

Ⓓ If you have a fair amount of tracks in your iTunes Library, it could take several hours for the scanning to complete.

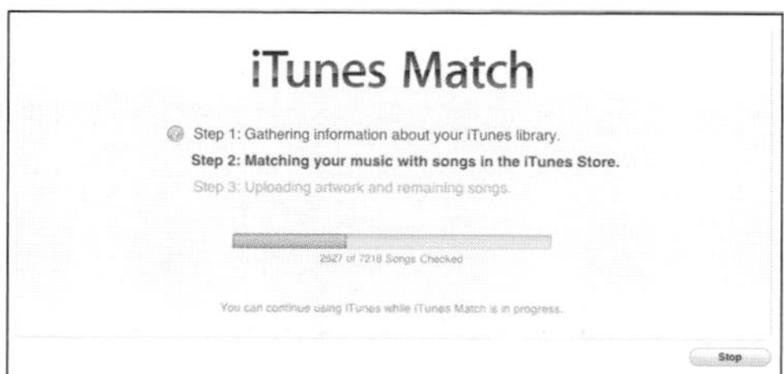

E Similarly, once the scan is complete, it could take quite a while to match your local files with files in the iTunes Store.

F When the process is complete, iTunes tells you how many songs are now available in iCloud.

G Once your songs are available in iCloud, an iCloud icon appears next to the Music entry in the iTunes sidebar.

4. Once iTunes has finished scanning your tracks, it begins matching your music with music on the iTunes Store **E**. Again, this is usually a lengthy process, but you don't have to stop using iTunes.

5. When iTunes finishes the matching, it automatically uploads unmatched songs and their artwork to iCloud. When the whole process is complete, iTunes lets you know in the iTunes Match screen **F**. In the sidebar, a cloud icon will also appear next to the Music, Movies, and TV Shows entries **G**.

continues on next page

TIP If you want to see the iTunes Match status of the items within your music library, in iTunes, choose View > View Options, then select the iCloud Download and iCloud Status checkboxes **H**, then click OK. In the Library list, iTunes will show you which items have been matched, which have been purchased, and which items are not on your current computer but are able to be downloaded from iCloud **I**. If there is no icon in the iCloud Download column, that means a copy of the track is already stored locally.

TIP To download items from iCloud, select the items in the iCloud Download column of the iTunes list with the download icon, then right-click and choose Download **J**.

TIP On a computer, if you play music that is on iCloud, iCloud will stream the music to you. On an iOS device, playing music stored on iCloud also downloads that track to your device.

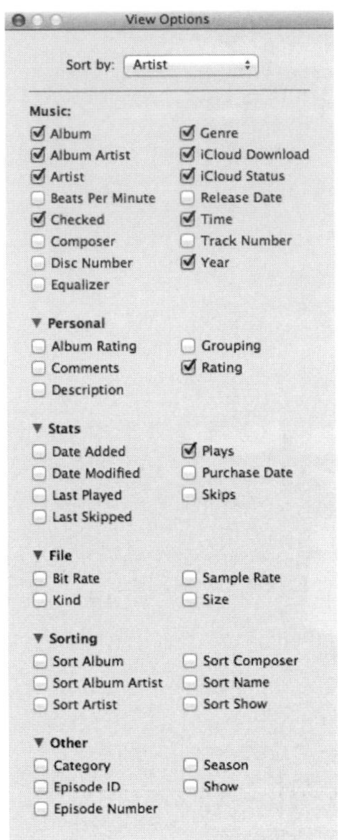

H To see what's going on with individual tracks, turn on iCloud Download and iCloud Status in iTunes' View Options.

I In the iTunes list, you can see which songs need to be downloaded to your local computer, as well as each track's iCloud status.

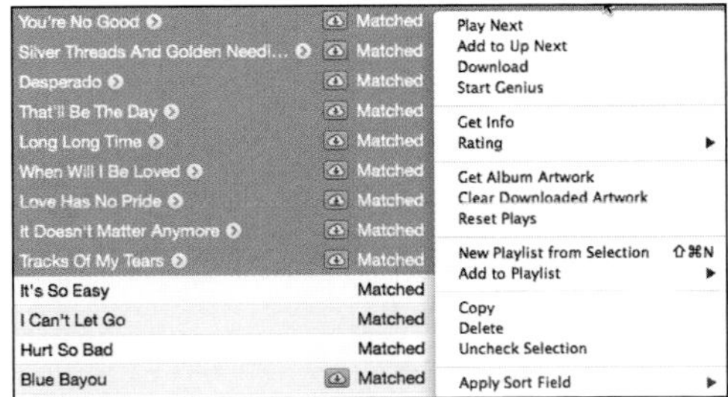

J Select all the files that need to be downloaded, then right-click and choose Download from the shortcut menu to download them to your computer.

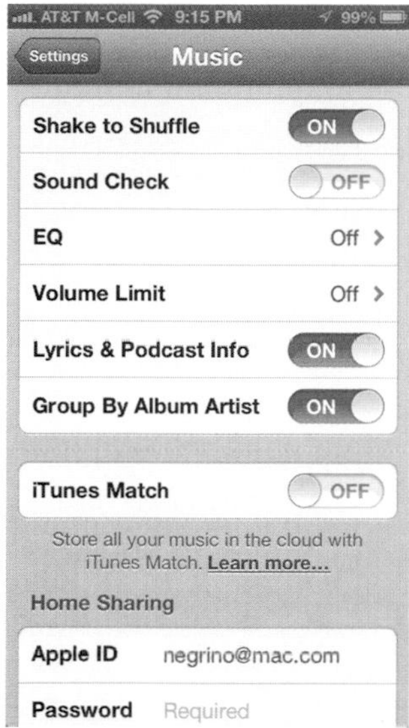

Ⓚ Begin enabling iTunes Match in the Music section of the Settings app.

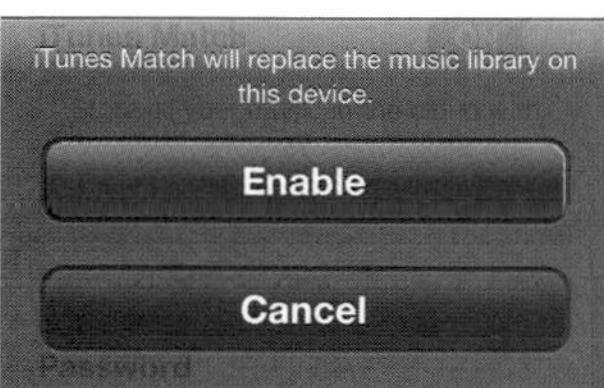

Ⓛ When you turn on iTunes Match, iOS warns you that it will replace the music library on the device.

To add an iOS device to iTunes Match:

1. On your iOS device, tap Settings > Music Ⓚ.
2. Turn on iTunes Match.
3. Your device will ask for your Apple ID Password. Enter it, then tap OK.

   The Music app warns you that iTunes Match will replace the music library on the device Ⓛ. However, any tracks already on the device that were previously synced from iTunes will still remain on the device.
4. Tap Enable.
5. Back in the Music screen, a new option, Show All Music, will appear. Turn this on to get access to your entire iCloud music library.

TIP When you know you won't have access to your online iCloud library (say, while you are on a plane flight), switching the Show All Music option to Off tells your iOS device to only show locally stored music.

To play or download music from iCloud to your iOS device:

1. In the Music app, the Playlists, Artists, Songs, and Albums tabs will now show everything in your iTunes Library. Navigate to music that you would like to download from iCloud to your device. You can tell that all or part of an album is not stored locally because it will have the iCloud Download icon next to the album name.
2. To play any song from iCloud, simply tap the song. After a brief pause, the song will start playing. It's being streamed from iCloud.

   or

   Tap the iCloud Download icon at the top of an album list to begin downloading the album. After a moment, the album will begin downloading, and a progress icon appears next to the tracks as they are downloaded **M**.

TIP If you want to download all the music by a particular favorite artist, tap Artists at the bottom of the Music app, find and tap the artist, then tap the Download All button below their list of albums N.

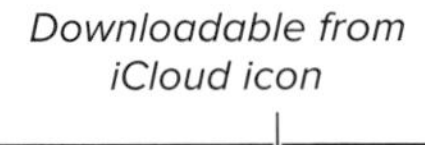

Download progress icon

M When you download a track from iCloud, it begins playing before it has completed downloading.

N To download all of an artist's albums to your mobile device, tap the Download from iCloud button below the album list.

iCloud Icons

The other icons that can appear in the iCloud Download column besides the Download icon are:

- **Ineligible** For songs that are too large, podcasts, audio books, and songs recorded at too low a bit rate.
- **Removed** Shown when a song has been removed from iCloud from a different computer. Songs deleted from iCloud are immediately deleted from iOS devices, but remain on other computers until they are manually deleted.
- **Error** Displayed when there was a problem matching the file.
- **Duplicate** You'll see this icon when a duplicate version of the song exists in your iTunes library. The icon will appear next to duplicates that weren't uploaded to iCloud.
- **Waiting** iTunes shows this icon when a song is in the process of being matched.

To manage iTunes Match devices:

1. In iTunes, click iTunes Store in the toolbar (or the sidebar if you have enabled it).
2. In the upper left corner of the iTunes window, click your Apple ID to access your account information.
3. Enter your Apple ID and password when prompted, then click View Account.
4. In the Account Information screen, there will be a section called iTunes in the Cloud **O**.
5. Click Manage Devices.
6. The resulting screen **P** will show you the devices associated with iTunes in the Cloud. If you want to remove one of these devices, click the Remove button next to it, then click Done.

TIP Apple allows you to associate a particular device or computer with a different Apple ID only once every 90 days.

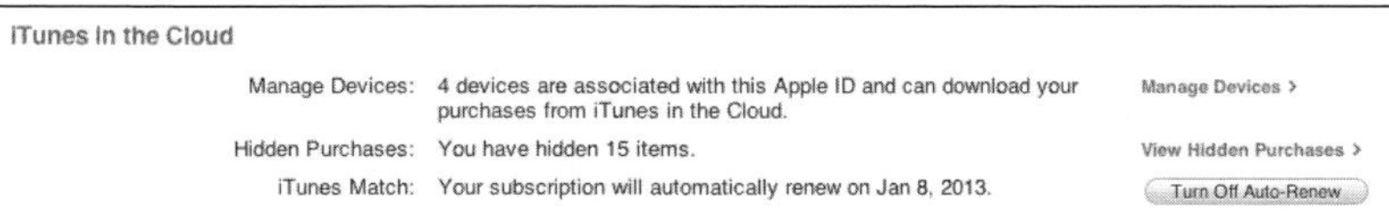

O Begin managing your iTunes Match devices in the iTunes Manage Accounts screen.

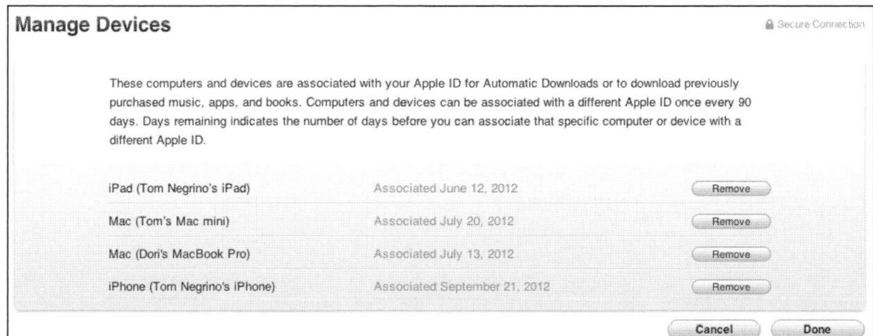

P On the Manage Devices screen, you can see which computers and iOS devices are associated with iTunes Match, and you can remove them if needed.

Updating Your Music with iTunes Match

As mentioned earlier, once iTunes Match scans your music library, it matches the songs that it finds with versions of the same track in the iTunes Store. You can then replace the versions on your computer (which may have been ripped from CD with old programs at lower-quality bit rates; I found a bunch of my music was originally ripped at 128 Kbps with SoundJam, the program Apple purchased and turned into iTunes back in 2000!) with new, higher-quality 256 Kbps AAC formatted files. If you previously purchased copy-protected music from the iTunes Store, the replacement tracks not only will be higher quality but will no longer have copy protection. If you don't want to invest in iTunes Match, Apple provides a service that allows you to update older-quality files you purchased from the Store to iTunes Plus (that 256 Kbps AAC format) for $.30 per track. Of course, if you want to upgrade more than 83 songs, it makes better financial sense to subscribe to iTunes Match.

To replace the older files with newer versions from the iTunes Store, you need to first find lower-quality versions of music in your library. A great tool to do that in iTunes is a Smart Playlist. Then you need to delete the old files from your library, and finally re-download the improved-quality versions from iCloud to your local library. I'd like to acknowledge Jason Snell, editorial director of *Macworld* magazine, for his excellent article detailing this process, which you can find at **`http://www.macworld.com/article/163620/2011/11/how_to_upgrade_tracks_to_itunes_match_fast.html`**. I've built on his work here.

TIP In the *Macworld* article referenced above, the author suggests you just replace all of your lesser-quality files in one massive operation. I don't recommend that, because in my experience, iTunes Match's matching, while quite good, isn't yet perfect. See the "It's Good, But It Ain't Gospel" sidebar.

Ⓐ Begin creating your Smart Playlist to root out your files that are good candidates for upgrading to higher quality.

Ⓑ These criteria look for lower-bit rate music.

To find matched songs that need upgrading:

1. Open iTunes.
2. Choose File > New Smart Playlist.

   The Smart Playlist window appears Ⓐ.
3. Change the first criterion. From the first pop-up menu, choose "Media Kind."

   The other two pop-up menus on that line will change to "is" and "Music." That's what we want.
4. Click the plus button at the right edge of the first criterion to add another criterion.
5. In the new criterion, change the first pop-up menu to "Bit Rate," the middle pop-up menu to "is less than," and enter "256" in the Kbps field Ⓑ.
6. Now we want to create a criterion group, where multiple criteria are treated as though they were one. To do that, hold down the Option key and click the Add criterion button for the criterion you created in Step 5.

   The new criterion group appears, with the pop-up menu set to "All" of the following are true, and one sub-criterion ready to be set.
7. In that pop-up menu, change "All" to "Any."
8. In the first pop-up menu of the sub-criterion, choose " iCloud Status."

   The other two pop-up menus of the sub-criterion will change to "is" and "Matched," which is what we want.
9. In the first sub-criterion, click its Add criterion button to add a new line to the group.

continues on next page

10. In the first pop-up menu of the new sub-criterion, choose " iCloud Status" again, leave the second pop-up menu set to "is," and change the third pop-up menu to "Purchased."
11. (Optional) Select the Match only checked items checkbox.
12. Select the Live updating checkbox.

    The settings for your Smart Playlist should now look like **C**.
13. Click OK.

    The new Smart Playlist appears in the iTunes sidebar with the name "untitled playlist."
14. Click the words "untitled playlist," and change the name of the playlist to "Better Quality on iCloud."

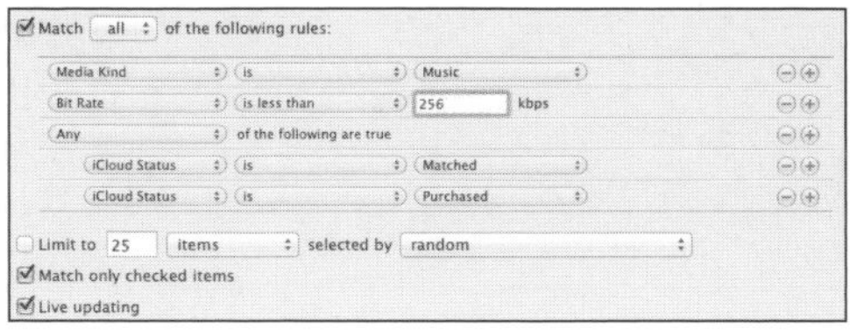

C The final Smart Playlist settings.

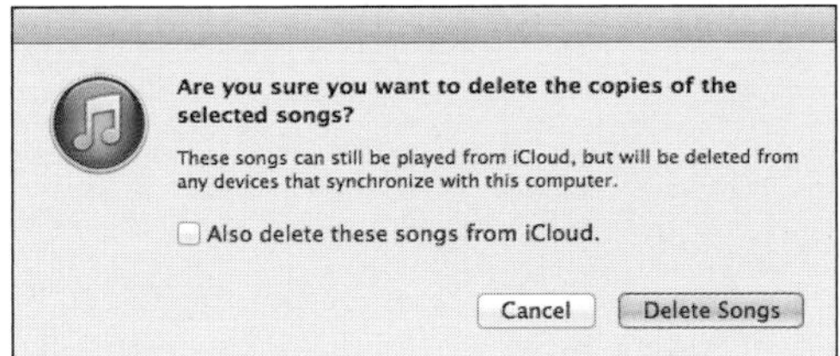

D iTunes always asks if you're sure you want to get rid of items.

E Here, you want to delete the local, lower-quality copies of your songs, so click Delete Files.

F Once you delete local files, the iCloud download icon appears next to them, indicating that the songs are waiting for you in the cloud.

To replace your lower-bit rate music with higher-quality versions from iCloud:

1. In the iTunes sidebar, click the "Better Quality on iCloud" Smart Playlist you just created.

   The playlist shows a list of lower-quality tracks that iTunes Match has matched and thinks are upgradable to better quality.

2. In the list, select one or more songs that you want to replace.

3. Press Option-Delete.

   iTunes will ask if you're sure if you want to delete the songs from your library **D**. Make sure that you *do* not check "Also delete these items from iCloud."

4. Click Delete Items.

   iTunes will ask if you want to keep the local files in the iTunes Media folder **E**. Scary as it may feel, yes, you do. The tracks are still available for you to re-download from iCloud, which you'll be doing soon.

5. Click Delete Files.

   iTunes deletes the local files, and marks the items with the iCloud download icon, showing that the files are now available on iCloud, rather than in your local library **F**.

6. Select the files you just deleted, then right-click and choose Download from the shortcut menu.

   iTunes downloads the higher-quality files from the iTunes Store.

It's Good, But It Ain't Gospel

iTunes Match is a surprisingly good service, but its matching (at this writing, at least) is far from perfect. It seems to often fall down on older and obscure albums, especially if they aren't in the iTunes Store.

Here are some examples from my own experience. In my iTunes Library, I have three CDs from a folk duo called The Williams Brothers that were made between 1987 through 1993. Only one of these three CDs is in the iTunes Store. Once you do a match, you can ask iTunes to show you the matched track on the Store. For one of these albums, it shows a match to a completely unrelated group called The Glass Brothers **G**. For another CD (the one that happens to be in the Store), it shows a match to The Williams Brothers, a famous vocal group of three black gospel singers **H**.

Online reports (corroborated by my own experience) suggest some other problems:

- Sometimes, songs within the same CD don't always match. This is puzzling, to say the least. iTunes will upload the tracks that don't match from your local copies, but it's still weird behavior.
- It's unclear what version of a track you may get if there are multiple versions of the track available on the Store (for example, original and remastered).
- Sometimes artwork isn't transferred to tracks that are downloaded.

Because of these issues, I recommend caution before trying a wholesale conversion of older files to your library to new versions. It's not a bad idea to spot-check that matched tracks are correct before upgrading them.

G These aren't the droids we're looking for.

H This was another incorrect iTunes Match. The folk singers on the left just don't have the gospel spirit of the group on the right.

Working with Documents in the Cloud

A real problem with using many devices is that it's surprisingly easy to work on a project and lose track of a document, or worse, its latest version. For example, I'm writing this chapter in Microsoft Word 2011 on the MacBook Pro on my kitchen table. Later, I'll save and close the chapter, go up to my office, and continue working on the Mac mini.

I can work on one document across all devices because my Word file is in a folder using the free Dropbox service, which automatically keeps it synchronized and available everywhere. But I still have to worry about where the document is (it has to be in Dropbox), and saving it. It would be even better if the document would auto-save and push its latest version to my devices. That's the aim of iCloud's Documents in the Cloud feature. It doesn't works with all apps, but for the ones it does work with, you can stop worrying about file locations and version, and focus on work.

In This Chapter

Configuring Documents in the Cloud 136

Storing and Working with Documents in iCloud 141

Working with iWork Documents on the iCloud Website 145

Configuring Documents in the Cloud

Before we get into the details of Documents in the Cloud, let's define what it is (and what it isn't), at least as December 2012, when I'm writing this.

- **What it is:** With the introduction of OS X 10.8 Mountain Lion, Documents in the Cloud inched closer to being a service that works with a variety of apps and their documents, making them easy to use between Macs, and between Macs and iOS devices. Primarily, the feature is a good way to work on iWork (Pages, Keynote, and Numbers) documents between iOS devices and (to a lesser extent) your Macs. As you work on an iWork document on iOS, it is, like all iOS documents, automatically saved in a mysterious location that you don't have explicit access to (because iOS hides the file system from the user). When Documents in the Cloud is enabled, iCloud automatically pushes the latest version to your other iOS devices, though you must manually download the changed version to your Macs from iCloud.com. Since the concept of a file system is foreign to iOS (each program has its private "bucket" of documents), we'll eventually have to see some standardized way that programs with both Mac and iOS versions can access the same files, but that doesn't exist yet.

  You can also think of Documents in the Cloud as an invisible and seamless way of backing up your iWork documents, since they are sent to iCloud as soon as you change them. As a facilitator of your work between iOS devices, Documents in the Cloud works quite well. You can start a document on your iPhone as inspiration strikes, then continue working on it on your iPad, and you'll pick up right where you left off.

  As more developers build Documents in the Cloud into their apps (as I write this, there are very few), it will become increasingly more useful beyond the iWork realm.

  Along with Mountain Lion, Apple introduced new Mac versions of the iWork programs, GarageBand, Preview, and TextEdit that were enabled for Documents in the Cloud. These programs allow you to choose from the Mac whether you want to save their documents locally, as you always have, or on iCloud. See "Storing and Working with Document in iCloud," later in this chapter.

- **What it isn't:** A general automatic file synchronization service. For Documents in the Cloud to work, the developer needs to enable it in their app, and it is really intended to support iOS, more than OS X or Windows. If you're more interested in a general sync service that works across many platforms, including OS X, iOS, and Windows, there are many, including Dropbox (`www.dropbox.com`), SugarSync (`www.sugarsync.com`), and Box (`www.box.com`). These services also allow you to set one or more individual folders for synchronization between devices, using the familiar file system metaphor of files and folders. What you don't get with a general service that you do get with iCloud is the automatic updating of documents (iWork or otherwise) across mobile devices (though some of these services offer automatic synchronization on desktop operating systems). That's a manual process if you use one of these services. Documents in the Cloud is also emphatically not a competitor to online document creation services like Google Docs. There's no website where you can create documents that then are synchronized via Documents in the Cloud.

Any documents that you synchronize using Documents in the Cloud count against your free 5 GB iCloud storage quota.

Documents in the Cloud also includes and synchronizes app data between your mobile devices. For example, a game that's been written to be universal (meaning it plays on both the iPad and smaller-screened iOS devices) and has been updated to take advantage of Documents in the Cloud can automatically synchronize its game data using iCloud, so you could play a few levels of the game on one device, and continue playing the game at the same point you left off on another device (many games use Apple's Game Center, which is part of iOS, to achieve the same goals).

TIP Because Keynote documents can contain large files, especially graphics, it's a good idea to make them as small as possible before you move them to iOS devices, in order to save both space on your devices and to minimize the impact on your iCloud storage quota. Before you upload a Keynote presentation from your Mac to iCloud.com (where it will be pushed automatically to your iOS devices), in Keynote for Mac, choose File > Reduce File Size. This command resamples the graphics in your presentation to screen resolution, greatly reducing their size.

TIP Don't forget that the versions of the iWork programs for iOS still have a subset of the features of iWork for Mac. So there could be some aspects of your documents (for example, certain slide builds or transition effects in Keynote) that don't survive a round trip journey from your Mac through iCloud to Keynote for iOS and back.

To enable Documents in the Cloud on Mac:

1. Choose System Preferences, then click the iCloud icon.

   The iCloud preferences appear **A**.

2. Click the checkbox next to Documents & Data.

A On the Mac, you'll turn on Documents in the Cloud in the iCloud preference pane.

Death Match: iCloud Versus Dropbox

The Dropbox service gives you 2 GB of free storage (you can purchase more storage, and the company makes it easy to get more free storage by completing some easy tasks and recommending friends) that you can access from all your devices, be they desktop, laptop, or mobile. The idea behind Dropbox is simple: when you install the program, it creates a Dropbox folder (typically on your desktop). Then, any file that you save to your is Dropbox automatically copied to all your computers, phones, and iPads (items are copied to mobile devices on demand to save bandwidth), and the Dropbox website. You can have any mix of files and folders inside your Dropbox folder, and you can choose to share any of those with anyone else, without them sharing all of your other stuff.

For me, Dropbox has become an integral part of my workflow. I keep all of my current project files in folders inside my Dropbox folder, and I know then that I'm always working with the latest version of my files. I even use Dropbox to transfer files between two machines that are physically right next to each other, because I don't need to worry about doing the transfer; it just happens by itself. Throughout this book, you've seen the results of this process; when I grab a screenshot of the iCloud control panel on Windows, my screenshot program is set to save the image to my Dropbox folder, and a couple of seconds after I snap the image, it automatically appears on my Mac a foot away, which is where I do cropping, add callouts, and the like. The Dropbox website also remembers past versions of documents, and I can revert to an older version, or restore a document that I inadvertently deleted.

Compared to the flexibility I get from Dropbox, iCloud's Documents in the Cloud isn't yet a serious competitor. It's nice that I can start working on a Pages document or Keynote presentation on my iPhone and have it automatically pushed to my iPad, but that's just not the same as being able to open a document on any computer or mobile device and know that I'm working with the latest version and that I don't have to worry about file management. Until Documents in the Cloud becomes more ubiquitous and flexible, I don't think that any of the general file synchronization services have that much to worry about.

B On iOS, you'll use the Documents & Data section of the iCloud Settings.

C When you switch Documents & Data on, iCloud will begin synchronizing your iWork documents to the iCloud servers. You can choose whether or not you want to use cellular data networks to synchronize your document and other data.

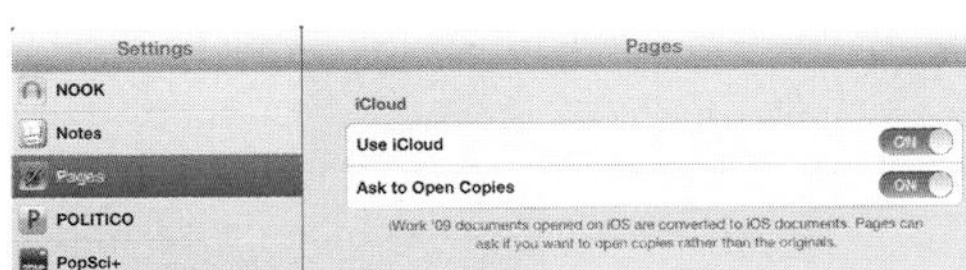

D The iCloud settings for the iWork applications are in the system Settings app (this one is for Pages).

To enable Documents in the Cloud on iOS:

1. Tap Settings, then iCloud.

   The iCloud settings appear **B**.

2. Tap Documents & Data.
3. On the Documents & Data screen, slide the Documents & Data switch to On **C**.
4. (Optional) If you want to allow your documents and data to synchronize over the cellular data network, slide the Use Cellular switch to On.

   If you have bandwidth caps and you regularly transfer a lot of cellular data, you might want to leave this option turned Off. I'm almost always within Wi-Fi range and have a bandwidth cap I share with my wife, so I leave it off.

5. (Optional) Some of your apps (for example, the iWork apps for iOS) may have Use iCloud switches in their sections in the Settings app **D**. You may need to turn these on. Other apps won't use the Settings app for their settings, but will contain their settings within the app itself **E**.

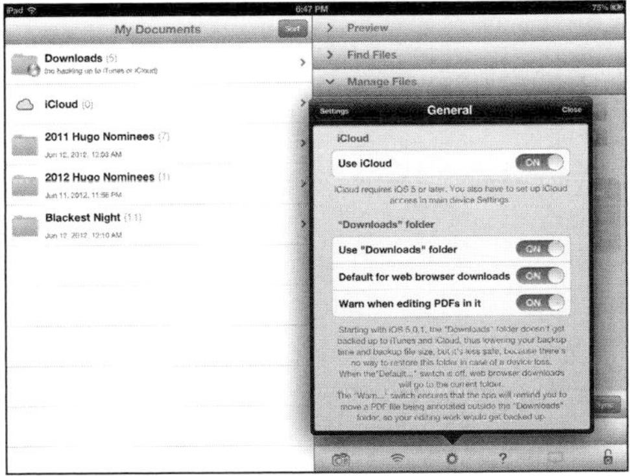

E Some app makers prefer to keep their settings inside their apps, as with the iCloud settings shown here for GoodReader, an excellent app that lets you read, annotate, and manage PDF, Office, iWork, and even image and video files.

TIP **After you turn on Documents in the Cloud, if you take a look at the Document Managers in the iWork programs, you can see the files being updated F. After updating, you can work with them as usual G.**

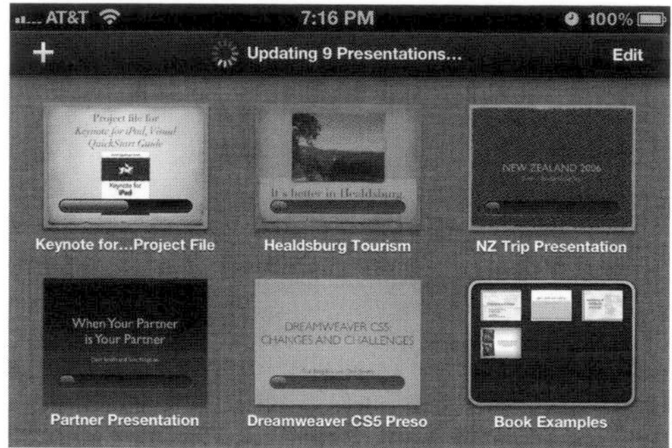

F Here are Keynote presentation files that were on my iPad in the process of being updated on my iPhone via iCloud.

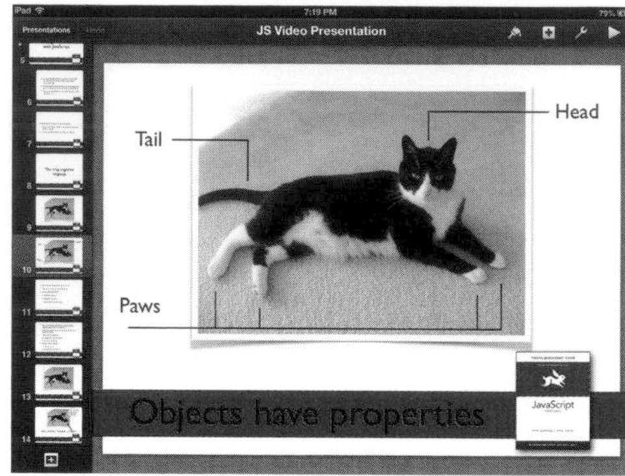

G This Keynote file started life on my Mac, then was transferred to the iPad, where it got a few touch-ups before the presentation.

Synchronizing Text Expansion Shortcuts

One really nice side effect of enabling Documents in the Cloud is that it also enables automatic synchronization of your text shortcuts between your iOS devices. Not using text shortcuts? You absolutely should be. It's a way for you to enter an abbreviation in any app, and have the system expand the abbreviation to a full word or phrase. For example, I often type "please" and "tomorrow" when I text. I've entered shortcuts for these as "pls" and "tmw," respectively. I type the shortcut, and when I tap the Space bar, the shortcut is automatically replaced. You can use shortcuts for longer phrases, too. I use "bts" for "Be there soon," for example. Or you might use shortcuts to build a library of alternative email signatures.

To add your own shortcuts, Tap Settings > General > Keyboard > Shortcuts. You'll find some shortcuts already created for you by Apple. Enter your own by tapping the Plus button, then entering the expanded phrase and the shortcut H.

Shortcuts can be incredibly helpful, and Apple's version of them are like training wheels compared to the far more capable TextExpander for Mac and TextExpander Touch for iOS, by Smile (`www.smilesoftware.com`). These programs allow you to share your shortcuts between all your devices via Dropbox, and many iOS app developers have built support for TextExpander Touch into their products.

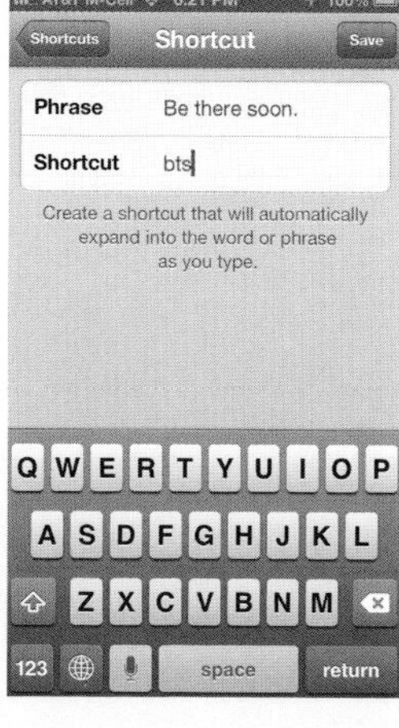

H Text shortcuts can save you a ton of time, freeing you from the need to type frequently used phrases.

Storing and Working with Documents in iCloud

On some Mac apps (most of them written by Apple), you now have your choice of saving them on your local hard drive or on iCloud. You'll usually make this decision the first time you save the document, then Mountain Lion will use its auto-save ability to continually save the document to your chosen location. Besides saving, the apps that save to iCloud also understand another Mountain Lion technology, Versions. The Versions feature works hand in hand with automatic saving to create snapshots of your documents. If you want to roll back to a previous version of your document, you can restore to any past version you want.

The benefit of saving documents to iCloud is that you can open and work on that document from either your Mac or your iOS apps, and because of the automatic saving, you can always be sure that you are working with the latest version of the document. It's nice to have the freedom to start a document on your iPad when inspiration strikes, save it to iCloud (actually, these iOS apps always save their documents to iCloud), and then open the document from iCloud on your Mac to put on the finishing touches.

Once you save a document to local storage or to iCloud, you're not stuck with that decision. It's possible to move documents between the two storage locations.

To save a document to iCloud:

1. In an app that is iCloud-enabled, create a document, then choose File > Save.
2. Give the document name, then from the Where pop-up menu, choose iCloud **A**.

   If you have already created folders on iCloud, those folders will also appear in the Where pop-up menu.
3. Click Save.

   The document is saved to iCloud.

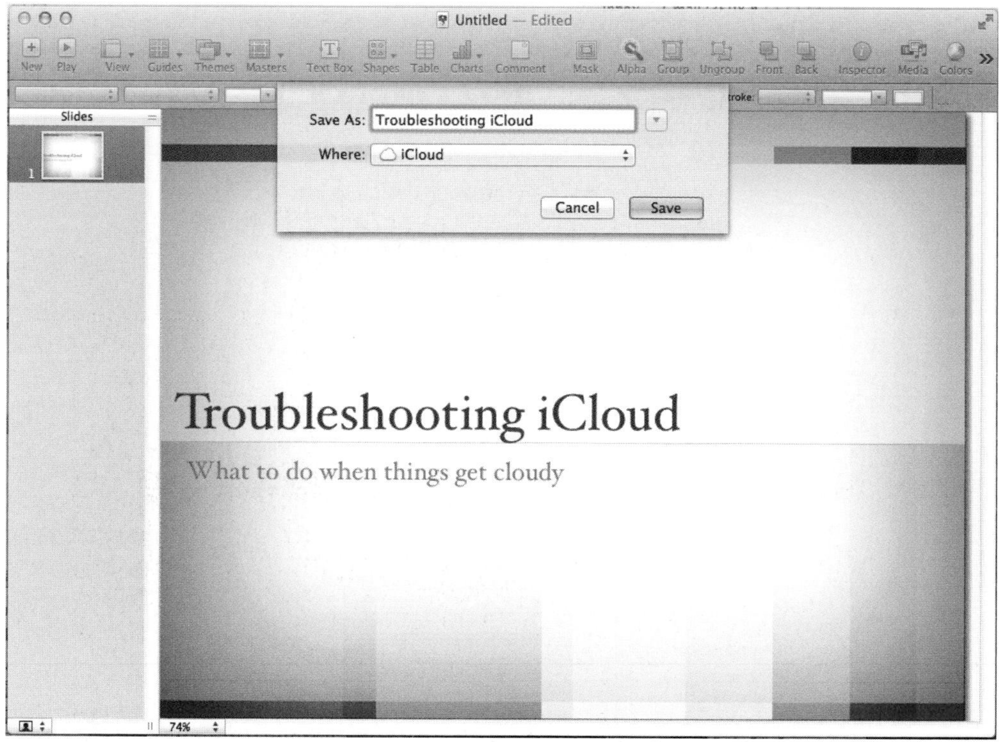

A To save a document to iCloud, choose iCloud from the Where pop-up menu.

To open a document from iCloud:

1. In an iCloud-enabled app, choose File > Open.

   The Open dialog now has two choices in its title bar: iCloud and On My Mac **B**. You can switch between the two to see files that are saved on iCloud or in your local environment, whether it be your own hard drive or a server on your local network.

2. (Optional) Just like in other Open dialogs, you can click the buttons at the bottom of the dialog to choose whether you want to view documents in icon or list view. In icon view, you'll see preview thumbnails of the documents.

3. Click to select the document you want to open, then click the Open button, or press the Return key.

TIP You can actually work on your iCloud documents while you are off-line, because the Mac keeps a cached local copy. Any changes you make don't update the copy of the file on iCloud until you reconnect.

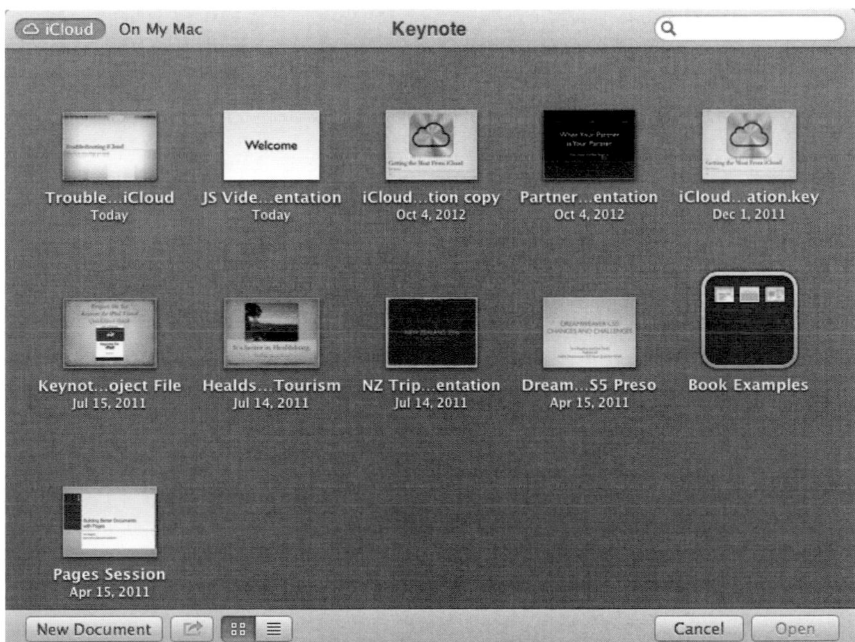

B The iCloud mode of the Open dialog shows you the iCloud-resident documents of the app you're working in.

To move a document between iCloud and your Mac:

1. In an iCloud-enabled app, open the document you want to move.
2. Choose File > Move To.

   The Save dialog appears **C**.
3. From the Where pop-up menu, choose the new location for the document.
4. Click Save.

   When you move the document to local storage (or vice versa), you are removing it from iCloud or your Mac; you're not making a copy. The file is physically being moved from one location to the other.

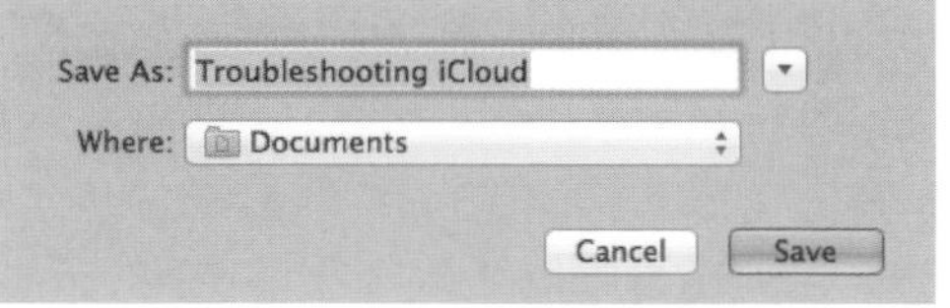

C To move a document from iCloud, choose a local destination from the Where pop-up menu.

When the Cloud Comes with Chains

Being able to save documents to iCloud can be convenient, but it also imposes some pretty hefty restrictions on the way you work with those documents. For one, it imposes the iOS way of working with documents onto the Mac, which is much less flexible than the way Mac users have been used to since, well, forever. On the Mac, you can start with a document on the desktop, double-click it, and the application opens and you can get to work. But on an iOS device, that idea gets stood on its head; first you open the app, then from within the app you can access your documents. Worse, it imposes the iOS security model onto the Mac. On iOS, there's no real conception of a file system; the user generally doesn't have to worry about where files are being saved or in what format they are being saved. On iOS, documents are saved into each app's separate, segregated file space, and generally files created by one app can't be accessed by another.

Documents in the Cloud brings this document silo idea to the Mac, often with unsatisfying results. For example, the Mac's Preview and TextEdit apps can both read text files. But if you create a text file in TextEdit and save it to iCloud, it can't be opened from iCloud by Preview, because the file is trapped within TextEdit's iCloud silo. Because of this wall between apps, you can't touch up an image file in Preview on the Mac, save it to iCloud, and then bring it into a Keynote presentation for either the Mac or iOS. Instead, you would have to take the extra step of saving the image file to a common data store (for example, like a Photo Stream), and only apps that understand how to access that common data store can make use of the image file.

It's understandable why Apple moved in this direction; people get confused by files and folders (I'd love to break my sister of her habit of saving everything onto her Mac's desktop, but I'm not hopeful). But segregating files so they can only be worked on by a single app robs users of much of the flexibility they need to get their work done efficiently. The current solution in Mountain Lion is unsatisfactory, and I hope that Apple improves its iCloud integration in the future.

Working with iWork Documents on the iCloud Website

To get iWork files from your Mac into iCloud, where they will then be automatically distributed to your iOS devices, you can also use the iCloud website. Conversely, you can access files that are already in iCloud on a computer through the web interface, and download them to your computer. The iCloud website allows you to download or upload the files onto your computers in one of the iWork formats (Keynote, Pages, or Numbers); Microsoft Office formats (PowerPoint, Word, or Excel); or as a PDF.

Remember that files that you get from iCloud via the website and then update on your computer are not automatically updated on iCloud and your mobile devices. To get that automatic updating, use the methods from "Storing and Working with Documents in iCloud," earlier in this chapter.

To manage iWork files on the iCloud website:

1. Go to the iCloud website, and login using your iCloud Apple ID and password.
2. On the iCloud Home screen **A**, click iWork.

   The iWork screen appears **B**.
3. At the top of the window, click the tab for the iWork program you wish to work with (Keynote, Pages, or Numbers).

A Begin managing your files on your computer on the iCloud website.

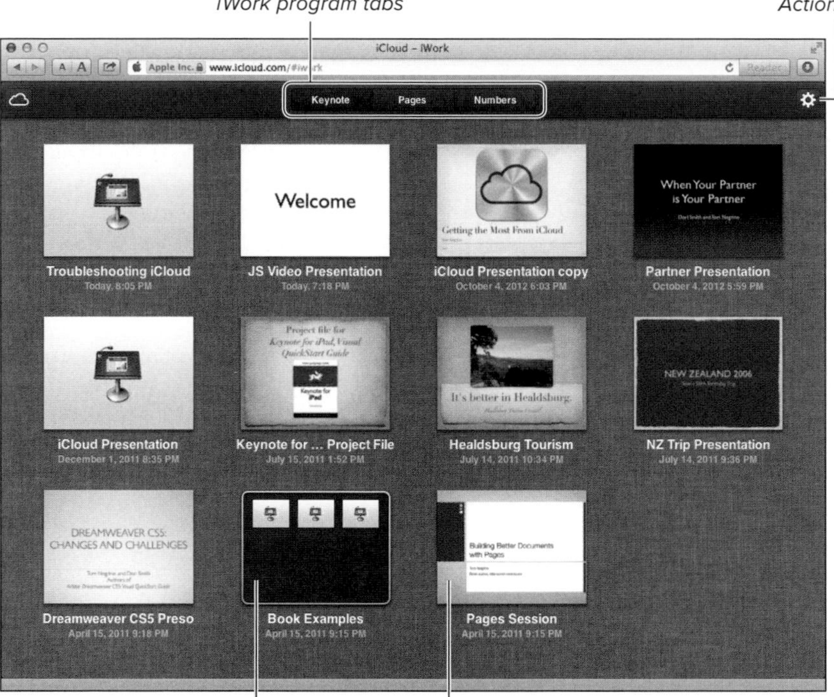

B The iWork screen shows you all of your iWork documents that have been uploaded to iCloud.

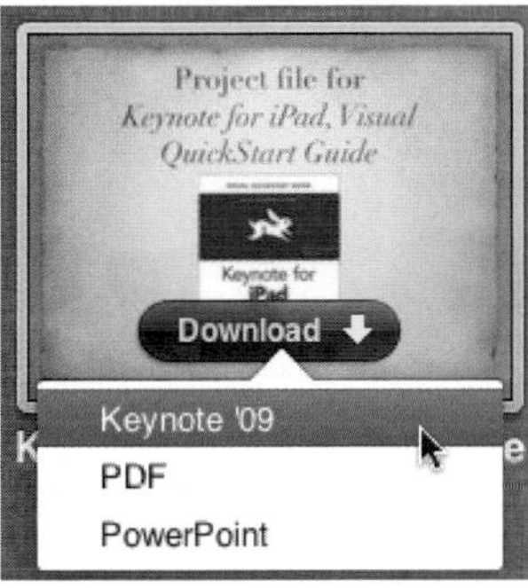

C Choose the download format you want.

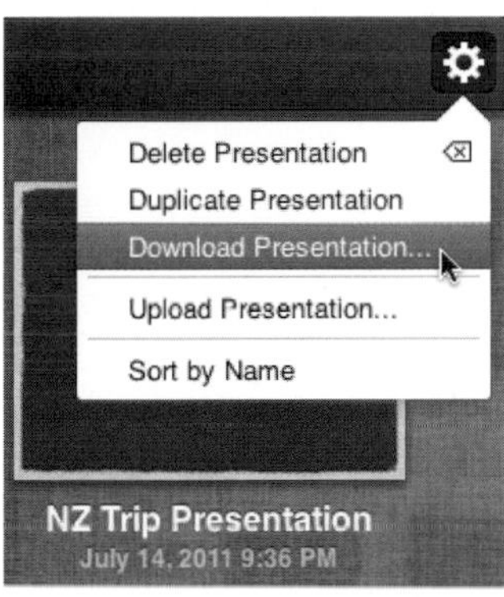

D You can also manage your iWork files with the pop-up menu from the Actions button.

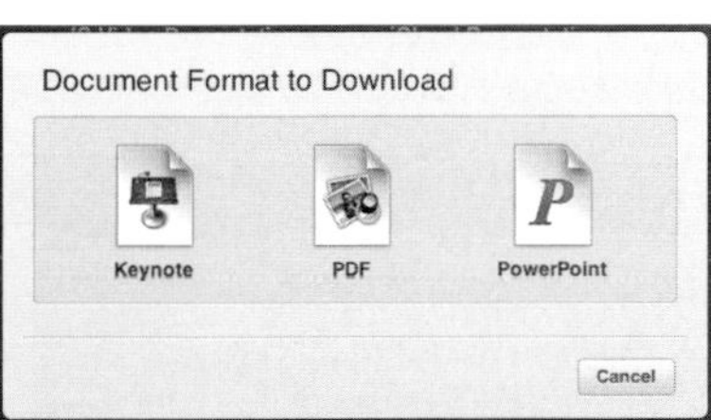

E This dialog allows you to choose your preferred download format.

F The iCloud web site lets you know if you have documents that aren't in sync across your different devices, and lets you download the version you want.

4. Do one of the following:

- To download a file to your computer, click on the file, and a Download button appears. Click the Download button, and choose the format you want the download to be in from the pop-up menu **C**. You can also download a file by selecting the file, clicking the Actions button, and choosing Download *filetype* from the pop-up menu **D**. You'll get a dialog that allows you to choose the download format **E**.

  Sometimes, you can have different versions of a file on different devices (usually because you started working on a file on one device, moved to a different device to continue work, and then never re-opened the iWork program on the original device to synchronize the changes). In that case, the iCloud website will ask you which version you want to download **F**.

continues on next page

- To upload a file from your computer to iCloud, drag the file from your desktop into the iWork website window **G**, or click the Actions button, and choose Upload *filetype* from the pop-up menu.
- You can create folders on the iWork website by dragging presentations on top of one another, then naming the resulting folder. The folder then appears in a similar way to folders on iOS **H**. Clicking the folder opens it and shows you its contents.
- To delete a document from iCloud, click to select it, then press Delete, Backspace, or click the Actions button and choose Delete *filetype* from the pop-up menu. As usual when you are destroying data, iCloud will ask you to confirm your choice **I**. Click Delete.

G Drag the iWork file you want to upload from your desktop into the iWork browser window.

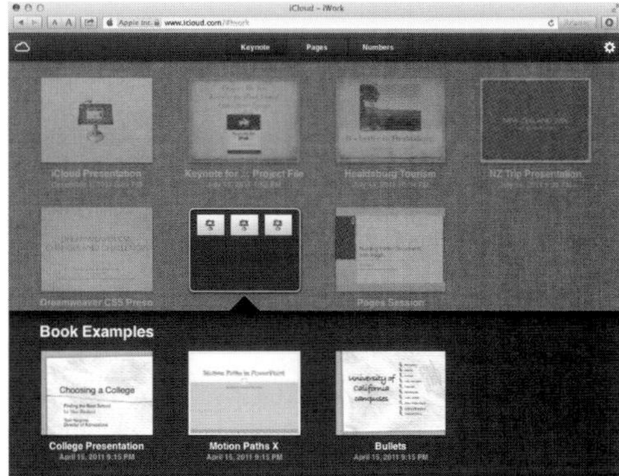

H Clicking a folder opens it, showing you the files within.

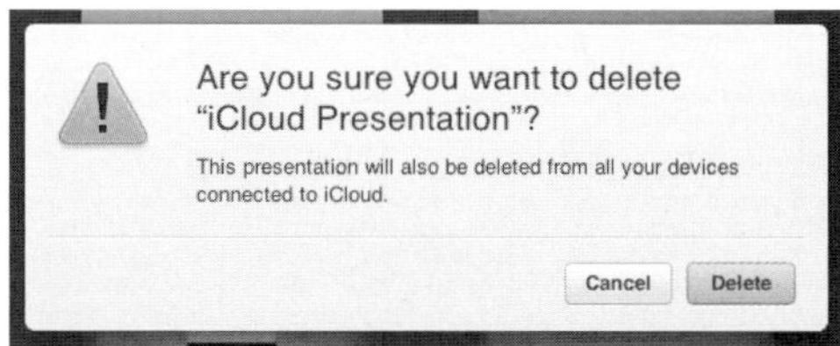

I You always have a last chance before you delete data.

Backing up to iCloud

Before the advent of iCloud, backing up an iOS device meant physically connecting it to a computer running iTunes via a USB cable, then letting that connection make a copy of the contents of the device onto your computer. iCloud eliminates the need for that cable, because it allows you to backup the data on your iOS device over a Wi-Fi connection to the iCloud servers. It's your choice: you can back up over Wi-Fi, or continue your backups via a direct connection to your computer. Naturally, if disaster strikes, you can also restore your data to an iOS device from a previous iCloud backup.

If iCloud's free 5 GB of storage aren't enough for you, you can manage the amount of data stored in the cloud, and even purchase more storage if needed.

In This Chapter

Understanding and Configuring iCloud Backup 150

Restoring an iOS Device from Backup 153

Managing Your iCloud Storage 154

Understanding and Configuring iCloud Backup

Everyone knows you should back up the data on your computers and mobile devices in case of hardware failure or theft. The problem is that unless the process is made incredibly easy (as in set it and forget it) most people simply don't back up their stuff. Apple has tried to solve the backup problem with the Mac with Time Machine, and with the introduction of iCloud, backing up your iOS device can now be done wirelessly and automatically, as long as you set it up once. So make sure you set it up that once!

As part of its synchronization process, iTunes has always backed up your data when you connect your iOS device with a USB cable. Now, Apple uses iCloud to backup your data over Wi-Fi, and all you have to do to make the backup happen is turn it on once, either in iTunes or on your iOS device, be on a Wi-Fi network, connect the device to a power source (which you have to do to recharge the battery anyway), and not be using the device for a while.

Before we jump into setting it up, let's talk for a moment about what gets backed up. Some of the items that are backed up count against the free 5 GB of storage you get with an iCloud account, and some items do not.

Items that count against the 5 GB of free iCloud storage:

- Data kept inside apps. For example, I have the Amazon Kindle app on my iPad. I have about 90 MB worth of books loaded in the app. That counts against part of my 5 GB storage quota. And some apps require a lot a data to begin with. For example, Navigon, the GPS app I use, keep about 300 MB of map data on my iPhone, with maps for just California, Oregon, and Washington loaded. If I downloaded and installed all the state maps for the entire U.S., that would require much more space.
- Photos and videos in the Camera Roll.
- Messages, such as SMS, MMS, iMessages, and Visual Voicemails.
- Device settings, such as Mail, Contacts, and Calendar accounts. Many apps you download from the App Store also keep data files on the iOS device. For example, my preferred note and info snippet keeper is Evernote, which I find indispensable. Evernote for iOS doesn't keep all of my Evernote data on my devices (the data is too large for that, but it's keeping about 100 MB of synchronized notes on my iPhone and iPad.)
- Home screen and app organization information.
- Ringtones.

You get unlimited free storage for:

- Music, apps, books, movies, and TV shows that you purchased from the iTunes Store. The apps part is especially important. I have a big first-person shooter game on my iPad. It takes up 2 GB. Yet because all that data is inside the app itself, it doesn't count against my 5GB iCloud storage quota.
- Items that are in your Photo Stream.

Things that *don't* get backed up to iCloud include:

- Music, movies, and TV shows you didn't buy from the iTunes Store (although if you subscribe to iTunes Match, music you didn't buy from the iTunes Store may still be available on iCloud, but it won't get backed up, and won't count against your storage quota).
- Podcasts and audio books.
- Photos that were originally synced from your computer (instead of using Photo Stream).

Your first backup could take a while, depending on how much data is on your mobile device that needs backing up. Because iCloud Backup is smart, subsequent backups only copy items that have been added or changed, so those subsequent backups go much quicker.

After the first backup, the backup happens automatically once a day, when the device is connected to the Internet over Wi-Fi, is connected to a power source, and the screen is locked.

So now we know what does and doesn't get backed up, and when the backups happen, let's set up your device for automatic backup, so you need never worry about it again.

TIP As of when I wrote this (December 2012), backups of purchased movies and TV shows are available in the U.S. only. It's also important to know that your previous purchases may not be restored if they are no longer in the iTunes Store, App Store, or iBookstore.

TIP I recently met someone who turned off their iPad every night, so naturally it wasn't being backed up. There's no reason to turn off an iOS device on a regular basis; just plug it in to recharge and let it go to sleep.

To turn on iCloud Backup on an iOS device:

1. Choose Settings > iCloud > Storage & Backup.
2. In the Backup section, turn on iCloud Backup Ⓐ.
3. In the resulting dialog, tap OK to confirm you want to use iCloud Backup.
4. (Optional) Scroll down on the Storage & Backup screen and tap the Back Up Now button to begin your first backup. Make sure you're connected to a power source and to Wi-Fi.

Ⓐ Turn on iCloud Backup on the iOS device to begin backing up your iOS device via Wi-Fi to Apple's servers.

TIP You can also use the Back Up Now button to perform a manual backup to iCloud any time you like, as long as you are connected using Wi-Fi. For example, you might want to run a backup just before you update the device's operating system or firmware.

To turn on iCloud Backup in iTunes:

1. Connect the iOS device to iTunes 11, then select the device in the toolbar.

   or

   If you are using iTunes a version of iTunes prior to iTunes 11, or if you have (as I recommend) chosen View > Sidebar in iTunes 11, select the device in the sidebar Ⓑ.
2. In the Backup section of the Summary screen, in the Automatically Back Up section, click the iCloud button Ⓒ.

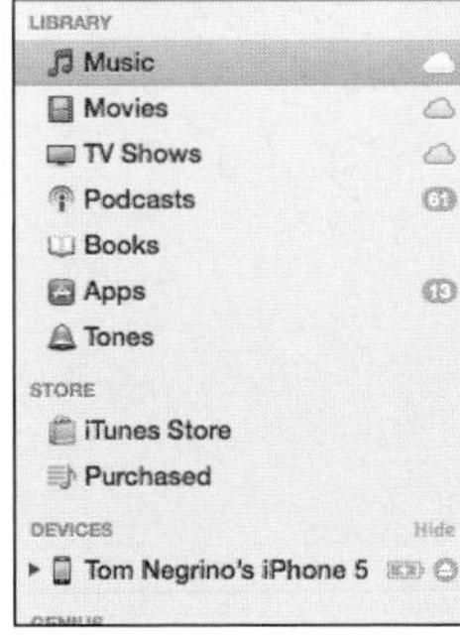

Ⓑ Select the iOS device in iTunes' toolbar (top) or sidebar (bottom).

TIP Once you turn on iCloud Backup, iTunes no longer backs up your iOS device when you sync; it all happens in the cloud.

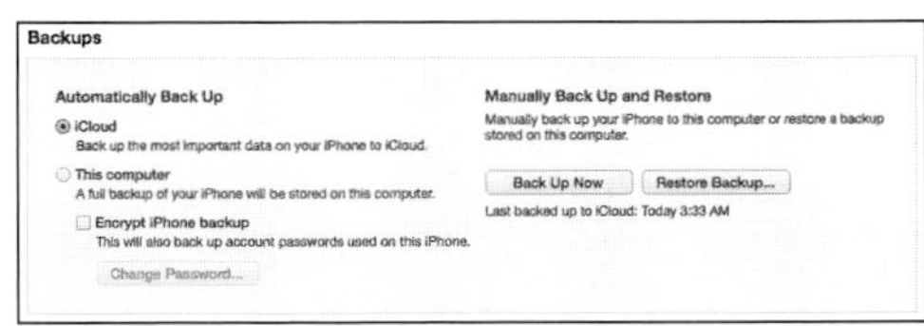

Ⓒ In iTunes, you can choose to either backup to iCloud or to the local computer.

A The Setup Assistant gives you the opportunity to restore from an iCloud Backup.

Restoring an iOS Device from Backup

Restoring an iOS device from a backup is a bit weird. You have very little control over the process. You can only restore to an iOS device that has been wiped clean or is brand new. The restoration happens as part of the Setup Assistant on a new iOS 5 or 6 device.

To restore from an iCloud Backup:

1. On an erased or new iOS device, turn it on. The Setup Assistant will automatically run.
2. When you get to the Set Up (*device name*) screen, you'll have the option to Restore from iCloud Backup. Tap that choice **A**, then enter your Apple ID and password.
3. From the next screen, which shows the three most recent backups for each of your backup devices, choose the backup you wish to use for the restore, then tap Restore.

   The backup will be downloaded, after which your device will restart and restore your settings and data.

TIP During the restoration process, you can restore a particular app sooner by tapping its icon.

TIP After the restore completes, expect to have to re-enter passwords for the various accounts on the device, such as email accounts and the App Store.

TIP Apple's terms and conditions state that it has the right to delete iCloud device backups that are more than 180 days old. That shouldn't be a problem once you've turned on backup, as it tries to perform the backup every evening.

Managing Your iCloud Storage

You have some control over the amount of storage that you're using with iCloud. From the iCloud preference pane on Mac or the iCloud control panel on Windows, you can view how much storage you're using from your free 5 GB allocation, choose to remove some data to free up space, and purchase more iCloud storage space.

Remember, music, apps, books, and TV shows that you purchased from the iTunes Store, and photos in your Photo Stream, don't count against your 5 GB of free storage.

A Begin managing your iCloud storage on the Mac in the iCloud pane of System Preferences.

To manage your iCloud storage on a computer:

1. Choose System Preferences > iCloud on the Mac.

   or

   Choose Start Menu > Control Panel > iCloud on Windows Vista or Windows 7. On Windows 8, begin on the Start screen and click the Desktop tile, which switches you to Desktop mode. Move your mouse to the upper- or lower-right corner of the screen to reveal the Charms bar, and then click the Settings charm. In the resulting settings bar, click the Control Panel link.

   The iCloud settings window appears **A**. At the bottom of the settings window, there is a bar graph showing you how much iCloud storage you have available.

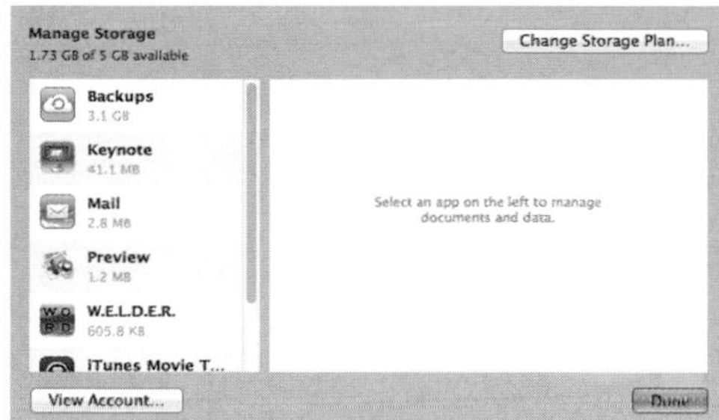

B You can see what is taking up room in your iCloud storage in the Manage Storage pane.

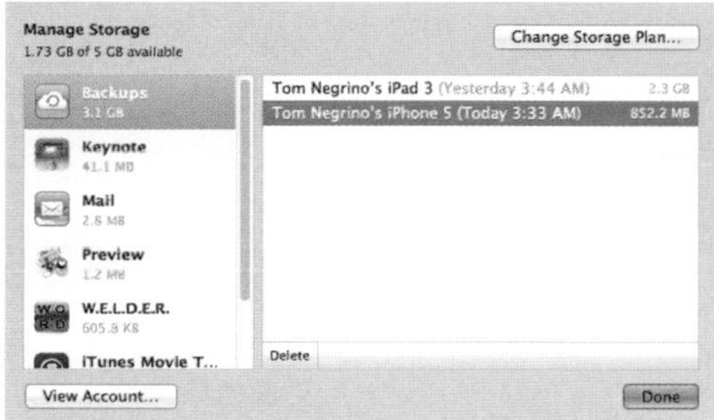

C Clicking one of the categories shows you its details.

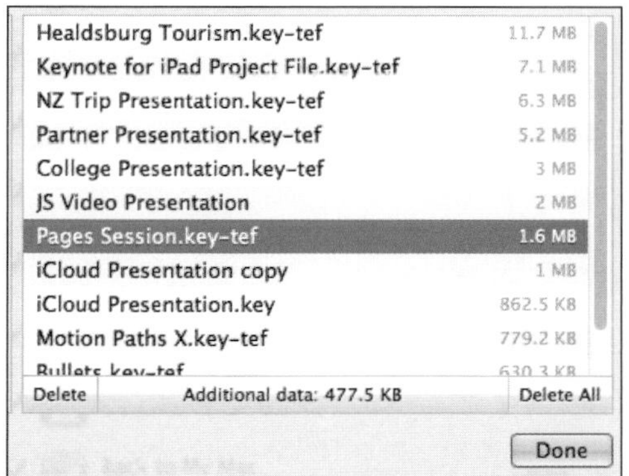

D Select an item and click Delete to remove it from iCloud.

2. Click Manage.

   The Manage Storage pane appears **B**. On the left, it lists the different categories of storage you are using in iCloud, and how much space each category is using.

3. Click a category to see the documents within it **C**.

4. If you want to delete one of the items within the category, click to select it, then click Delete **D**.

   or

   If you want to delete all of the items within the category, click Delete All.

   iCloud asks if you are certain you wish to delete, and warns you that the item will be immediately deleted from iCloud and your devices **E**.

5. Click Delete.

   The item is deleted and you'll return to the Manage Storage pane.

6. Click Done.

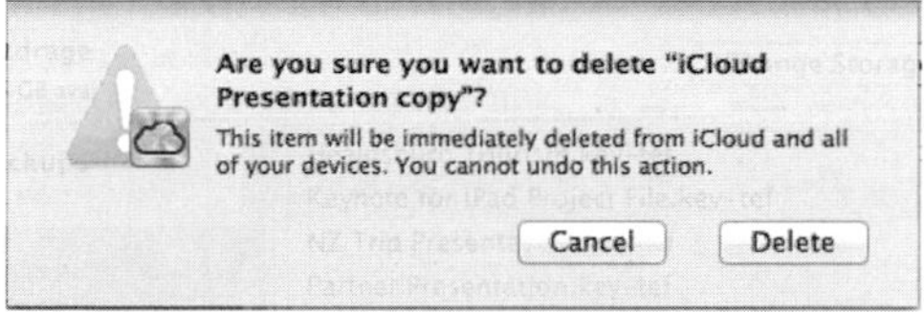

E If you're not sure you want to get rid of that item, this is the time to click the Cancel button.

To manage your iCloud storage on an iOS device:

1. Tap Settings > iCloud.
2. At the bottom of the list, tap Storage & Backup **F**.
3. On the Storage & Backup screen **G**, tap Manage Storage.

   On the Manage Storage screen, the categories of storage you're using appears **H**.

F On an iOS device, begin managing your storage in the iCloud screen of Settings.

G Next, in the Storage & Backup screen, tap Manage Storage.

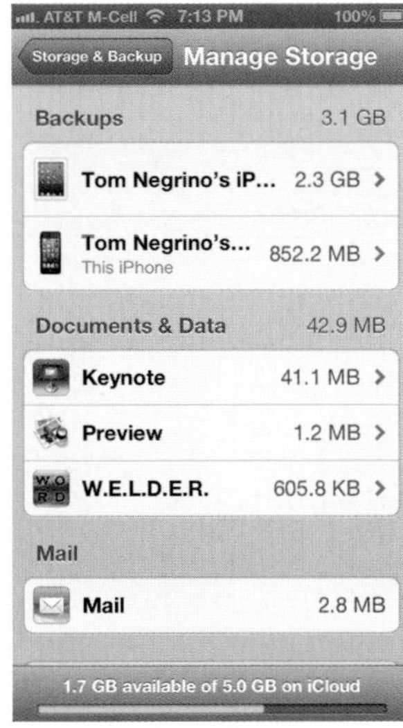

H The Manage Storage screen shows you how your iCloud storage is distributed.

I You can turn back up on or off for individual apps on your device.

J If you like, you can delete individual files from iCloud.

4. (Optional) On an iOS device, you have a bit more granular control over the storage used for backups on that particular device. In the Backups section of the Manage Storage screen, tap the backup for the iOS device you are working with to choose backup options for the apps you are backing up **I**. If you want to stop backing up data for a particular app, simply turn it off under the Backup Options section.
5. Tap a category to see the documents within it.
6. To delete a particular item, swipe a finger to the right on the item to make the Delete button appear **J**, then tap Delete.

To purchase more iCloud storage:

1. Choose System Preferences > iCloud on the Mac.

   or

   Choose Start Menu > Control Panel > iCloud on Windows.

   The iCloud settings window appears.

2. Click Manage.

   The Manage Storage pane appears.

3. Click Buy More Storage.

   In the resulting dialog **K**, choose the amount of storage upgrade you wish, then click Next.

   Your storage upgrade will be charged to your iTunes account and go into effect immediately, and will automatically renew each year unless you downgrade to the free storage plan before your renewal date. Once you upgrade your plan, if you decide you made a mistake, you can get a full refund within 15 days of an upgrade, or within 45 days after a yearly payment.

TIP To purchase more iCloud storage on an iOS device, tap Settings > iCloud, then tap the Buy More Storage button. In the resulting dialog L, you'll get the same storage upgrade options. Choose the option you want, then tap the Buy button.

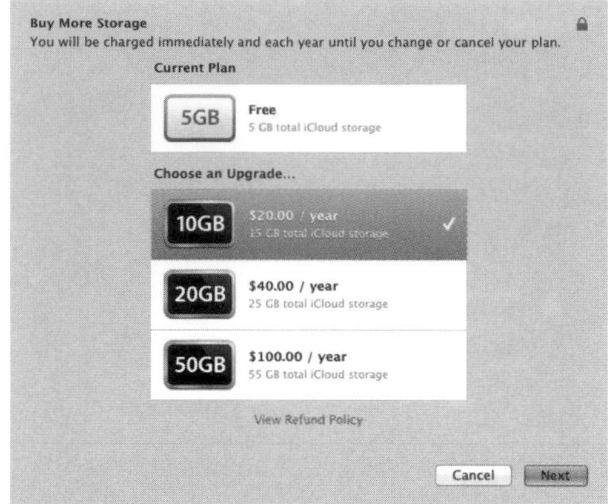

K You can use the iCloud preference pane on a Mac or the iCloud control panel on Windows to purchase more storage.

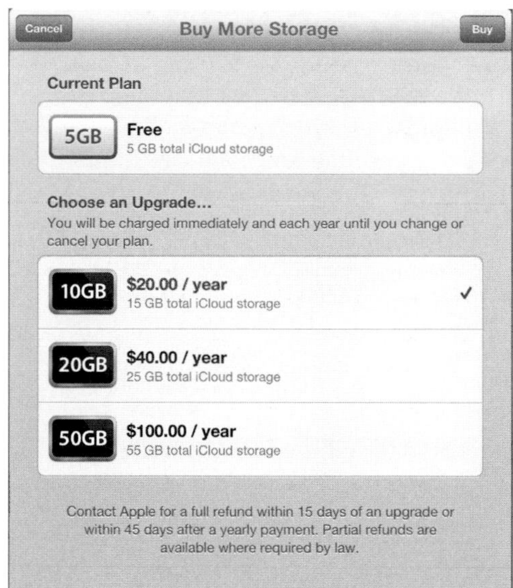

L You can also purchase more iCloud storage on an iOS device.

9

Working with Safari

We all use bookmarks to make our web browsing experience easier, but it can be kind of a pain to be working on one device, and realize that you bookmarked a particular site on another device. Relax; iCloud has you covered. It can synchronize browser bookmarks across four different browsers: Safari for Mac and Windows, Safari for iOS, and Microsoft's Internet Explorer for Windows.

And a new feature in OS X 10.8 Mountain Lion and iOS 6, iCloud Tabs, allows you to also synchronize open tabs in Safari between your Mac and iOS devices. Another new feature, Reading List, lets you save the content of a page you are browsing for later reading. The contents of your Reading List are also synchronized via iCloud.

In this chapter, you'll see how to turn on bookmark synchronization and learn a little about the best ways to manage bookmarks, and how you can work with iCloud Tabs and Reading List. As a bonus, I'll point you to some useful bookmarklets, which are little, handy JavaScript programs masquerading as everyday bookmarks.

In This Chapter

About Bookmark Management 160

Configuring Bookmark Syncing with iCloud 161

Using iCloud Tabs and Reading List 163

Useful Bookmarklets for iOS 169

About Bookmark Management

If you're anything like me, you have a huge selection of bookmarks that you've created over the years, on different computers and different devices, and the thought of having iCloud merge them all together onto all of your devices is a bit daunting. That's why I think it's a good idea to do a little preparation before you turn on browser synchronization.

- **Do some spring cleaning.** If possible, get all your devices in one place. This is a good time to compare and review bookmarks on your devices and get rid of duplicates and outdated bookmarks. Your goal is to keep only the bookmarks that are still useful. If you bookmarked a particular page that has an article on it that you want to read, go ahead and read it, or save it to one of the read-later services, such as Instapaper (`www.instapaper.com`) or Readability (`www.readability.com`). After you've dealt with the article, delete the bookmark.
- **Decide which devices you want to synchronize.** After thinking about it a little, I realized that I had no real interest in synchronizing all of the bookmarks on my desktop and laptop computers with each other, much less with my mobile devices. I tend to use the desktop in my office for different purposes than the laptop, and I use Safari on my iOS devices (my iPad and my iPhone) in similar ways, but differently than how I use bookmarks with my Macs. So I decided to merge and synchronize my bookmarks only between my mobile devices, leaving the feature turned off on my Macs and on my Windows machine.

A On a Mac, you turn on Safari synchronization from the iCloud preference pane.

B On Windows, you use the iCloud control panel.

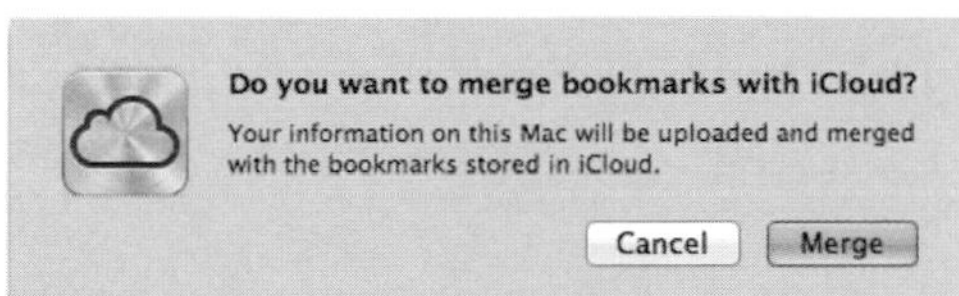

C As usual, iCloud warns you before you do something that might change data across many devices.

D On Windows, you can choose whether you want to use iCloud bookmarks with Internet Explorer or Safari for Windows.

Configuring Bookmark Syncing with iCloud

Once you've cleaned up your bookmarks and decided which devices you want to synchronize, turning bookmark synchronization on is easy. Just follow these steps:

To enable bookmark synchronization on a Mac or Windows machine:

1. On the Mac choose System Preferences, then click the iCloud icon.

   The iCloud preferences appear **A**.

   or

   On Windows Vista or 7, Choose Start Menu > Control Panel, click the Network and Internet section, then click iCloud. On a Windows 8 PC, begin on the Start screen and click the Desktop tile, which switches you to Desktop mode. Move your mouse to the upper or lower right corner of the screen to reveal the Charms bar, and then click the Settings charm. In the resulting settings bar, click the Control Panel link.

   The iCloud control panel appears **B**.

2. Click the checkbox next to Safari (Mac) or Bookmarks (Windows).

   iCloud asks if you're sure you want to merge bookmarks **C**.

3. Click Merge.

TIP On Windows, there is an Options button in the control panel; clicking this allows you to choose if you want to merge your bookmarks from Internet Explorer, or Safari for Windows D.

To enable bookmark synchronization on an iOS device:

1. Tap Settings, then iCloud.

   The iCloud settings appear **E**.

2. Slide the Safari switch to On.

   Your device warns you that you're about to merge your bookmarks with iCloud **F**.

3. Click Merge.

   After the merge is complete, the same bookmarks will appear on all enabled devices. Changes made on one device will be replicated on the other devices on your iCloud account.

TIP Some folders' contents are synchronized, but the folders can't be deleted, notably the History, Bookmarks Bar, and Bookmarks Menu folders. That's true even on the iPhone and iPod touch, which don't have a Bookmarks Bar.

E You turn Safari synchronization on in the iCloud settings on iOS.

F On a mobile device, you get the same warning that your data will be merged.

Using iCloud Tabs and Reading List

By enabling browser synchronization through iCloud, you also get synchronization of two other Safari features; iCloud Tabs and Reading List. The former is simple: as you open tabs in Safari on the Mac or the iPad, Safari tells iCloud behind the scenes the URLs of the open tabs. Thus, if you leave one device with open tabs, you can pick up another device, tap an icon, and see the open tabs on the original device.

Reading List is useful for when you start to read a page, then realize that you don't have the time to finish it, and you want to save it for later. Rather than a simple bookmark, when you send a page to your Reading List, it grabs and sends the entire contents of the page (including text, images, styles, and scripts) up to iCloud, and then those pages are synced down to your devices. Because the page contents are cached on your devices, you can access the items in your Reading List even if you are offline, with no access to the Internet.

To use iCloud Tabs:

1. Open one or more tabs in Safari on your iCloud-enabled device.
2. In Safari's toolbar, click or tap the iCloud Tabs button.

   On the Mac, you'll see a menu showing the other devices and their open tabs. On the iPad and iPad mini, a popover with that information appears **A**.

   or

   On an iPhone or iPod touch, tap the Bookmarks button in the bottom bar, then tap the iCloud Tabs folder on the Bookmarks screen.

A On iOS, you can use iCloud Tabs to see your other devices and their open tabs.

3. In the popover, tap the name of the tab you want from the other device.

   The page opens in your local copy of Safari, replacing any page you might already have had displayed **B**.

TIP If the iCloud Tabs button isn't visible in the toolbar, most likely you don't have Safari synchronization enabled in iCloud's settings.

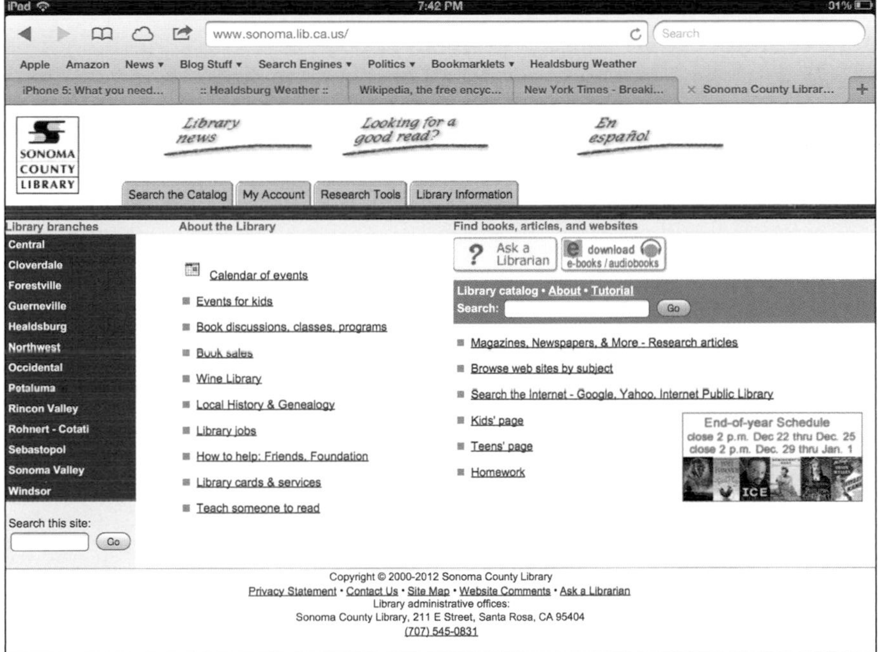

B Loading a tab open on a remote device makes it appear in your local Safari app.

The Chrome Alternative

If you prefer to use Google's Chrome browser, rather than Safari, it has you covered as far as sharing. Once you sign into your Google Account, Chrome shares your open tabs, bookmarks, passwords, search, and history data between all instances of Chrome running on any supported platform, including Mac, Windows, Linux, iOS, and Android. Because Safari doesn't have Linux or Android versions, if you use OS X or iOS and those other operating systems are part of your computing mix, Chrome is a better choice as your main browser. Another benefit on the Mac and Windows of using Chrome and Chrome syncing is that it also syncs the Chrome extensions available from the Chrome Web Store. There are many useful extensions that you can download for free to improve your web browsing experience, but extensions aren't available for Chrome for iOS (blame Apple's restrictions, not Google).

On Chrome for iOS, you can see which tabs are open in Chrome on other devices by choosing Other Devices from the menu at the right edge of the Chrome toolbar **C**.

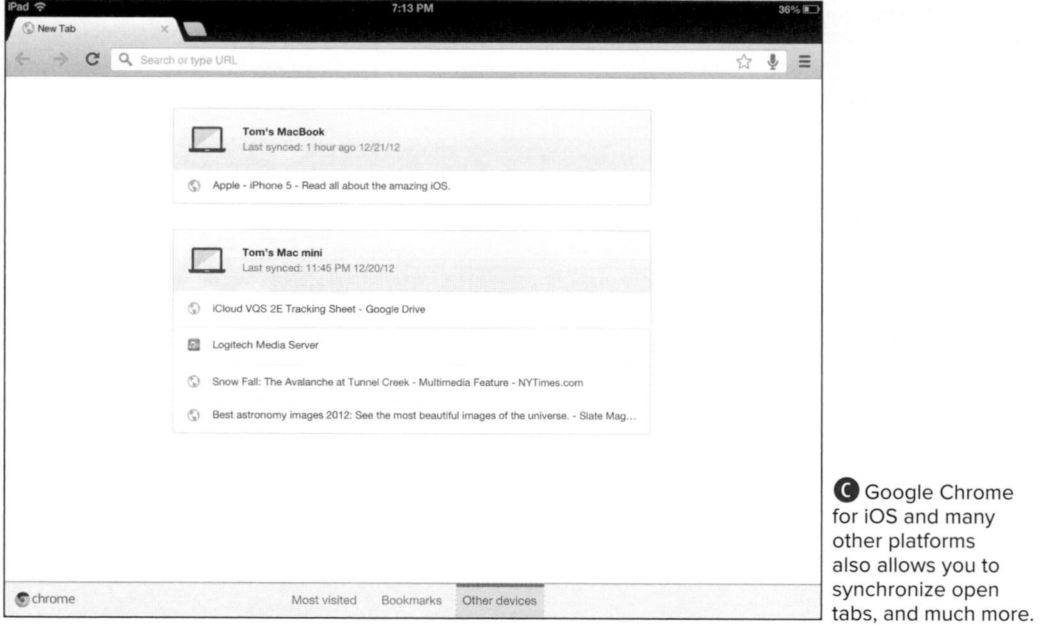

C Google Chrome for iOS and many other platforms also allows you to synchronize open tabs, and much more.

D From the Actions popover on iOS, tapping Add to Reading List saves the current page for later.

To use Reading List:

1. Open any Web page.
2. In the Safari toolbar, tap or click the Actions button, then from the popover (iOS) or pop-up menu (Mac) choose Add to Reading List **D**.

   Safari takes a moment to save the page to iCloud.

continues on next page

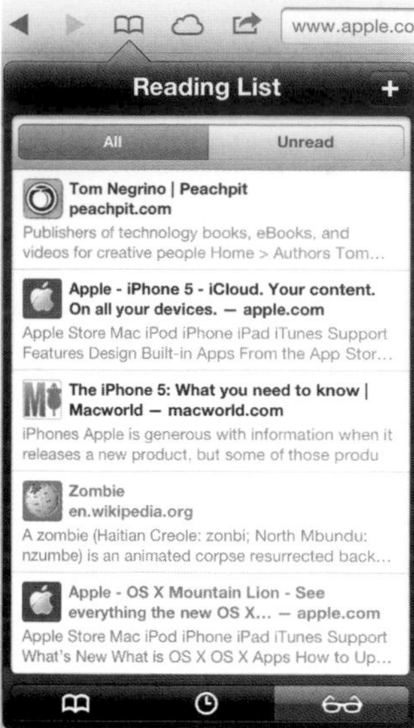

E You can switch between All or Unread items in your Reading List.

3. To retrieve and read a page from your Reading List, do one of the following:
   - On the iPad and iPad mini, tap the Bookmarks button on the toolbar, then tap the Reading List icon (it looks like a pair of reading glasses) at the bottom of the resulting popover **E**. The pages in your Reading List appear. Tap the page you want from the Reading List, and Safari loads it.
   - On the iPhone or iPod touch, tap the Bookmarks button on the toolbar, then tap the Reading List choice in the Bookmarks list. The pages in your Reading List appear. Tap the page you want from the Reading List, and Safari loads it.
   - On Safari for Mac or Windows, choose View > Show Reading List, which opens a sidebar containing the Reading List pages. Click the page you want from the list, and Safari loads it.

TIP One of the popular features in Safari is Reader, which makes pages easier to read by removing the clutter of ads, sidebars, navigation menus, and all the other stuff that gunks up a page. Unfortunately, you can't first invoke Reader and then send the cleaned-up version to your Reading List, the version that gets saved is the original. To save cleaned versions of Web pages for later, you'll need a third-party service such as Readability (`www.readability.com`) or Instapaper (`www.instapaper.com`). Both of these services have bookmarklets for Safari on iOS to make it easier to get content into their services (see the "Useful Bookmarklets for iOS" section later in this chapter for more on bookmarklets).

Useful Bookmarklets for iOS

Bookmarklets are bookmarks (or favorites, if you prefer Internet Explorer's terminology) that contain a small JavaScript program, rather than a URL. When you tap the bookmarklet, it executes the JavaScript program.

I like to use bookmarklets on my iOS devices because they can often substitute for a feature that most desktop browsers (including Safari for the Mac) have and mobile Safari does not: browser extensions. For example, on the desktop I have browser extensions installed that clip web content to my snippet manager of choice, Evernote (from the company of the same name; **`www.evernote.com`**), and re-style pages that are designed in such a way that I find them difficult to read (what is it with designers who like little white type on dark backgrounds?).

In this section, I'm going to point you to three bookmarklets that you'll be able to download from the book's page at **`icloud.negrino.com`**, and show you how to install them into your iCloud-enabled browsers. There are, of course, many more bookmarklets available.

- **Unicode Symbols** gives you a new browser window or tab that allows you to copy and paste useful symbols that are not possible to type from the iOS keyboard.
- **Black Text** makes the background of a web page white and the text on the page black. I use it to make overly designed pages more legible.
- **Clip to Evernote** brings up a window that allows you to send the current selection to the free Evernote clipping service.

Safari for Mac, iPad, and iPad mini have a Bookmarks Bar that allow easy access to frequently used bookmarks. With their smaller screen real estate, the iPhone and iPod touch lack the Bookmarks Bar.

Something you should know about installing bookmarklets: it's *way* easier to do it on the Mac or PC, then synchronize it with your mobile device via iCloud. On a computer, all you need to do is drag a link containing the bookmarklet to the Bookmarks Bar, then name the bookmarklet. On an iOS device, it's a complicated procedure, which I've detailed below on an iPad. Follow it carefully, and here's hoping that Apple makes it easier to add bookmarklets in the future.

To add a bookmarklet on an iOS device:

1. In Safari on your mobile device, go to the book's web page at icloud.negrino.com.
2. On the page, the JavaScript code for each bookmarklet is in a text box **A**. Tap inside a text box, pause for a second, then tap again. In the Edit popover, tap Select All **B**, then tap Copy **C**.
3. In the toolbar, tap the Actions button, then tap Bookmark from the resulting popover **D**.

In Mobile Safari, copy and paste the contents of the boxes below, according to the detailed instructions in the book:

Unicode symbols:

```
javascript:(function()
{symbols=%22&#161;&#162;&#165;&#169;&#171;&#172;&#174;&#176;&#177;&#180;&#181
;&#187;&#189;&#191;&#247;&#248;&#710;&#711;&#916;&#937;&#946;&#960;&#8217;&#8
220;&#8221;&#8222;&#8224;&#8225;&#8226;&#8249;&#8250;&#8253;&#8356;&#8364;&#8
482;&#8592;&#8593;&#8594;&#8595;&#8630;&#8634;&#8635;&#8670;&#8671;&#8676;&#8
677;&#8679;&#8682;&#8734;&#8776;&#8800;&#8804;&#8805;&#8963;&#8984;&#8986;&#8
987;&#8996;&#8997;&#8998;&#9003;&#9099;&#9166;&#9167;&#9312;&#9313;&#9314;&#9
315;&#9316;&#9317;&#9318;&#9319;&#9320;&#9674;&#9728;&#9729;&#9730;&#9731;&#9
732;&#9733;&#9742;&#9745;&#9746;&#9754;&#9755;&#9756;&#9757;&#9758;&#9759;&#9
760;&#9763;&#9764;&#9765;&#9770;&#9773;&#9774;&#9775;&#9785;&#9786;&#9787;&#9
788;&#9789;&#9790;&#9792;&#9794;&#9812;&#9813;&#9814;&#9815;&#9816;&#9817;&#9
818;&#9819;&#9820;&#9821;&#9822;&#9823;&#9824;&#9825;&#9826;&#9827;&#9828;&#9
829;&#9830;&#9831;&#9832;&#9833;&#9834;&#9835;&#9836;&#9837;&#9839;&#9842;&#9
850;&#9872;&#9873;&#9888;&#9986;&#9991;&#9992;&#9993;&#9996;&#9997;&#9999;&#1
0002;&#10004;&#10006;&#10013;&#10017;&#10025;&#10026;&#10037;&#10042;&#10045;
&#10046;&#10047;&#10048;&#10049;&#10070;&#10086;&#64257;&#64258;%22.split(%22
;%22);outStr=%22<br />
<table cellpadding='10' style='font-size:1.2em;'>
<tr>%22;for(i=0;i<symbols.length-1;i++){outStr+=(i%252)?%22
<td bgcolor='#CCC'>%22:%22
<td>%22;outStr+=symbols[i]+%22<\/td>%22;if(i%259==8)outStr+=%22<\/tr<br />
<tr>%22;}symWin=window.open('','sWin','');symWin.document.body.innerHTML=outStr
+%22<\/tr>
```

A In order to use a Bookmarklet on iOS, you'll need to copy the code in this text box.

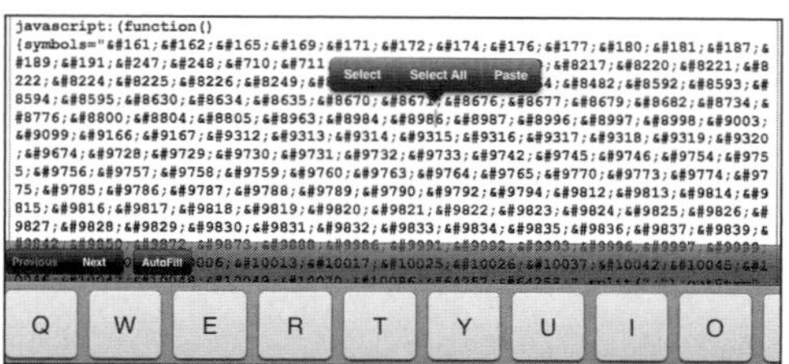

B Tapping twice brings up the Edit popover so you can tap Select All.

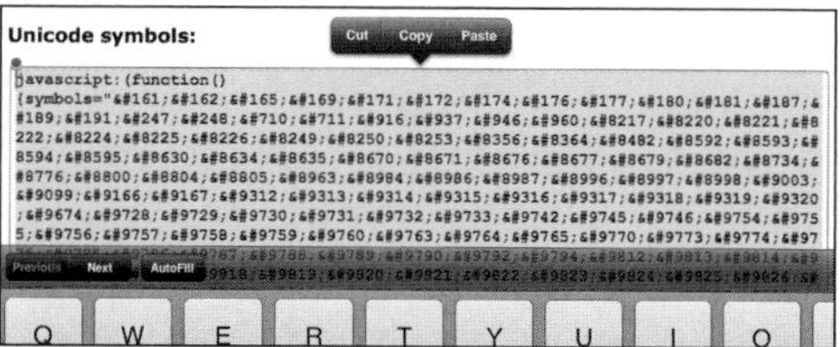

C After the selection, the Edit popover changes to show you the Copy option.

D You need to add a bookmark from the Actions button.

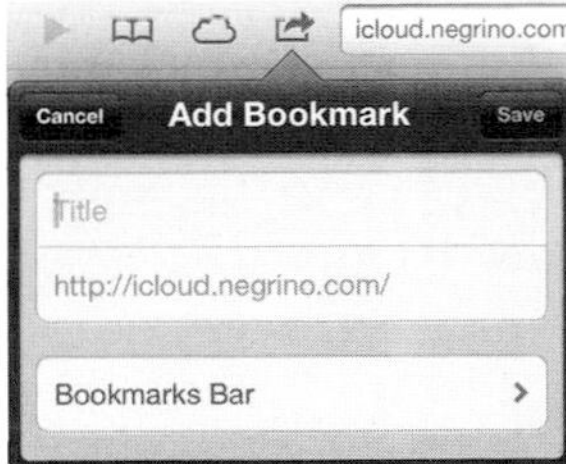

E Change the default Title name to the name of the bookmarklet you are creating.

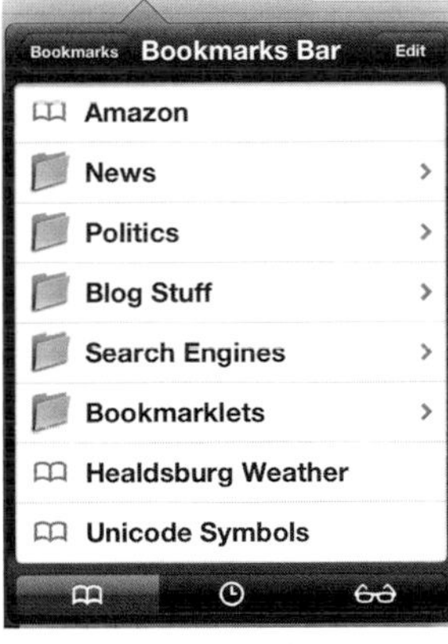

F After finding the bookmark you just created, tap Edit.

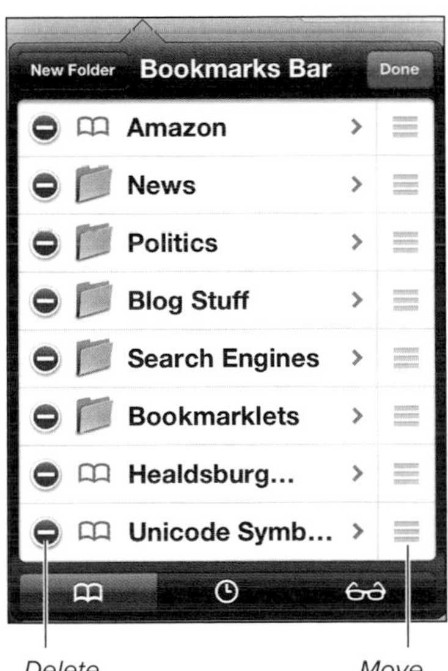

G Tap the name of the bookmark to edit it.

4. In the Add Bookmark popover E, tap the X "Clear-contents" control (so the field contains "Title"), then type in the name of the bookmarklet you are creating.

   The address for the bookmark below the name shows the URL of the book's page. We'll change that in a moment; it can't be changed yet.

5. Below the URL, choose the location where you want the bookmarklet (I usually use the Bookmarks Bar), then tap Save.

6. Tap the Bookmarks button in the toolbar, and locate the newly created bookmark. Tap Edit F.

   The screen changes to the edit mode G.

7. Tap the bookmark name (make sure not to tap the "Delete" or "Move" controls) to select it for editing.

   The popover changes to Edit Bookmark, with the URL of the source site.

continues on next page

8. Tap the URL, then tap the X "Clear-contents" control, tap again in the Address line to invoke the Edit popover, then tap Paste H.

   The JavaScript code you copied in Step 2 is pasted in the Address line.

9. Tap outside the Edit Bookmark popover to save your changes. The new bookmarklet appears in the Bookmarks Bar I on the iPad, or wherever else you put it in your Bookmarks.

10. To run the bookmarklet, tap it in the Bookmarks Bar, or choose it from your Bookmarks.

    For the Unicode Symbols bookmarklet, the symbols appear in a new tab J; you can copy a symbol from the window and paste it wherever you need it.

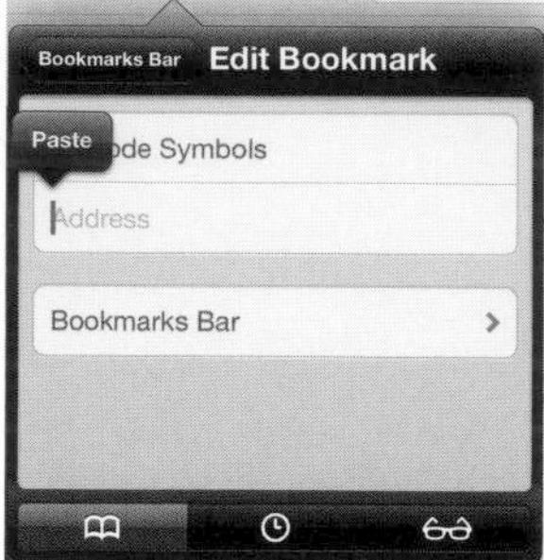

H You need to clear the placeholder URL so you can paste in the JavaScript code, then tap the Paste control.

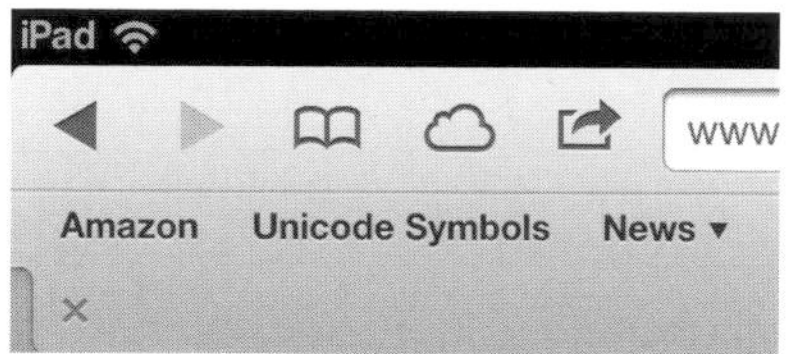

I The new bookmarklet appears in the Bookmarks Bar on the iPad.

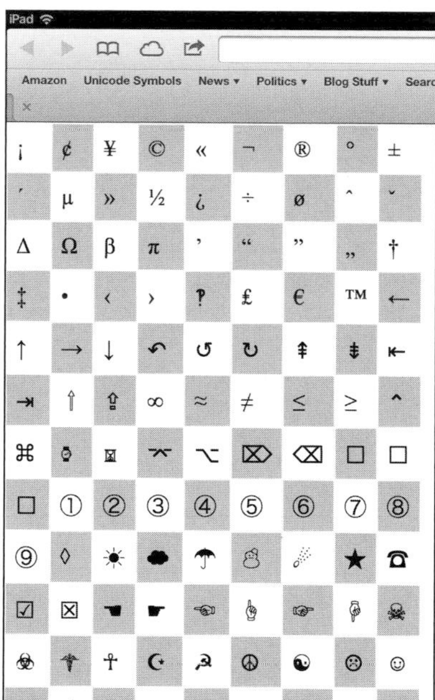

J For the Unicode Symbols example, copy the symbol you want from the page, then paste it in to any other application.

Using iCloud to Find People and Devices

Need to find your iOS devices? How about your friends or family members? Or maybe your Mac? iCloud can help you with that. iCloud has a rich suite of services that allow you to find your iOS devices or your Macs, and locate them on a map. Once you've found them, you can send an audio signal, a text alert, remotely lock and add a passcode to the device, and even remotely wipe the device in the event of theft or loss.

Finding your iOS device isn't just useful in case of nefarious action. You can use the audio signaling feature to track down your iPhone after it has slipped out of your pocket and in between the couch cushions.

To find devices, you can use the iCloud website, or you can use Apple's Find My iPhone app, which runs on any iOS device. Another Apple app, Find My Friends, allows you to permanently or temporarily locate your friends (as long as they are carrying an iOS device).

In This Chapter

Configuring iCloud Locating on the Mac 174

Finding and Working with Your Devices 178

Using Find My Mac 187

Using Find My Friends 193

Using Back to My Mac 199

Configuring iCloud Locating on the Mac

With OS X 10.7 Lion and later, applications and websites can get and use information based on the current location of your Mac. For example, a web browser like Safari may ask for your location while browsing a shopping website in order to find good deals near you, or to determine nearby movie showtimes. Actually, the website you're browsing is asking Safari for your geolocation and Safari is passing the request on to you. You have to give your permission before the application or website can use your location information, which is handled by a part of the OS called Location Services (see the "Understanding Location Services" sidebar).

The Find My Mac service in iCloud uses Location Services, which in turn determines the approximate location of your Mac based on nearby Wi-Fi networks. You have to turn on the Find My Mac feature before you can, well, find your Mac.

If your Mac doesn't have Wi-Fi capabilities (like my old Mac Pro) or has Wi-Fi turned off, but is still connected to the Internet via Ethernet, you won't be able to use the iCloud website or the Find My iPhone app to locate that Mac on a map, but you can still activate the other features, such as Remote Lock and Remote Wipe, discussed in the "Using Find My Mac" section, later in this chapter.

A You'll need to enable Find My Mac in the iCloud pane of System Preferences.

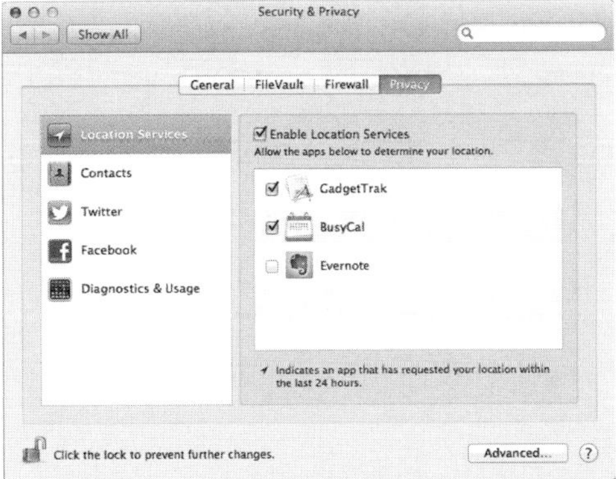

B Location Services are enabled by default, but you can control them in the Security & Privacy pane of System Preferences.

To activate Find My Mac:

1. From the Apple menu, choose System Preferences.
2. In the Internet & Wireless section, click iCloud.
3. In the iCloud Preference pane, click the checkbox next to Find My Mac **A**. While you're at it, click the checkbox next to Back to My Mac. We'll be using that later in this chapter.
4. Close the System Preferences window.

There are two other places in System Preferences where you can deal with Location Services, if you're using a Mac with Wi-Fi. On all Macs running Lion or later, choose System Preferences > Security & Privacy > Privacy **B**. If you want to turn off Location Services (it's enabled by default), deselect the Enable Location Services checkbox. You'll probably have to click the padlock icon at the bottom of the window and enter your admin password before you can make this change. The list in this preference pane shows the applications that have requested your location. The checkbox next to an application name in this list indicates whether or not you have granted that application permanent location-finding ability. If the checkbox is unselected, the application will ask you each time it wants to use your location (for privacy reasons, that's the setting I actually recommend).

If Location Services is enabled and Wi-Fi is turned on, your Mac can set its time zone automatically using the current location. Choose System Preferences > Date & Time > Time Zone **C**. Select the checkbox next to Set time zone automatically using current location. Location Services will work its magic, put a red pushpin near your current location, and set the time zone.

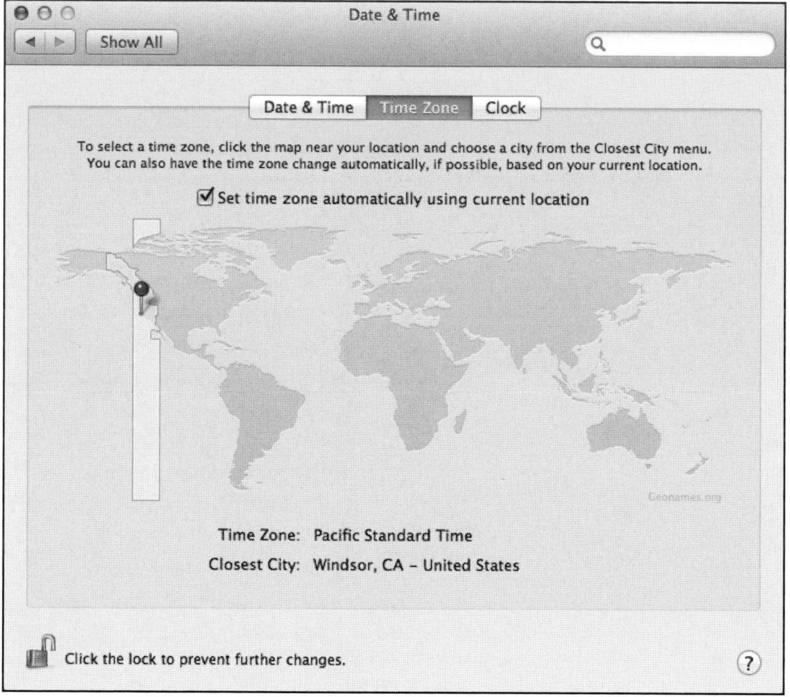

C Location Services can automatically set your Mac's time zone.

Understanding Location Services

Location Services is a part of OS X and iOS that allows applications such as iCloud, Find My Friends, Camera, and Maps to determine your approximate location. Location Services uses information from the GPS (Global Positioning System) chips in some iOS devices, cellular tower triangulation in iPhones and iPads with 3G, 4G, and LTE, and a database Apple maintains of public and private Wi-Fi hotspots. Your devices send location information to Apple continuously, but Apple says it does so in an anonymous fashion, so there is no way to personally identify and track you.

To determine your location, your device first tries to use GPS, if your device has it (because it offers the greatest accuracy). If you're not within a clear line of sight to the GPS satellites, the device tries to determine your location by looking for nearby Wi-Fi hotspots (you don't have to be connected to the hotspot; as long as your device can see it and it's in Apple's database, that's enough). If you're not in range of Wi-Fi, and you have a device with an active cellular connection, Location Services will try to calculate your approximate location by triangulating the distance to nearby cell towers (naturally, the exact location of every cell tower is known by the cellular carriers, and is shared with Apple).

Location Services often does a pretty good job of finding your iOS device, especially your iPhone (as long as it is equipped with GPS). It's less accurate with Macs. For more about accuracy, see the "Let's Talk Accuracy" sidebar, later in this chapter.

Finding and Working with Your Devices

You can use the iCloud website or the Find My iPhone app, running on an iOS device, to find an iPhone, iPad, iPad mini, iPod touch, or Mac (see the next section for specific information about finding a Mac). It's important to note that you can only find the devices that you have already set up for use with Find My iPhone. Set those devices up now, so you can find them later.

To use the finding features, your iOS device must be using iOS version 3.1.3 or later. So you're not limited only to iOS devices eligible for iCloud (and therefore capable of running iOS 5 or later); even the oldest iPhone or iPod touch will work, as long as it was updated to the latest iOS version it could handle.

In this section, we'll be using the iCloud website to find and work with your devices. The Find My iPhone app, running on an iOS device, works similarly to the website, with minor differences because it's running on a mobile device with differently sized screens.

If you lose track of your mobile device, you will first want to try to find it by sending it a signal that triggers the device to make a loud noise. If it turns out that you didn't simply misplace the device and it appears to have been stolen, you can put it into Lost Mode, which immediately locks the device and adds a passcode, preventing someone else from using it, and also begins tracking it. The passcode must be entered before the device can be used. As part of Lost Mode, you can try sending a message to the device. If all else fails, you can remotely wipe the device, which erases all the information on it, preventing a thief from seeing or using your information.

Don't Be Lulled into Complacency

If your iOS device or Mac really is stolen, you have a limited window of opportunity to use Find My iPhone's features. If you remotely set a passcode or wipe the device, those events will only occur if the device is online and findable. If the thief is smart enough to quickly power the device down, turn off Find My Device, or turn on Airplane Mode, there's nothing you can do.

As usual, one good way to deter a criminal is to slow things down. And the best way to do that (and give you time to determine whether or not the device has actually been stolen or just misplaced) is to set a passcode for the device before you lose it.

On iOS, tap Settings > General > Passcode Lock, then tap the Turn Passcode On button. It's also a good idea to set the Require Passcode time to a short interval, and on the prior screen to set Auto-Lock to a short amount of time (I use one minute for both values).

On OS X, choose System Preferences > Security & Privacy > General, then check Require password [*pick a time from the pop-up menu*] after sleep or screen saver begins.

A On your iOS device, turn on Find My iPhone in Settings > iCloud.

To configure your iOS device for location:

1. Tap Settings > iCloud.
2. Scroll down the list, then turn on Find My iPhone or Find My iPad or Find My iPod touch, depending on your device **A**.
3. Press the device's button to close the Settings app.

To find your device:

1. Using a web browser, sign in to your iCloud account at `http://www.icloud.com`.
2. If the iCloud website brings you to the last application you are working in, rather than the iCloud home screen, click the cloud button at the upper left corner of the window **B**.

   The website brings you back to the home screen.
3. Click the Find My iPhone icon **C**.

   The application launches, and the website displays a map with dots for each of the devices you have activated with iCloud **D**.

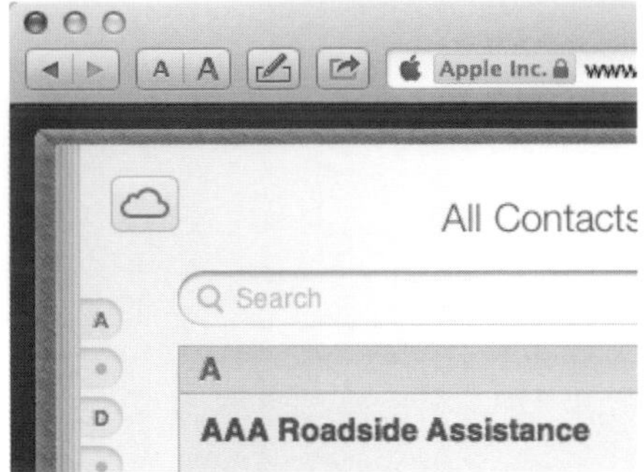

B If necessary, click the cloud icon in one of the other iCloud website applications to bring you back to the iCloud homepage.

C On the iCloud homepage, click the icon for Find My iPhone.

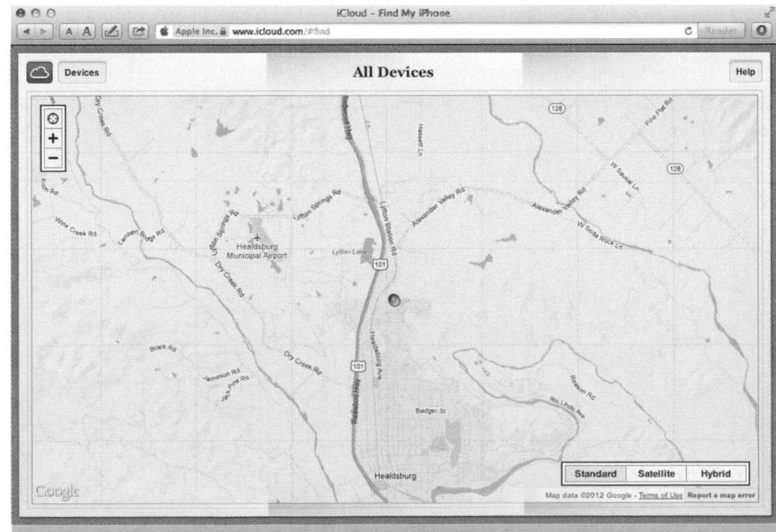

D Your device appears on the map as a green dot.

E You can select any of the devices in the My Devices list to display its location.

F When you select a device, a popover shows its name, when it was located, and the blue Info icon.

4. Click the Devices button, then in the resulting popover **E**, click the device you wish to find.

   or

   If more than one device dot is shown on the map, you can click the dot to show what device it is **F**.

6. (Optional) As usual with online maps, you can use the controls in the window to zoom in or out, and switch from a standard map view to a satellite view, or a hybrid view that overlays street and location names over the satellite view.

TIP In the Devices list, a colored dot will appear next to each device. A green dot means the device was recently located or signaled to the iCloud servers that it was online. A gray dot means that Find My iPhone is trying to connect to the device or that it can't be located.

To play a sound on your device:

1. On the map, your device will appear with its name, when it was last located, and a blue I (for Information) icon F.
2. Click the blue icon, or select the device in the Devices list.

   An Info dialog appears G.
3. Click the Play Sound button.

   A banner appears on the Web site confirming the sound was sent. Usually within a minute, the device will play the loud pinging sound (even if the device's Mute switch is on) and display the message H.

   The iCloud website will send a confirmation email to the address associated with your Apple ID I.

TIP You can manually update the location of your devices by clicking its dot; if the location is old, the blue Information icon will be replaced by a Refresh button.

G The Info dialog allows you to work remotely with your device.

H Besides playing a sound, a message appears as a notification on the lock screen of your iOS device.

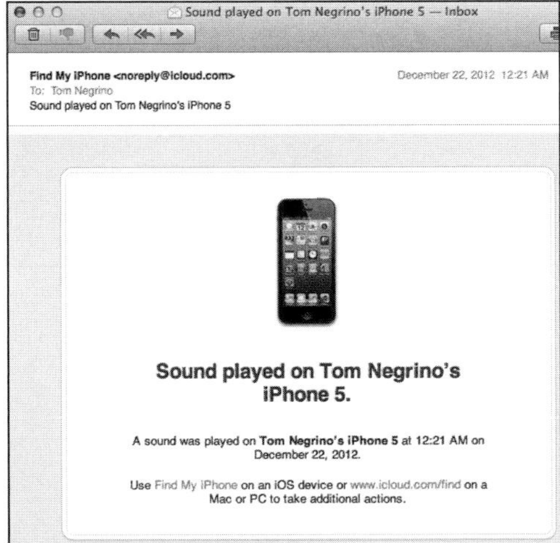

I The iCloud website also sends you an email confirmation whenever it interacts with one of your devices.

J To begin the Lost Mode process, enter a four-digit passcode.

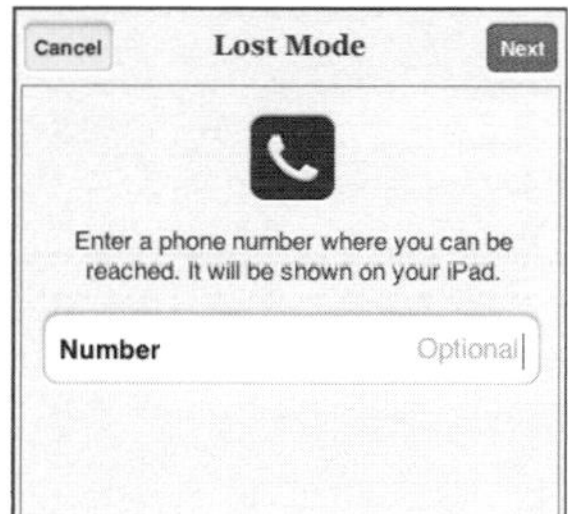

K Enter a phone number that will appear on the device's lock screen.

To remotely lock and add a passcode to your iOS device:

1. On the iCloud website or with the Find My iPhone app, find your device.
2. Click the blue icon in the popover, or select the device in the Devices list.

   The device's Info dialog appears **G**.
3. Click the Lost Mode button.

   The Lost Mode dialog appears **J**.
4. Enter a four-digit passcode.

   After you enter the passcode, the screen will automatically change to another screen asking you to reenter the passcode.

   If the device already used a passcode for lock security, it will immediately lock using the existing passcode, and you won't be asked to enter one.
5. Reenter the passcode.

   The screen changes to allow you to add a phone number where you can be reached in the event the device has been lost, and not stolen **K**.

continues on next page

6. Click Next.

   The screen changes to allow you to add a personalized message **L**.

7. Enter a message if you do not want to use the default message, then click Done.

   The iOS device immediately locks, the dialog on the iCloud website will show the device has been locked and is in Lost Mode **M**, and the iCloud website will send you a confirmation email. To use the device again, the passcode will need to be entered.

8. To stop Lost Mode or to change the phone number or lock message, click Lost Mode again and make the changes in the dialog **N**. When you stop Lost Mode, the passcode lock is removed from the device, though the passcode will still need to be entered the first time the device is used again.

TIP If the iCloud website could not contact the device when you send the Lost Mode command, the lock and tracking will occur when it next connects to the Internet.

L Enter a message for the lock screen here, then click Done.

M After the device has been successfully placed into Lost Mode, the Info dialog lets you know the process was successful.

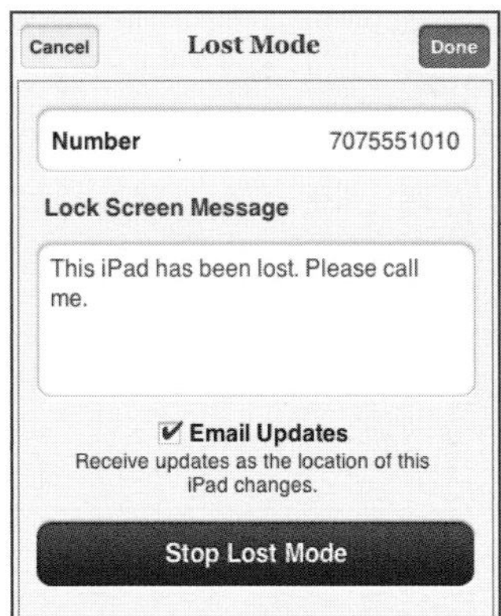

N Use this dialog to modify or stop Lost Mode.

O Are you sure you want to erase your device? I sure wasn't; I chickened out and clicked Cancel.

To remotely wipe your iOS device:

1. On the iCloud website or with the Find My iPhone app, find your device.
2. Click the blue icon in the popover, or select the device in the Devices list.

   The device's Info dialog appears **G**.
3. Click the Erase button.

   A confirmation dialog appears **O**.
4. Enter your Apple ID password, then click Erase.

   The data is wiped immediately, if the device is online. Otherwise, the device will be wiped when it reconnects to the Internet.

TIP Once you remotely erase a device, it can no longer be found from the iCloud website or the Find My iPhone app. If you are truly convinced that the device has been stolen, wiping it can protect your important data (and then you'll be able to restore to a replacement device using either your iCloud backup or your iTunes backup). But if you think you have merely misplaced the device and you may be able to retrieve it, think twice about sending the Erase command.

Let's Talk Accuracy

When you find your device, you should not necessarily expect pinpoint accuracy. The best accuracy will come from iOS devices that contain GPS chips. In my testing, I found that the reported location of my iPhone 5 could sometimes be within a few feet of where the device really was. My third-generation iPad (Wi-Fi-only model) usually didn't provide as much location accuracy, but the reported location was typically within 50 feet of the actual location. The iPhone gave better results outdoors, where its GPS chip had a clear view of the sky. But even then, refreshing the website often showed the devices in a different location, even though they had not actually moved at all.

When GPS is obstructed (or the device doesn't have GPS at all), and the device falls back to Wi-Fi hotspot location or cell tower triangulation, you will usually see a large circle around the reported location of the device, indicating that the device is somewhere in that area **P**. Sometimes, as in the figure, that radius is quite large, and wouldn't be very useful in tracking down that wayward MacBook.

Using Find My iPhone can provide excellent results, but that depends on the device, whether it is outdoors, and other factors. It's a good service to have, but it's not a panacea.

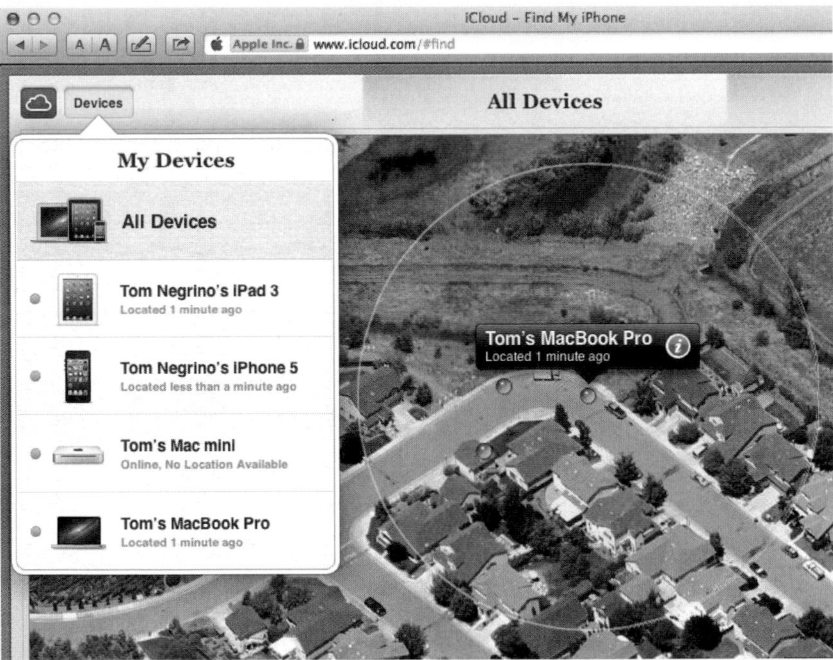

P The error radius when using Wi-Fi positioning can be pretty large; it's true that my MacBook Pro is somewhere within that big green circle, but the circle is a bit too big to be truly useful.

Using Find My Mac

When you're using the iCloud website to work with a Mac, some things work in much the same way as with an iOS device, but with other things there are some differences. Finding and signaling your Mac work the same way as with a mobile device, so I refer you to the instructions earlier in this chapter to accomplish those tasks.

Things work a little differently if you want to Lock or Erase a Mac from the iCloud website or from the Find My iPhone iOS app. First, it's important to note that Find My Mac is only available on Macs running iCloud, which is to say a Mac running OS X 10.7.2 Lion or later.

A Mac is a bit harder to misplace than a mobile device, but the iCloud website still allows you to play a loud sound through the Mac to find it. Naturally, the sound only plays if the computer is on. For example, if you send the Play Sound command to a notebook computer, the sound won't play until the lid is open and the Mac is in use.

All Macs running Lion (or Mountain Lion) have a feature called Lion (or Mountain Lion) Recovery, which is normally intended to let you repair your boot disk or reinstall OS X without the need for a physical install disc. The way that Recovery works is that during the installation of OS X, the installer program creates an invisible read-only boot volume on your hard drive, called Recovery HD, which contains a variety of utilities that allow you to download and reinstall OS X; use Disc Utility to repair or erase your hard drive; restore from a Time Machine backup; or browse with Safari to get online help.

The Lock and Erase features in iCloud make use of this bootable Recovery HD. When you invoke Lock from the iCloud website, you are asked to set a four-digit passcode. If your Mac is online, it immediately restarts and reboots from the Recovery HD volume, presenting a screen requiring the passcode. If the Mac is offline, the passcode lock happens the next time it's online.

As a last resort, you might want to use Erase. If your Mac is online, it immediately restarts from the Recovery HD volume, and begins erasing your boot disc, destroying all of its information. If the Mac is offline, the erasure happens the next time it connects to the Internet.

TIP Interestingly, if you execute Lock or Erase on your Mac, it's possible that you'll still be able to find it later with Find My Mac, because OS X also stores your iCloud credentials and the status of the Find My Mac feature on the Recovery HD.

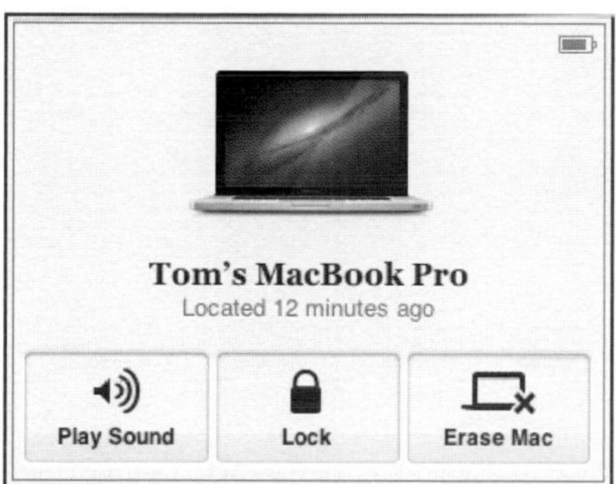

Ⓐ To begin the Play Sound process for your Mac, you'll start in its Info popover.

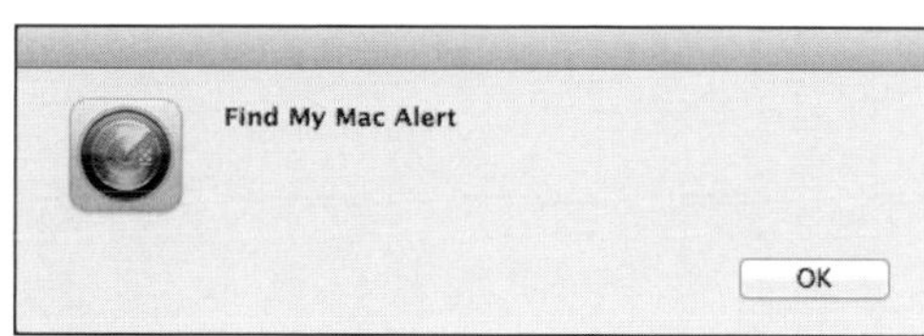

Ⓑ When the sound plays, you also get an alert on the Mac screen. Enter a four-digit passcode for the Remote Lock.

To play a sound on your Mac:

1. On the iCloud website or with the Find My iPhone app, find your Mac.
2. Click the blue icon in the popover, or choose the Mac in the Devices list.

   An Info dialog appears Ⓐ.
3. Click the Play Sound button.

   A banner appears on the Web site confirming the sound was sent. Usually within a minute, the Mac will play a loud pinging sound (even if the Mac's volume is turned down) and display the message Ⓑ.

   The iCloud website will send a confirmation email to the address associated with your Apple ID.

TIP If the iCloud website could not contact the Mac when you send the Play Sound command, the website will report "Pending: Play Sound" and the sound will play when the Mac next connects to the Internet.

To remotely lock your Mac:

1. On the iCloud website or with the Find My iPhone app, find your Mac.
2. Click the blue icon in the popover, or choose the Mac in the Devices list.

   The device's Info dialog appears Ⓐ.
3. Click the Lock button.

   A confirmation dialog appears Ⓒ. It reminds you that if you lock the Mac, you can't wipe it (because the machine will immediately lock and reboot from the Recovery volume).
4. Confirm you want to lock the Mac by clicking Lock.
4. Enter a four-digit passcode Ⓓ.

   After you enter the passcode, the screen will automatically change to another screen asking you to reenter the passcode.
5. Reenter the passcode.

   The screen will automatically change to another screen that allows you to enter a message that will be shown on your Mac's screen after it's been locked Ⓔ. For example, you might want to enter your contact information so that someone who finds your Mac and is inclined to return it can easily do so.

Ⓒ The iCloud website warns you that a locked Mac can't be wiped. You can enter a message that will appear on the boot screen of your Mac after it has been locked.

Ⓓ Enter a four-digit passcode that will be required to unlock the Mac.

Ⓔ You can enter a message that will appear on the Mac's Lock screen.

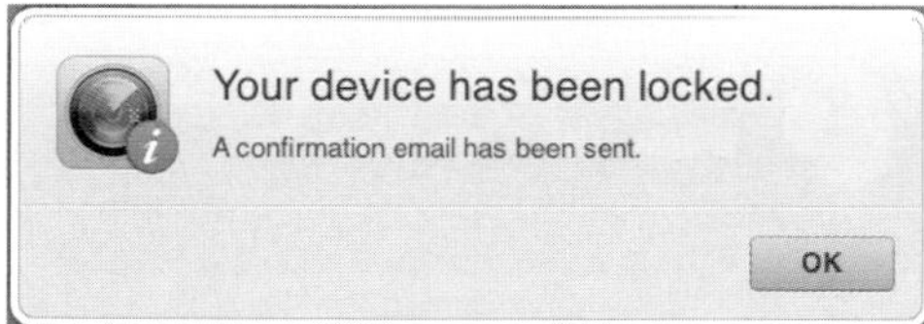

F The iCloud website confirms the Mac has been locked.

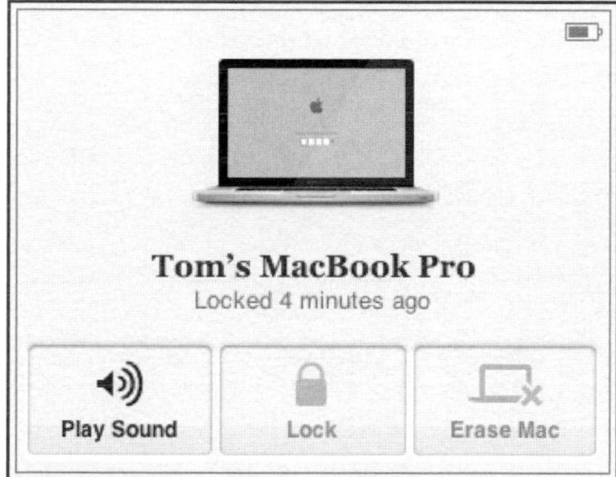

G After the deed has been done, the Info popover lets you know your Mac has been locked and rebooted into the lock screen.

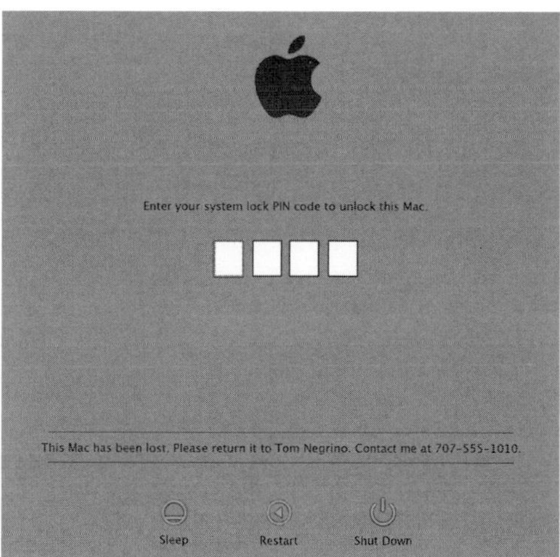

H This photo illustration shows what my MacBook Pro's screen looked like after it was locked.

6. (Optional) Enter a message.
7. Click the Lock button.

   The Mac will immediately lock and reboot using the Recovery HD, an alert on the iCloud website confirms the locking **F**, the Info dialog on the iCloud website will reappear showing you the device has been locked **G**, and the iCloud website will send you a confirmation email. To use the device again, the passcode will need to be entered **H**.

To remotely erase your Mac:

1. On the iCloud website or with the Find My iPhone app, find your device.
2. Click the blue icon in the popover, or choose the Mac in the Devices list.

   The device's Info dialog appears **A**.
3. Click the Erase Mac button.

   A confirmation dialog appears **I**. It reminds you that everything on the Mac will be erased, and that it could take up to a day to complete the job.
4. Enter and reenter a four-digit passcode.

   The passcode will be needed to unlock the Mac even though the boot disc has been erased. The popover will automatically change to another screen that allows you to enter a message that will be shown on your Mac's screen after it's been locked and wiped. This might allow you to recover the hardware, even though you'll have to restore your data from a backup.
5. (Optional) Enter a message.
6. Click the Erase button.

   The Mac will immediately lock, reboot using the Recovery HD, and begin erasing the regular boot drive.

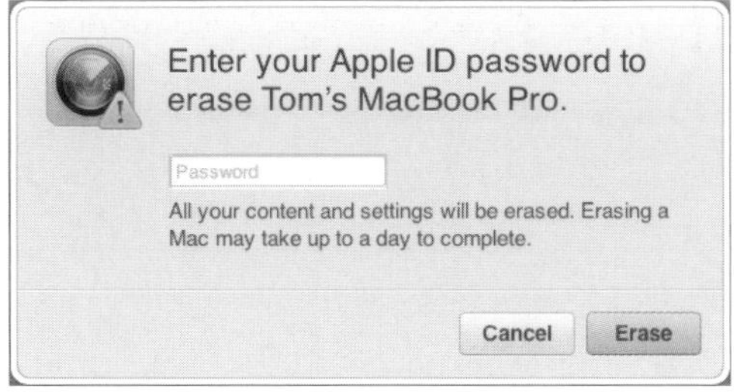

I Enter your Apple ID password to begin the remote Erase.

Using Find My Friends

At the same time Apple released iCloud and iOS 5, they also released a free new iOS app called Find My Friends. With this app, you can locate the iOS devices (presumably being carried by your contacts), as long as they've given you permission to locate them.

You can use Find My Friends in two ways. You can set up a list of contacts that you can locate all the time (for example, your close family members) and you can also set up temporary events to which you can invite people and that automatically expires at a set time. You might want to set up and use temporary events when you and a group of colleagues are attending a conference, or when extended family members are at a vacation spot, or when you and some friends are attending a concert or sporting event.

For privacy purposes, Find My Friends allows anyone who has authorized you to find their location to revoke that authorization at any time, and it also allows you to hide your location from all followers whenever you want.

Find My Friends requires iOS 5 or later, and all the participants must have downloaded the app to their mobile device. You can only use the Find My Friends features from the app; you can't use the iCloud website for this purpose.

To set up Find My Friends for the first time, download it from the App Store, then tap Find Friends on your iOS device **A**. Enter your Apple ID (which is the same as your iCloud account name) and password. Tap Sign In, then confirm the app is allowed to use your location.

TIP In the instructions below, I'm using the version of Find My Friends running on an iPhone. The iPad version is similar, but some specific instructions are different, thanks to the larger screen size.

A Tap the Find Friends app to get started.

To add contacts permanently:

1. On the All tab of the Find My Friends app, it will initially show that you have yet to add any contacts, and that you can use the app to suggest iCloud contacts who already use Find My Friends, and who might be amenable to allow you to add them **B**. Tap Friend Suggestions, or tap the Add button (+).

   The Add Friends screen appears **C**.

2. Type a friend's Apple ID, or tap the blue Add Contact button (+) to bring up your Contacts list. If you want, you can send a request to multiple people at the same time. You can also enter a personalized message.

   You can also still access the Friends Suggestions from this screen by tapping that button. The screen will then change to Invite Friends, and show you a list of people in your contacts who are using Find My Friends. I'm not showing that because of privacy concerns.

3. Tap Send.

   The app will show you a message explaining that after your friend has approved your request, he or she will appear in your friends list.

TIP Just because you've sent someone a request and they approved it, it doesn't mean that they can also see your location. For that, they'll need to send you a location request as well.

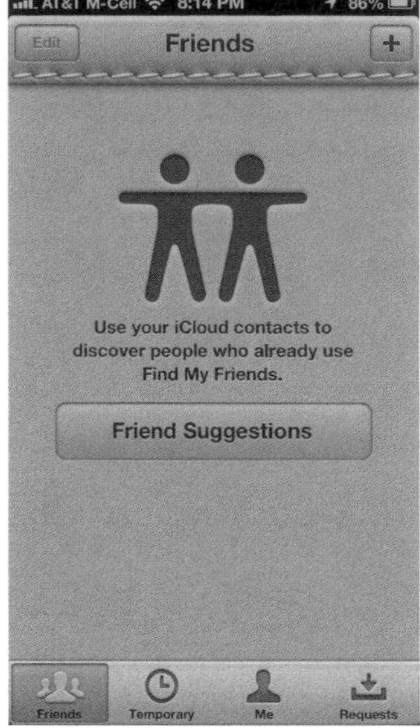

B Sadly, you don't have any friends yet. Better click that Friend Suggestions button.

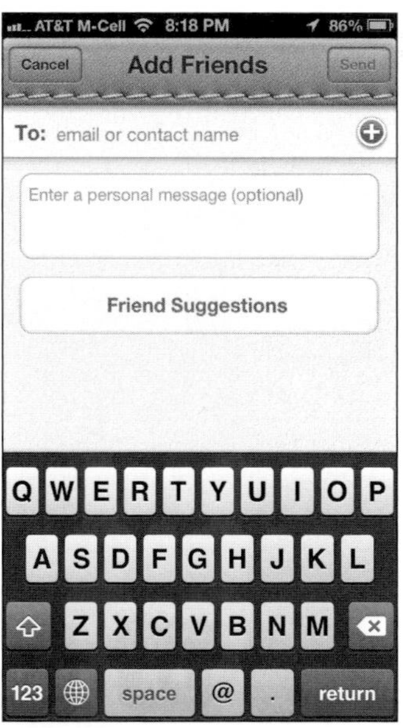

C You need to enter your friend's Apple ID in the screen, and optionally send them a personalized invitation message.

D The Friends tab shows the friends you've permanently added, and their approximate distance from you.

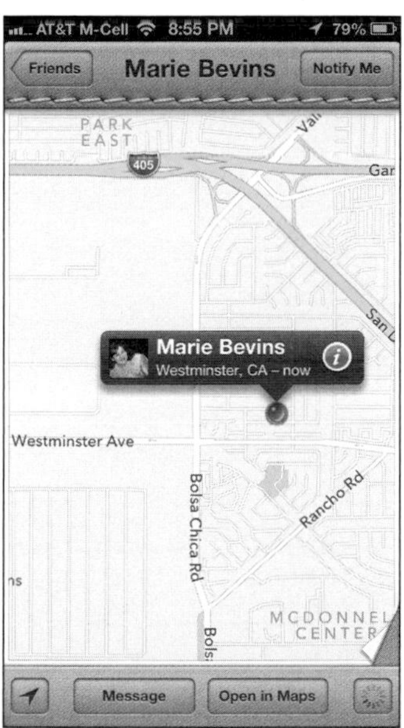

E You can get a map of your friend's location, and as usual that map can be a standard street view, a satellite view, or a hybrid of the two.

To accept location requests:

1. Usually, a location request will appear as an iOS notification on the home screen. Tap the notification to launch the Find My Friends app.
2. Tap the Requests button at the bottom of the screen **A**.
3. Click Accept.
4. (Optional) If you're not already following the person who requested your location, and you want to add them to your friends list, tap the Ask To Follow button, which sends a request back to the person.

To locate friends:

1. Tap the Friends button at the bottom of the screen **D**, which shows a map and list of each friend and their general location. On the map, your location will show a blue dot, and everyone else's map pins will be purple.

   or

   Tap a friend in the list to see a zoomed-in map, with a popover pointing to their location **E**.

continues on next page

2. (Optional) To contact your friend, tap the blue I information icon on their popover, and their Info screen appears with their location and some contact info. Do one or more of the following:

   Tap the Send Message button to send a text message (you'll be prompted for which phone number or address to use; choosing your friend's iCloud address will send an iMessage, and choosing their mobile phone number will send a regular SMS).

   or

   Tap the FaceTime button to initiate a video conference (if the recipient has a capable FaceTime device).

   or

   Tap an email address to open the Mail app and compose an email.

TIP You can also tap the Directions button, which opens Maps and routes turn-by-turn instructions from your location to theirs.

F To begin setting up a temporary event, you'll need to invite one or more friends.

Setting Up Temporary Events

If you only want to share your location with other people for a limited period of time, setting up a temporary event is just what you want. Find My Friends allows you to invite friends with a specified ending date and time, after which the location sharing automatically ends.

To set up a temporary event:

1. In Find My Friends, tap the Temporary button, then tap the Invite Friends button **F**.
2. Add the people you want to invite, give the event a name, and then tap the Ends field to choose a date and time the event will end.
3. Tap Send, and Find My Friends sends your invitation. If one of your recipients isn't already using Find My Friends, they'll get an email with the invitation (with instructions on how to download the app); recipients already using Find My Friends will receive an iOS notification, which they can accept or decline in the app.

continues on next page

4. During the event, you can tap the Temporary button in the app to show a list of the event's participants **G**. You can tap Send iMessage to send everyone a text message, or tap View Map to display a map with all the participants locations marked.

TIP Unlike permanent location sharing, when someone joins an event, they can automatically see everyone else who is part of the event, without each person having to exchange location authorization with every other person.

TIP If you are part of an event and wish to leave it, just tap the event name in the Temporary tab, then tap Leave Event.

TIP If you created the event, you can change the event name and ending time, remove or add participants, or delete the event.

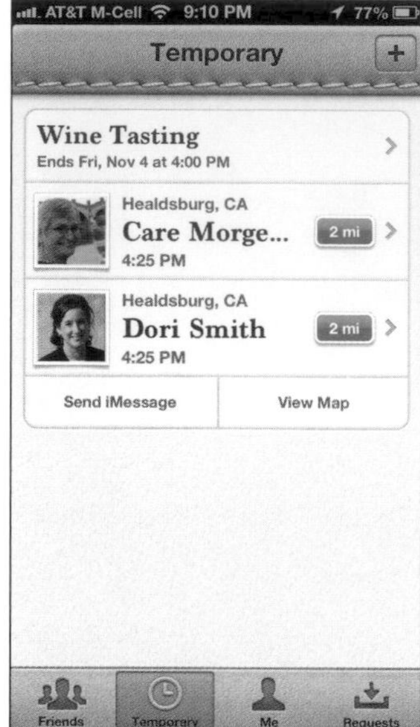

G During the event, tapping the event's name shows you its participants and their approximate distance from you.

Using Back to My Mac

Back to My Mac allows you to connect to one of your Macs from another Mac over the Internet. Once you are connected using Back to My Mac, it's just like being connected on a local network. You can mount volumes on the remote Mac for file sharing, or you can initiate a Screen Sharing session to control the remote Mac directly.

Imagine that you're on a business trip, and you're working in your hotel room on your Mac laptop when you realize that you left a vital file on your iMac at home. Naturally, you're not connected to your home network. But as long as you have turned on Back to My Mac before you left on your trip, you will usually be able to reach it from your room's Internet connection. You'll be able to mount the home Mac's hard disk as if it were just another network volume, and copy files back and forth between your local hard disk and your hard disk at home.

In the last paragraph, I said you could usually connect, because sometimes, due to poor or outdated network configuration in the location where you're staying, Back to My Mac just can't make the connection. That kind of failure to connect has become increasingly rare (Back to My Mac was originally introduced in 2007), but it still occasionally occurs.

In this section, we'll first show you how to configure your Mac so it can be accessed remotely, then show you how to use file sharing with your remote Mac, and finally show you how to start up a Screen Sharing session with the remote Mac.

TIP Besides connecting one Mac to another over the Internet, you can also use Back to My Mac to connect to a Time Capsule or AirPort Disk.

To set up your Mac so it can be remotely accessed:

1. On the Mac you will want to access remotely, open System Preferences > iCloud, then make sure that the checkbox next to Back to My Mac is selected **A**.
2. In the Sharing pane of System Preferences, select the checkboxes for Screen Sharing and File Sharing **B**.

   With both these types of sharing, you'll ensure better security if you click the radio button for Only these users in the Allow access for section, click the Plus button, and add your own username.
3. You will also need to enable Back to My Mac in the iCloud pane of System Preferences on the Mac that you are taking with you on the road.

TIP You must be signed in to iCloud with the same Apple ID on both computers for Back to My Mac to work.

A The first thing you need to do is make sure that Back to My Mac is checked in the iCloud preference pane.

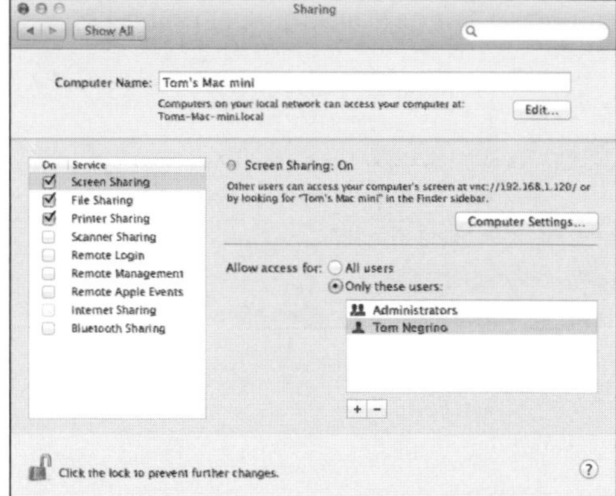

B You need to make sure that Screen Sharing and File Sharing are enabled on the Mac you'll be accessing before you leave home.

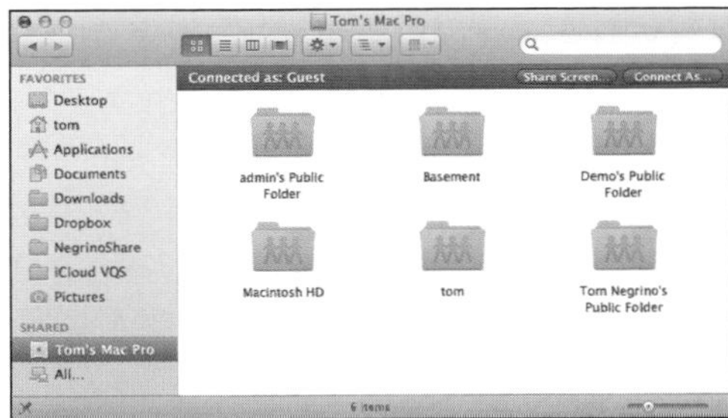

C When you click the remote Mac in the sidebar of a Finder window, its available volumes appear.

D You can sign in for File Sharing as either a registered user, or you can use your Apple ID.

To use file sharing on your remote Mac:

1. Open a window in the Finder. In the window's sidebar, the Shared section will show your remote computer, using its Computer Name that is set in its Sharing preference pane.
2. Click the remote computer in the Finder window sidebar. After a moment, the volumes that you have allowed to be shared will appear in the Finder window **C**.
3. By default, you will be connected as a Guest, which will prevent you from accessing files in your home folder. Click the Connect As button in the Finder window, then enter your username and password (to authenticate as a registered user), or click the Using an Apple ID button, which uses your iCloud credentials **D**.
4. You can now work with the remote files as if they were on any other file server.

The Technical Stuff

In order for you to use Back to My Mac, your router for the network attached to the Mac you are trying to reach must support either UPNP (Universal Plug-And-Play) or NAT-PMP (NAT Port Mapping Protocol), and one of those services must be enabled. Virtually all modern routers support both or at least one of these protocols, and they are turned on by default, so you shouldn't need to adjust your router configuration.

Back to My Mac uses a combination of Bonjour (a protocol that allows services on a computer or device to advertise themselves on a network so other equipment can discover them), Wide Area Bonjour (which extends Bonjour to work over the Internet), and IPsec (a security protocol that creates a encrypted "tunnel" between the two computers).

To share the screen of your remote Mac:

1. Open a window in the Finder. In the window's sidebar, the Shared section will show your remote computer.
2. Click the remote computer in the Finder window sidebar.
3. By default, you will be connected as a Guest. Click the Share Screen button in the Finder window, then enter your username and password (to authenticate as a registered user), or click the Using an Apple ID button, which uses your iCloud credentials **E**.
4. Screen Sharing will start, and a window displaying the screen of your remote Mac will appear **F**. You can click inside and work on objects in this window with your mouse, trackpad, and keyboard as if you were sitting in front of the remote Mac.

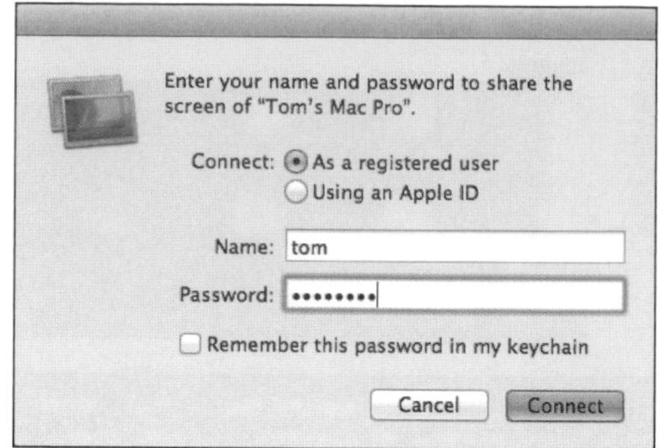

E You can sign in for Screen Sharing as either a registered user, or you can use your Apple ID.

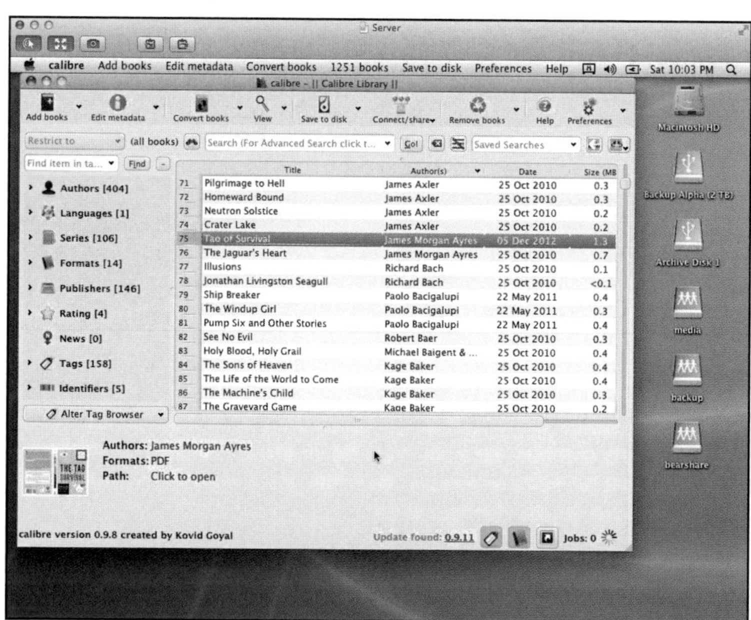

F Once Screen Sharing is started, you can see and work with the screen of the remote Mac as if you were sitting in front of it.

Index

Numbers

1Password website, 5
10.7 Lion app names
  Address Book, 21
  iCal, 21
  iChat, 21
  Mail program, 21
10.8 Mountain Lion app names
  Calendar, 21
  Contacts, 21
  Game Center, 21
  Messages, 21
  Notes, 21
  Reminders, 21

A

Address Book app equivalents, 21
AirPrint, using with notes, 41–42
alarms versus reminders, 93
albums, downloading, 128
alerts versus banners, 94
aliases, using with mail, 36. *See also* email aliases
Aperture library, importing Photo Stream items into, 107
Aperture program, using Photo Stream with, 108
app names and equivalents, 21
Apple IDs
  associating user account with, 10
  multiple, 10
  password, 10
  requirement, 9
  signing in with, 11–12
Apple Mail program. *See also* Macs
  account setup, 19–20
  actions button, 25
  application window, 19
  equivalents, 21
  Folders list, 25
  hiding Folders list, 26
  hiding Mailboxes list, 26
  hiding message list, 26
  on iCloud website, 25
  mail headers, 19
  mailboxes, 25
  message area, 19, 25
  message list, 19, 25
  refreshing messages, 26
  resizing Folders list, 26
  resizing Mailboxes list, 26
  resizing message list, 26
  search box, 19, 25
  toolbar, 19, 25
  viewing, 26

B

Back to My Mac. *See also* Macs
  Bonjour protocol, 201
  explained, 199

Back to My Mac. (*continued*)
File Sharing, 200–201
IPsec protocol, 201
NAT-PMP support, 201
router support, 201
Screen Sharing, 200, 202
setting up remote access, 200
UPNP support, 201
using, 199–202
Wide Area Bonjour, 201
Back Up Now button, 152
backing up to iCloud. *See* iCloud Backup
banners versus alerts, 94
Bcc field, including in messages, 37
Black Text bookmarklet, 169
Bonjour protocol, use with Back to My Mac, 201
bookmark synchronization
configuring, 161–162
enabling, 161–162
explained, 159
bookmarklets for iOS
adding, 170–172
Black Text, 169
Clip to Evernote, 169
Edit popover, 170
explained, 169
installation, 169
running, 172
saving changes to, 172
Unicode Symbols, 169
Box website, 136
browser bookmarks, 4
browser synchronization, preparing for, 160
BusyCal calendar, 66

C

Calendar app
alternatives, 66
BusyCal alternative, 66
Calvetica alternative, 66
to-do items, 61
equivalents, 21
events, 60
Fantastical alternative, 66
reminders, 61
views, 60
Calendar preferences
Advanced, 84
Alerts, 83
Appearance, 83
Event Updates, 84
Format, 83
General, 83
Invitations, 84
Old Events & Reminders, 84
Scheduling, 83
Time Zone, 84
calendar sharing
checking status of, 79
features, 77
ownership, 79
removing someone from, 79
stopping, 79
turning on, 78–79
Calendars app, 4
calendars. *See also* public calendars
creating on iOS devices, 64
creating on Macs, 63
editing on iOS devices, 65
editing on Macs, 65
sharing, 62

calendars on iCloud website
Actions pop-up menu, 68–69
adding, 70
Calendar view buttons, 68
Calendars list, 68–69
changing date views, 71–72
color picker, 70
creating, 68–69
Date selector, 71–72
deleting, 70
editing, 70
events, 73–75
Go to Today button, 68
hiding, 69
naming, 69
New Event button, 68
notifications, 68
viewing, 69
Year and Month selector, 68
Calvetica calendar, 66
canonical data, 14
Chrome browser versus Safari, 166
Clip to Evernote bookmarklet, 169
Clock app, using Alarm function on, 93
Composing preferences, setting for mail, 37
contact addresses, displaying maps of, 51
contact groups
adding, 55
adding members to, 55
displaying members of, 55
features, 54
removing, 55
removing members from, 55
renaming, 55
contacts
adding, 52
adding fields, 52
adding from incoming mail, 34
adding to Find My Friends, 194
deleting, 53
editing, 52–53
searching, 51
selecting multiple, 53
sending email to, 51
viewing, 50
Contacts app Action menu items
contact cards, 56
Delete, 56
Import vCard, 56
Make This My Card, 56
New Contact, 56
Print, 56
Contacts app, 4, 21
Contacts app Preferences
Address Layout, 57
Automatically Format Phone Numbers, 57
Display Order, 57
Sort Order, 57
control panel, downloading for Windows, 15, 100

D

deleting
calendars on iCloud website, 70
events on iCloud website, 76
folders, 31–32
items from iCloud storage, 157
iWork documents from iCloud, 148
messages, 35
notes on Macs, 44
photos, 113–114
reminders, 87–88
saving sent, 35
subscribed calendars, 82

devices. *See also* iOS devices
  charging, 3
  finding, 173
documents, synchronized, 4
Documents in the Cloud. *See also* iWork documents
  adding text shortcuts, 140
  benefit, 141
  configuring, 136–140
  versus Dropbox, 138
  enabling on iOS, 139–140
  enabling on Macs, 138
  features, 136–137
  Keynote documents, 137
  moving on iCloud website, 144
  opening, 143
  restrictions, 144
  saving, 142, 144
  synchronizing text shortcuts, 140
  updating files, 140
Dropbox
  versus Documents in Cloud, 138
  website, 5, 42, 136

E

email. *See also* Mail app; messages
  adding contacts from, 34
  adding signatures to, 37
  Archive icon, 28
  Compose icon, 28
  composing, 29
  Delete icon, 28
  filing, 31
  forwarding, 30, 35
  Move to Folder icon, 28
  Reply icons, 28
  replying to, 30
  sending to contacts, 51
  toolbar, 28
email accounts. *See* mail accounts
email aliases, number of, 18. *See also* aliases
Erase feature, invoking, 188
Erase Mac button, clicking, 192
events
  creating on iCloud website, 73–75
  deleting on iCloud website, 76
  editing on iCloud website, 76
  handling, 85
  moving on iCloud website, 76
  versus reminders, 61
  saving on iCloud website, 75
  setting up for Find My Friends, 197–198
Evernote website, 42, 169

F

FaceTime button, using with Find My Friends, 196
Fantastical calendar, 66
Find My Friends app
  accepting location requests, 195
  adding contacts permanently, 194
  contacting friends, 196
  Directions button, 196
  explained, 193
  FaceTime button, 196
  Friends tab, 195
  locating friends, 195–196
  opening Maps, 196
  requirements, 193
  setting up, 193
  temporary events, 197–198
  using, 193
Find My Mac services
  accuracy of, 186
  activating, 175–176
  Erase feature, 188, 192
  errors in Wi-Fi positioning, 186

explained, 174
Lock feature, 188
locking Macs remotely, 190–191
message for Lock screen, 190
playing sounds, 189
using, 186–192
using for stolen devices, 178
using passcodes, 190
finding devices, 173, 180–181
finding features, using, 178
Flickr website, 5
folders
adding, 31
deleting, 31–32
dragging, 31
naming, 31
forwarding email, 30, 35
friends. *See* Find My Friends app

G

Gallery, discontinuation of, 5
Game Center app, equivalent, 21
Google Chrome browser, 166
Groups mode, using with contacts, 54–55

H

hardware requirements, 7–8

I

iCal app equivalents, 21
iChat app equivalents, 21
iCloud
and Apple TV, 12
benefits, 2–3
browser bookmarks, 4
Calendars, 4
charging devices, 3
configuring on iOS devices, 11–12
configuring on Mac, 13–14
configuring on Windows PC, 15–16
Contacts, 4
control panel for Windows, 15
email, 4
explained, 2
features, 4
location services, 4
music, 4
Photo Stream, 4
preference pane, 13
Reminders, 4
safety, 3
services, 14
setup process, 13
signing into, 11
storage space, 149–151
synchronized documents, 4
System Preferences, 13
iCloud Backup, 148
restoring iOS devices from, 153
Setup Assistant, 153
turning on, 152
iCloud documents. *See also* iWork documents
adding text shortcuts, 140
benefit, 141
configuring, 136–140
versus Dropbox, 138
enabling on iOS, 139–140
enabling on Macs, 138
features, 136–137
Keynote documents, 137
moving on iCloud website, 144
opening, 143
restrictions, 144
saving, 142, 144
synchronizing text shortcuts, 140
updating files, 140

iCloud mail. *See also* mail accounts
email aliases, 18
versus MobileMe mail, 18
iCloud storage
backup options, 157
deleting items, 157
purchasing, 158
iCloud Tabs, using in Safari, 159, 163–165
icloud.com
account, 4
addresses, 10
email, 18
iDisk, discontinuation of, 5
IMAP email protocol, 18
iMessages. *See also* messages
delivery confirmations, 48
features, 46
sending on iOS devices, 47
sending on Macs, 47–48
versus text messages, 48
using with iPads, 48
using with iPod touch, 48
verifying conversations, 47
Instapaper read-later service, 160, 168
inviting versus sharing, 77, 79
iOS apps
Calendar, 21
Contacts, 21
Game Center, 21
Messages, 21
Notes, 21
Reminders, 21
iOS devices. *See also* devices
adding passcodes to, 183–184
configuring for locations, 179
configuring iCloud on, 11–12
finding, 180–181
finding devices, 173, 186
finding features, 178
finding with Location Services, 177
locking remotely, 183–184
Lost Mode process, 183
mail accounts, 22–24
playing sounds on, 182
restoring from backups, 153
setting passcodes for, 178
updating locations of, 182
wiping remotely, 185
working with remotely, 182
iOS requirements, 7–8
iPhoto in Photo Stream, 104–107
iPsec protocol, use with Back to My Mac, 201
iTunes, turning on iCloud Backup in, 152
iTunes in Cloud
automatic downloads, 117–118
configuring, 116–121
Download All button, 121
re-downloading items, 119–121
iTunes Match. *See also* music
adding computers to, 124–126
adding iOS devices to, 127
configuring, 122
cost, 122
creating Smart Playlists, 131–132
device management, 129
Download icons, 129
downloading music, 128
Duplicate icon, 129
Error icon, 129
features, 122
finding matched songs to upgrade, 131–132
Ineligible icon, 129
limitations, 123, 134
playing music, 128

Removed icon, 129
replacing lower-bit rate music, 133
requirements, 123
seeing status of items, 126
subscribing to, 124
updating music, 130–133
Waiting icon, 129
iWeb site publishing, discontinuation of, 5
iWork documents. *See also* Documents in the Cloud
creating folders for, 148
deleting, 148
downloading, 147
managing on iCloud website, 146–148
opening folders, 148
uploading, 148
iWork programs for iOS, 137
iWork screen
actions, 146
folders, 146
Keynote presentation file, 146
program tabs, 146

J

Junk mailbox, retrieving mail from, 32

K

Keynote documents, file sizes, 137

L

Lion app names
Address Book, 21
iCal, 21
iChat, 21
Mail program, 21
Location Services, 4
controlling, 175
determining locations, 177
explained, 174
finding iOS devices with, 177
overview, 177
setting time zones with, 176
turning off, 175
Lock button, clicking, 191
Lock feature, invoking, 188
Lock screen, entering message for, 190
locking devices remotely, 183–184
locking Macs remotely, 190–191
Lost Mode process
beginning, 183
modifying, 184
stopping, 184

M

Macs. *See also* Apple Mail program; Back to My Mac
configuring iCloud on, 13–14
connecting over Internet, 199
erasing remotely, 192
locking remotely, 190–191
mail accounts, 18–21
playing sounds on, 189
using Notes app on, 43–44
mail accounts. *See also* iCloud mail
IMAP email protocol, 18
setting up on Macs, 18–21
setup on iOS devices, 22–24
Mail app. *See also* email; messages
account setup, 19–20
actions button, 25
application window, 19
equivalents, 21
Folders list, 25
hiding Folders list, 26
hiding Mailboxes list, 26
hiding message list, 26
on iCloud website, 25

Mail app. (*continued*)
- mail headers, 19
- mailboxes, 25
- message area, 19, 25
- message list, 19, 25
- refreshing messages, 26
- resizing Folders list, 26
- resizing Mailboxes list, 26
- resizing message list, 26
- search box, 19, 25
- toolbar, 19, 25
- viewing, 26

Mail preferences
- Accounts, 36
- aliases, 36
- Composing preferences, 37
- forwarding email, 35
- General, 34–35
- message previews, 35
- Rules, 38
- Vacation, 39

maps
- showing for contacts' addresses, 51
- using with Find My Friends, 196

messages. *See also* email; iMessages; Mail app
- adding recipients, 29
- deleting, 35
- getting, 29
- marking, 32
- moving, 31
- moving deleted, 35
- printing, 34
- refreshing in Mail app, 26
- saving as drafts, 29
- searching for, 33
- selecting, 31
- Show Bcc field, 37
- sorting, 33
- UTF-8 Unicode, 37
- viewing, 26

Messages app, equivalents, 21

mobile devices. *See* iOS devices

MobileMe conflicts, 14

MobileMe mail
- email aliases, 18
- versus iCloud mail, 18

MobileMe services
- demise of, 5–6
- Gallery, 5
- iDisk, 5
- iWeb site publishing, 5
- OS X system synchronization, 5
- third-party software synchronization, 6

Mountain Lion app names
- Calendar, 21
- Contacts, 21
- Game Center, 21
- Messages, 21
- Notes, 21

music, 4. *See also* iTunes Match
- downloading, 128
- playing, 128
- updating with iTunes Match, 130–133

N

Notes app
- accessing folders, 41
- Accounts screen, 40
- alternatives, 42
- configuring on iOS devices, 41
- creating notes on Macs, 44
- creating on iOS devices, 41
- default account, 41

deleting notes, 41, 44
editing notes on Macs, 44
emailing, 41
equivalents, 21
Evernote, 42
fonts, 41
printing, 41
Send button, 41
synchronized, 40
using on iCloud website, 45
using on Macs, 43–44
Notification Center, 95
notifications
alerts, 94
banners, 94
configuring on iOS devices, 98
configuring on Macs, 96–97
managing, 94–98

O

OmniFocus, 6
OS X system synchronization, discontinuation of, 5

P

passcodes, setting for devices, 177, 183–184, 190, 192
PC
configuring iCloud on, 15–16
requirements, 8, 16
people. *See* Find My Friends app
Photo Stream, 4
automatic upload from iOS devices, 105
disabling, 106
drawbacks, 103
enabling, 106
enabling on Macs, 101–102
enabling on PCs, 101–102
features, 99
importing items, 107
in iPhoto, 104–107
photo storage in cloud, 100
removing from iOS devices, 103
setting preferences, 106
setting up on iOS devices, 103
sharing, 109–112
supported formats, 100
system requirements, 100
using with Aperture, 108
viewing on Apple TV, 12
Photobucket website, 5
photos, deleting, 113–114
pictures. *See* Photo Stream
printing
messages, 34
notes, 41–42
Printopia 2 website, 42
public calendars. *See also* calendars
deleting subscribed, 82
finding, 82
subscribing to, 80–82

R

Readability read-later service, 160, 168
Reading List
All items, 168
Unread items, 168
using in Safari, 163, 167–168
read-later services
Instapaper, 160
Readability, 160
recipients, adding to email, 29
Reminder lists
adding on iCloud website, 89
editing on iCloud website, 89
sharing, 89

Reminders, 4
reminders
- adding, 85–89
- adding on iCloud website, 86–89
- adding to calendar, 61
- versus alarms, 93
- editing on iCloud website, 86–89
- handling, 85
- making as completed, 88
- setting on iOS devices, 90–92

Reminders app
- assigning due dates, 87
- deleting reminders, 87–88
- Details popover, 87
- Edit Reminder list, 86
- equivalents, 21
- features, 92
- New Reminder list, 86
- priority levels, 87–88
- Reminder lists, 86
- reminders area, 86
- search box, 86
- searching lists, 88
- Show/Hide Calendar, 86

remote access, setting up, 200
replying to email, 30
restoring iOS devices from backups, 153

S

Safari browser
- bookmark management, 160
- bookmark synchronization, 159, 161–162
- bookmarklets for iOS, 169–172
- versus Chrome, 166
- iCloud Tabs, 159, 163–165
- Reader feature, 168
- Reading List, 163, 167–168
- viewing devices, 163

searching
- contacts, 51
- for messages, 33

services, turning off, 12
sharing
- calendars, 77–79
- versus inviting, 77, 79
- Photo Stream, 109–112
- Reminder lists, 89

shortcuts, adding in Documents in the Cloud, 140
Show Bcc field, including in messages, 37
signatures, adding to outbound mail, 37
Smart Playlists, creating in iTunes Match, 131–132
SMS text messaging, 46
Snell, Jason, 130
software requirements, 7–8
songs, playing from iCloud, 128
sorting messages, 33
sounds
- playing on devices, 182
- playing on Macs, 189

stolen devices, finding, 178
storage space, 149–151
- checking availability, 154
- managing, 154–157

SugarSync website, 136
system requirements, 7–8
- iTunes Match, 123
- for Macs, 13
- Photo Stream, 100
- for Windows PCs, 16

T

tabs. *See* iCloud Tabs
task managers, 92
text messaging, 46, 48
text shortcuts, adding in Documents in the Cloud, 140
TextExpander website, 140
to do items, adding to calendar, 61
tracks, downloading from iCloud, 128

U

Unicode Symbols bookmarklet, 169
UTF-8 Unicode, using with messages, 37

V

Vacation preferences, setting for mail, 39

W

websites
- 1Password, 5
- Box, 136
- control panel for Windows, 15
- Dropbox, 5, 42, 136
- Evernote, 42, 169
- Flickr, 5
- Instapaper read-later service, 160, 168
- Photobucket, 5
- Printopia 2, 42
- Readability read-later service, 160, 168
- read-later services, 160
- SugarSync, 136
- TextExpander, 140
- Weebly, 5

Windows PC
- configuring iCloud on, 15–16
- requirements, 8, 16